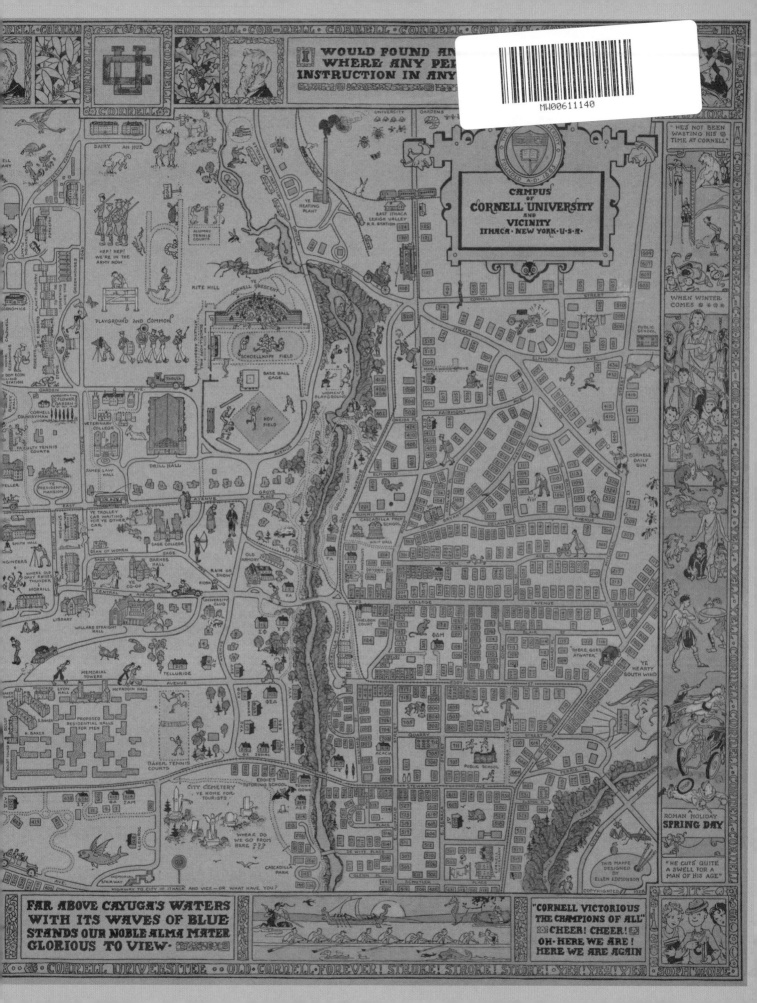

CORNELL

Glorious to View

Cornell

Carol Kammen

CORNELL UNIVERSITY LIBRARY
ITHACA, NEW YORK

First edition
10 9 8 7 6 5 4 3 2

Second printing, 2011

Library of Congress Control Number: 2003111767
ISBN: 0-935995-03-X

Images: from Rare and Manuscript Collections, Kroch
  Library, Cornell University; from Dale Corson; and
  from the author
Frontispiece: Commencement, ca. 1928

Photo editor: Susette Newberry
Design: John Hubbard
Produced by: Marquand Books, Inc., Seattle
  www.marquand.com
Printed and bound by C&C Offset Printing Co., Ltd.,
  Hong Kong

For my Cornellians

      Daniel Merson Kammen '84
      Douglas Anton Kammen '89, Ph.D. '97

And for Michael, who since 1965 has taught
history at Cornell

ALMA MATER

. . . .

Far above Cayuga's waters,
With its waves of blue,
Stands our noble Alma Mater,
Glorious to view.

Far above the busy humming
Of the bustling town,
Reared against the arch of heaven,
Looks she proudly down.

Sentry like o'er lake and valley
Towers her regal form,
Watch and ward forever keeping,
Braving time and storm.

So through clouds of doubt and darkness
Gleams her beacon light,
Fault and error clear revealing,
Blazing forth the right.

To the glory of her founder
Rise her stately walls.
May her sons pay equal tribute
Whene'er duty calls.

When the moments, swiftly fleeting,
Ages roll between,
Many yet unborn shall hail her:
Alma Mater, Queen.

In the music of the waters
As they glide along,
In the murmur of the breezes
With their whispered song,

In the tuneful chorus blending,
With each pealing bell,
One refrain seems oft repeated:
Hail, all hail, Cornell!

Here, by flood and foaming torrent,
Gorge and rocky dell,
Pledge we faith and homage ever
To our loved Cornell.

May time ne'er efface the memory
Of her natal day
And her name and fame be honored
Far and wide away!

Lift the chorus, speed it onward,
Loud her praises tell,
Hail to thee, our Alma Mater.
Hail, all hail, Cornell.

—Archibald Croswell Weeks '74 and
Wilmot Moses Smith '74, 1872

CONTENTS

1. Ezra Cornell
2. Andrew D. White
3. Theodore W. Dwight
4. Willard Fiske
5. Evan W. Evans
6. William C. Cleveland
7. Burt G. Wilder
8. Joseph H. Whittlesey
9. Lewis Spaulding
10. James Law
11. Eli W. Blake
12. Charles F. Hartt

13. Louis Agassiz
14. George C. Caldwell
15. Jo. Morgan Hart
16. Homer B. Sprague
17. Ziba H. Potter
18. John L. Morris
19. William D. Wilson
20. William C. Russel
21. Goldwin Smith
22. James Russell Lowell
23. George William Curtis

FOUNDER & FACULTY
OF
CORNELL
UNIVERSITY,
Photographed
BY
PURDY
AND
FREAR
ITHACA, N.Y.

This group was made in the Spring of 1869. Unrepresented are: 24 James M. Crafts 26 Albert N. Prentiss
25 T. F. Crane 27 Albert S. Wheeler
28 John Stanton Gould

their pictures have since been added, from photographs of the same date as the rest

copyright & license

I FIRST BECAME INTERESTED IN THE CORNELL UNIVERSITY
Archives in the early 1980s through a story in the *Cornell Alumni News*. An interest in Cornell's photographic history soon led to my meeting with Gould Colman, University Archivist; Tom Hickerson, then Chairman of the Department of Manuscripts and University Archives; and Dale Corson, Cornell President Emeritus. We shared a common belief that knowledge of the riches of the university's history was vital for Cornell students, alumni, faculty, and staff. Although Morris Bishop's *History of Cornell* is outstanding and treasured by all, it carries Cornell's history only to the early 1950s. Since this coincided with my own graduation from Cornell, in 1951, I knew well that much had happened at Cornell since then, and that the Cornell University Archives had continued to add valuable, exciting documents, even for the earlier period.

Dale Corson convinced me that I should join him and Cornell Trustee Robert Purcell in supporting archival arrangement and indexing of the papers of recent Cornell presidents, a project that would support the writing of a new history. With this goal in mind, I continued to work closely with the staff of the Archives, including the new University Archivist, Elaine Engst. Through my frequent visits to the library, I became ever more enthusiastic about bringing the Cornell story up to the twenty-first century. Cornell Presidents Dale Corson, Frank Rhodes, and Hunter Rawlings all provided necessary encouragement.

Creating a new history of Cornell has, not surprisingly, proven to be a complex task. That it is finished today has required the talents and dedication of numerous people. Without the enthusiasm of my friends in the University Archives and the support of University Librarians Sarah Thomas and Alain Seznec, this endeavor could have never reached completion. Through Tom and Elaine, I met Carol Kammen, the ideal person to author this work. Carol had been writing books, articles, and newspaper columns about Cornell and the Ithaca region for many years. Additionally, she teaches an undergraduate course on Cornell's history that has generated a spirit of excitement about Cornell among her students. Now she has completed a work that will extend knowledge of this unique history to generations of Cornellians to come. Carol's wonderful work opens with an eloquent foreword from Professor Walter LaFeber, one of Cornell's great historians, and includes brief reflections by Dale Corson, Frank Rhodes, and Hunter Rawlings.

PREAMBLE

Commencement, ca. 1928.

Cornell is so in my blood because my father, Sidney G. Kay, was class of 1922; I was class of 1951; and I have two sons who are Cornellians: my eldest, L. William Kay, III, is from the class of 1974, and my youngest, Henrik L. Werring, from the class of 1991. My wife Brit and all of my children have generously shared, and sometimes graciously endured, my devotion to Cornell and pleasure in my many associations there.

The publication of *Cornell: Glorious to View* coincides with the inauguration of Jeffrey Lehman as Cornell's eleventh president. It is a fitting time to look back to Cornell's origins in the nineteenth century, to reflect on the challenges and achievements of the twentieth, and to look forward to its future in the twenty-first.

L. William Kay, II
October 2003

ALTHOUGH THE UNITED STATES, BORN IN 1776, WAS ONE OF the youngest of countries, its stunning economic development, social pluralism, and political reform made it the first twentieth-century nation. Much the same can be said of Cornell University. It is among the youngest of the world's major universities. As this superb book succinctly reveals, however, Cornell's physical development, openness to cutting-edge research and teaching, and institutionalization of pioneering educational reforms marked it as an initial twentieth-century, and now twenty-first-century, university.

This history is even more astonishing given Cornell's upstate New York location, where isolation is matched by magnificent scenery (which has the cultural equivalent, we learn from one essayist with tongue firmly in cheek, of "five full professors"). Such isolation has, however, been made to work to the university's advantage. For Cornell is not only a campus but, because of its location, a compressed academic hothouse in which the community's students, faculty, and administration necessarily interact to germinate ideas that have shaped world affairs while also shaping and reshaping the relationships within the community itself. The remarkable commitment and generosity of Cornell alumni, who consistently rank at or near the nation's top in terms of both dollar contributions and personal participation in the university's myriad activities, no doubt come in part from the memories of having lived in, and intellectually prospered from, that unique academic hothouse.

In the mid-1990s, the spouse of a Cornell alumnus making her first visit to Ithaca was awed by traveling for miles through rural, Appalachian countryside and then, as she phrased it, "suddenly encountering an Athens," complete with hills, surrounding villages bearing Greek names, and a roaring local democracy. Her remark in part echoed that of the university's third president, Jacob Gould Schurman: Cornell combined "the idealism of ancient Athens with the industrialism of modern America."

When Ezra Cornell uttered his famous claim that he would found an institution where any person could study any subject, both parts of his claim were revolutionary. In 1865 mostly white males inhabited college classrooms, where they largely studied required courses in ancient languages, the humanities, and some basic science. Equally revolutionary was the belief of Cornell, Schurman, and especially the cofounder, Andrew Dickson White, that Athenian humanism and modern

American industrial science and technology did not divide into two cultures, but instead formed two sides of a single mission that aimed to create a nation whose society would be more open and equal as its economy provided ever-greater material benefits.

The history of Cornell, as of increasing parts of the world, has been largely the struggle to keep those two sides in balance, even as industrial and scientific change resembled an out-of-control kaleidoscope. Some of the university's most dangerous moments arose in the 1870s to 1880s, and more recently during the 1950s to 1980s, when it remained committed to upholding the founders' principles in a violently changing world that sometimes tried to destroy openness and pluralism. In the earlier era, one of intense Protestant religious evangelicalism, White and his successors insisted that Cornell be a nonsectarian institution open to those of all religious faiths. In the later era, Cornell's officials successfully protected the faculty against McCarthyism. Not every American university, unfortunately, could claim such success.

The informal motto of Cornell has been "freedom and responsibility," the phrase offered by the distinguished historian, Carl Becker, on the university's seventy-fifth birthday. But in truth, as Carol Kammen's work reveals, a great university's freedom is actually restricted by its responsibilities. And that is where the major tension arises. Being in the world but not wholly of it has been an even more difficult, complex proposition at Cornell and other institutions of higher learning than it can be at a seminary or convent. By definition, intellectuals work on the margins of the society so that they can see it whole and not be trapped in the whirling vortex of the center, but—as Andrew Dickson White and especially Ezra Cornell understood—they nevertheless have to be in that society (the result of being in a publicly supported institution), while contributing to and, if necessary, fundamentally, constructively criticizing it (a responsibility that comes with the privilege of having tenure). Such responsibility runs the gamut, from conducting state agricultural extension work and creating international science laboratories to training responsible citizens and professionals, including public servants. This responsibility is renewed each spring in the laudatory decision to use Commencement not as a platform for a visiting speaker (or to bestow honorary degrees not earned at Cornell), but as a forum for the university's president to give a major speech in which he accounts for his and the campus's activities of the past year.

Carol Kammen tells this story superbly because she has the ideal combination of experience and disciplinary background. A longtime teacher at Cornell who has offered innovative research and writing courses in the History Department, she intimately knows the university, its environment, and its traditions after living nearly four decades in Ithaca. She is also a distinguished, pioneering practitioner in the discipline of local history, perhaps the fastest growing of all historical fields. "One of the nation's leading exponents and instructors in local and community history," as one reviewer described her, she understands that hothouse—the necessarily close relationship between Cornell and the central New York region that has become internationally known for the realization of Ezra Cornell's vision. She comprehends the fascinating complexity of the only American university that has both private, endowed colleges and state-supported colleges while being simultaneously committed to the dual humanistic and science-industrial vision of its founders.

Above all, Carol Kammen understands the enormous tension in this community between freedom and responsibility, and how the former is necessarily besieged by the latter. She quotes an early distinguished alumnus, David Starr Jordan, who declared that the "only tradition of which Cornell was proud was that [it] had no tradition." But she observes that traditions indeed took root: the traditions "of tolerance and freedom of expression—and freedom from the rule of force—would be tested again and again." This is an important, highly revealing account of the tests faced by a university committed to melding into a single mission the advancement of humanistic idealism and modern economic and scientific development.

Walter LaFeber
Andrew Tisch and James Tisch University Professor
Cornell University

THIS BOOK OBSERVES THE DISTINCTION BETWEEN A FLOCK and a bird—appropriately enough for a history of a university with a world-famous Laboratory of Ornithology. Birds have individual histories. A flock has its own history, even as the many individual stories continue on their own. Essentially, this book is the history of the flock.

Parts of the individual stories of Cornell University can be found here. But this book is not just the story of the founders, the faculty, the students, buildings, the curriculum, the athletic program, or other worthy and interesting subjects. This book is about Cornell as a university. The university is a private institution, yet it administers and runs four colleges funded by New York State. It is an undergraduate institution with graduate and professional schools. Its teaching mission is located on farm and field, in laboratory and library, in Ithaca and Arecibo, New York City, Buffalo, Geneva, and even Qatar.

A university is partially the land on which it sits and the buildings in which it functions, and place is important. Cornell's campus is one of the most beautiful anywhere. But its location was also thought to be daunting. When asked about various attractive features of the university he was creating, Ezra Cornell is reported to have said, in effect, Well, wait until you see where we are going to put it! A university is also a state of mind. A university reflects the culture of its time and it boasts of its traditions; at the same time a university is always changing.

Cornell began with no traditions and that became a tradition in itself. But a tradition of democracy of studies and of students, a tradition of freedom of thought, a tradition of inquiry defined this institution even while there were those who said traditions be damned. A university is of the world and out of it; it is a retreat that focuses on the condition of the world and attempts to understand it, and perhaps, if we are lucky, to influence it for the better. A university can be no one thing.

We all owe L. William Kay, II, class of 1951, a great debt for making this project possible, and for having the patience to wait for its completion. It was his vision to have a new history of Cornell. It is my hope that this book will please him. Tom Hickerson, Associate University Librarian, and Elaine Engst, Director of the Rare and Manuscript Collections and University Archivist, asked me to take on this project, wanting a short history that would feature the richness of the Cornell Archives so wonderfully housed in the Carl A. Kroch Library. They have been unfailingly supportive. I have had the most perfect situation in which to work, and

PREFACE

xv

if this volume has taken longer than expected, it might be because I have been so comfortably perched in a study in Kroch Library near all the sources I need, working among people who have been encouraging and helpful. It is a pleasure to say thank you.

My debt to Elaine Engst is great: her understanding of Cornell history and of the collections has been invaluable. I am also very grateful to Susette Newberry, who has been the picture editor for this book, for her knowledge of the vast resources in the Cornell Archives and for selecting the images that appear here. Others from the department have aided me, too. My appreciation goes to Rhea Garen, C. J. Lance-Duboscq, Katherine Reagan, Petrina Jackson, Nancy Dean, Laura Linke, Julia Parker, David Corson, and especially to Cheryl Rowland, whose cheerfulness and knowledge I have relied on and appreciated. Also Ken Baitsholts, Margaret Nichols for her editorial skills, and especially Eileen Keating, who has shared her knowledge of the history of Home Economics and who has aided with numerous problems. Peter Martinez and Bryan Vliet have helped dig me out of the numerous computer problems I managed to create. Librarians are indeed the true friends of historians. My appreciation extends to those who work on the reference desk in Olin Library, who are unfailingly helpful, cheerful, and kind.

I appreciate those who read draft chapters, including Elaine Engst, Michael Kammen, Robert J. Smith, Sally Atwater, Gould Colman, Dale Corson, Joel Silbey, and Walter LaFeber. I benefited from their comments and questions.

There were people all over the university who answered phones, gave out information, and answered questions, often without giving their names. They made tracking down information easy and pleasant. Some of them are Jeri A. Wall of the College of Veterinary Medicine, Pat Avery, Jane MtPleasant, Kathy Alvord, Brenda Bricker, Donald Schnedecker, Esther Baker, Marti Dense, Isaac Kramnick, Michael Busch, Darla McCoy, David Curtis, Tina Snead, Robert Richardson, and most especially David Fontanella, Barbara Krause, and Ann Huntzinger.

Others who helped include Martha Armstrong of the Tompkins County Area Development Agency, Deborah Levin, Ann Reilley, Justin Manzo '03, Deborah Brunner, Lou Robinson, and Sally Atwater, whose advice is always so welcome.

Writing of Cornell, Morris Bishop noted, "The historian is almost bound to be a plagiarist. He is expected to be scrupulous and exact, to tell only what has been securely reported; how, then, can he be blamed for saying precisely what has been said before?" This applies *especially* if those who have gone before are Carl Becker and Morris Bishop, in whose footsteps I humbly follow.

CORNELL

Chapter One

Of her natal day

Cornell began as a university in a country of colleges. Its student body was large from the start when other schools were considerably smaller. Cornell was democratic where others prided themselves on being elite places that educated the sons of the well enough off. Cornell was nonsectarian when most colleges had been founded by one religious denomination or another. Cornell was at the beginning complex, diverse, and somewhat contrary—words that still fit the institution we know today. Some observers have feared that the loss of these qualities would mean that Cornell was slowing down, losing its distinctive edge, that Cornell would no longer be an educational leader. Without these qualities, some say, Cornell would become like other institutions, when in fact, it is the much more the other way around. Looking at universities in the United States today, in a number of key respects we might observe that they look amazingly like Cornell. Yet whether copied or part of academic trends, Cornell remains unique.

Cornell arose from three distinct impulses present at one time. The marvel is that these three generative forces connected in such a way that the result became greater than the separate currents from which it sprang. These origins could be called the governmental, the utilitarian, and the intellectual; their confluence occurred at a time when older ideas about higher education were proving inadequate and restrictive, when a new American educational system was needed to meet the emergence of what we consider modern and scientific. Cornell University provided an early answer to this need and served as a model of what might constitute an academic program and who might qualify to be a student.

Governmental support for education came only slowly, as Cornell's distinguished historian Carl Becker has shown. No federal role in education was specifically noted in the United States Constitution. Although there were schools for learning to read and write, and colleges that taught classical subjects such as mathematics and the ancient languages, no college offered to teach Americans to become more efficient farmers or more clever engineers. The idea of governmental aid to education is often said to have originated with Vermont Sen. Justin S. Morrill, for whom the first federal education act, passed in 1862, was named. Many people before the 1860s, however, had urged state governments to encourage agricultural education. As early as 1819 Simeon DeWitt, the New York State surveyor general and the man who laid claim to 1,400 acres at the headwaters of Cayuga Lake where

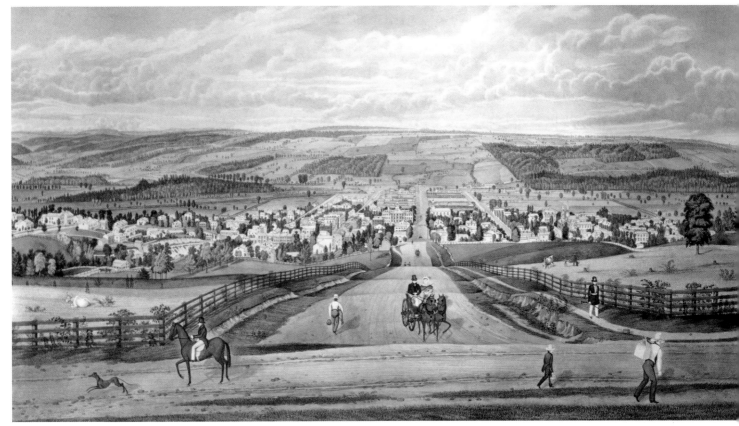

Henry Walton,
"East View of Ithaca,
Tompkins County,
New York," hand-
colored lithograph,
1836.

he created the village of Ithaca, published a tract extolling progressive agricultural training for the children of the wealthy. On his East Hill farm in Ithaca, DeWitt kept a special strain of Merino sheep in the hope of improving his own stock and that of his neighbors. County fairs, too, were as much about agricultural education as they were about hucksters and picnics. By the 1820s, several New York lawmakers had endorsed the idea of teaching the agricultural and mechanical arts, although at the time the state took no action.

The germ of the land grant college idea, according to Becker, can be traced to ideas developed by Jonathan B. Turner of Illinois. In reaction against the classical education available at the colleges of his day, Turner believed the federal government should foster a practical education that would teach the latest principles of agriculture and the mechanic arts—subjects that would be of value to the young men of the expanding nation. Newspapers wrote about the idea, congressmen talked about it, and it picked up traction.

Practical subjects were not the usual stuff of university curricula at mid-century, nor were the young men then in our colleges—and they were almost all men at the time—likely to have been much interested in such earth-bound topics. The origins of the Western university can be found in Roman Catholic schools begun a thousand years ago, and at first the Church dictated what was taught. The universities of Bologna and Paris expanded somewhat, adding other subjects, as did Oxford and Cambridge, founded in England in the twelfth and thirteenth centuries. In the colonies, college founders up to the mid-nineteenth century followed English university patterns, with local variations. This was the mold from which emerged Harvard, William and Mary, Yale, Princeton, Dartmouth, Kings (renamed Columbia), and Queens (later Rutgers). But despite expanding beyond select subjects (by adding surveying, for example) and prescribed ways of teaching, the American college offered a classical curriculum through the first half of the nineteenth century. Education served those with elevated needs—the pious who sought to become preachers, the wealthy who had the time and means to study (but not so much as to cut into their social life or to make it appear that courses and grades mattered). In contrast, the Morrill Land Grant Act of 1862 would create seventeen academic institutions to educate men from all economic backgrounds and meet the needs of a developing nation—an entirely new and utilitarian justification for higher education, and one greeted with some disdain by the older institutions.

The Morrill Act stipulated that money derived from the sale of federal lands should be treated as a perpetual fund whose interest was to be appropriated by each state to support and maintain at least one college whose object was, without excluding other scientific and classical studies, to teach branches of learning related to agriculture and the mechanical arts. To this was added a requirement that these colleges also teach military science, a subject much on the minds of legislators at the time. In 1862, of course, Congress consisted only of members from the northern and western states, whose young men—the intended beneficiaries of

AN ACT DONATING PUBLIC LANDS TO THE SEVERAL STATES AND TERRITORIES WHICH MAY PROVIDE COLLEGES FOR THE BENEFIT OF AGRICULTURE AND THE MECHANIC ARTS

Be it enacted by the Senate and House of Representatives of the United States of America in Congress assembled, That there be granted to the several States, for the purposes hereinafter mentioned, an amount of public land [for] support and maintenance of at least one college where the leading object shall be, without excluding other scientific and classical studies, and including military tactics, to teach such branches of learning as are related to agriculture and mechanic arts, in such manner as the legislatures of the State may respectively prescribe, in order to promote the liberal and practical education of the industrial classes in the several pursuits and professions in life.

—The Morrill Act, July 2, 1862
(U.S. Statutes at Large, Vol. XII, 503)

this act—were by and large engaged in the Civil War. On July 2, 1862, even as the cannons boomed from gunboats on the James River and the Confederates were withdrawing from the Peninsula Campaign, Abraham Lincoln signed the Morrill Land Grant Act into law.

On its own, the Morrill Act only offered opportunity. It required each state to accept its terms and provide for implementation. It required, above all, vision and will. The source of the funding was federal land. This plan worked well in Ohio, Indiana, Illinois, Michigan, Wisconsin, and states west of the Mississippi River carved from the Louisiana Purchase—places where the land belonged to the federal government, which allocated acres to veterans and encouraged settlement. Despite homesteading, however, some tracts of land had remained in the government's hands. These parcels neither generated tax monies nor, more importantly, enlarged the population—necessary if a state was to increase its power in Congress. The offer made by the Morrill Act was enticing—colleges were believed to attract settlers, something that interested all frontier states—but in 1862, land prices were low, an acre sometimes selling for as little as 53 cents. Even as late as 1869 Ezra Cornell was warned by a land broker in the Midwest that the "demand for [land] Script is so very light I cannot make you a good offer for cash." There was a glut of land out west, and the country was at war.

New York, on the other hand, had no federal land. New York had begun as a royal colony, claiming as its own all the land within its borders. Following the Revolutionary War, New York held meetings with Connecticut, Vermont, and Pennsylvania to settle contested state lines, and it treated with the few thousand Iroquois who remained within the state, finally restricting them to reservation areas. The act therefore provided that New York be given access to federal land in another state. In our governmental system, however, one sovereign state may not hold land in another, so the federal government gave New York the right to sell scrip to individuals who would locate, survey, and sell land in other states, the proceeds of those sales to be used to fund practical education as outlined in the Morrill Act. This bypassed the problem of state ownership of land but necessitated a person or persons with enough money to buy the scrip to make the scheme work. The state, for its part, would receive approximately 60 cents for each acre, and the resale of the scrip would benefit education—all without the state having to spend any of its own funds. Those states with ample federal land, such as Wisconsin, also welcomed this aspect of the Morrill Act because it put more of their federal land up for sale; future settlement would increase the population and consequently the state's power in Washington.

It was the population of each state that determined the amount of land that the state would receive. As the most populous state in the Union in 1862, New York received the most land. On May 5, 1863, the Senate and Assembly of the State of New York enacted legislation to accept and implement the Morrill Land Grant Act.

The state Senate designated that the proceeds from the sale of its scrip support the People's College in Havana, now Montour Falls, an institution sponsored by Sen. Charles Cook. The People's College had a handful of tutors and a stone building standing ready; what students it might have had, however, were at war. According to the conditions imposed by the state, within three years of receiving the Morrill designation, the trustees of the People's College were to hire ten competent professors to give instruction in agriculture, the mechanic arts, and military tactics, and to have adequate land and buildings to accommodate 250 students, with a library, a farm of at least 200 acres with farm buildings, implements and stock, and suitable shops, tools, machinery, and other arrangements. All this was to be owned by the college free and clear of debt. The state's regents would make an unannounced inspection to see that the conditions had been met.

In 1864, the New York State Comptroller acknowledged receipt of 6,187 pieces of scrip, each for 160 acres, making a total of 989,920 acres. This was 80 acres shy of the 990,000 due to New York according to the terms of the land grant. Morris Bishop, Cornell's historian, did not understand where the missing acres went, nor do I; we must chalk the discrepancy up to the vagaries of the federal government.

———

The second force that led to the creation of Cornell University was Ezra Cornell, an unlikely man to become the founder of a university. Cornell was born in 1807 to Quaker parents, in Westchester Landing, New York. The family moved about— to New Jersey, then back to Westchester, finally on to DeRuyter, in Cortland County. They were, like most Americans at the time, in search of prosperity, which remained elusive. Ezra attended school sporadically, going to classes for two or three years from late October to the end of March. His book learning was limited but he excelled at understanding the nature of mechanical devices and construction. As the eldest son, he assumed responsibilities for the family, and in 1826, with nine dollars in his pocket, he set out to make his fortune, walking first to Syracuse, where he found work but was robbed of his wages, then on to Homer to live with relatives. In 1828, Ezra made his way to Ithaca, where he found work as a carpenter, then as a mill worker, at which time he acquired the nickname Plaster Cornell,

Ezra Cornell,
chalk drawing after
a daguerreotype,
ca. 1845.

because of the wheat dust that clung to his clothing. He also met Mary Ann Wood of Dryden, who became his wife.

As their Ithaca family grew, Ezra worked at Colonel Beebe's mill, tended store, farmed a bit, tinkered, sold plow franchises in Maine and Georgia, and because he was in the right place at what ended up being the right time, found himself involved in the developing telegraph industry. Cornell learned what he could about the new technology, took chances, and acquired the rights to short telegraph lines, which seemed doomed to failure because of his lack of funds. Just when reasonable men would have given up, Cornell held on, only to emerge with locations central to the creation of a national telegraph company. After years of juggling payments, struggling with untrustworthy business partners, and facing debt and impending ruin, Ezra Cornell emerged—mostly because he was in the way—as a partner in the newly created Western Union Company. Within a short time he had a fortune at his disposal.

It is at this point that Ezra Cornell veered from the pattern of other nineteenth-century self-made or newly rich men. With money beyond most men's dreams, Ezra Cornell did something unusual, something unexpected. With an annual income of many thousands of dollars, at a time when laborers earned but a dollar a day, Cornell counted his money and set out to do with it "the most good."

In a bound book that young Ezra had begun in 1823 as a mode of self-education in mathematical principles, where he had written out his multiplication tables, figured the mysteries of compound interest, and copied questions of volume, fractions, and profit, he made several notations of significance. In 1860 he picked up his Cyphering Book and under the heading "Loss & Gain" summarized his personal battle against debt, noting that the credit side seemed to have triumphed.

In 1861 the citizens of Tompkins County elected Ezra Cornell to serve a two-year term in the New York State Assembly, followed by two terms in the Senate. At the same time, as president of the New York State Agricultural Society, he joined the board of trustees of an agricultural college in Ovid, Seneca County, overlooking Seneca Lake. The school was to be called the New York State Agricultural College; it was sometimes known as the Ovid Agricultural College.

On August 29, 1864, Ezra Cornell made another entry in his Cyphering Book, noting that he now expected an income in excess of one hundred thousand dollars. "My greatest care," he wrote, "is how to spend this Large income, to do the most good to those who are properly dependent on [me]—to the poor and to posterity."

Ezra Cornell's first act of philanthropy was to endow a free public library in Ithaca for the citizens of Tompkins County. This was, at the time, an extraordinary gift because where there were libraries at all, most were private; membership was by invitation, and annual fees of ten dollars or more put them beyond the means of most working people. Cornell's library was to be free and open to all residents of Tompkins County. On the board of the Cornell Library were members of the local clergy and some businessmen. The building Cornell erected was large enough that the rents were thought to be enough to maintain the library.

We now have two of the elements in place: in addition to the Morrill Land Grant Act, there was also Ezra Cornell, a wealthy man desiring to do good. Had only these two—that is, government money and a philanthropist interested in useful education—come together without the third, they might have created a satisfactory, even a good, practical college—which is what Cornell and other members of the board of the nascent agricultural college probably had in mind.

THE CYPHERING BOOK
LOSS & GAIN
. . . .

In 1844, there was a balance perhaps of a couple thousand dollars on the cr side. In 1854 the contest was a doubtful one, and a debt with which I was then incumbered amounting to $50,000 would probably have swept the board if the game had been stoped at that period, but the contest has been continued, with increasing success for the side of gain and at the present period Feb. 1, 1860, that mountain of debt has mostly been paid at the rate of 100 cents on a dollar with 7 per ct interest added, and a yearly income of $15,000, seems to be a reliable guarenty that the cr. Side, has won the victory.

Forest Park Ithaca, Tompkins Co. N.Y.
February 1, 1860
Ezra Cornell

That something so much greater emerged from this opportunity is one of the accidents of history, enough to cause one to wonder about that which is not planned, about that which happens because of circumstances. In this case, the unforeseen was that the Cornell Library in Ithaca, as a corporation, needed the approval of the state, and so the library charter was sent off to Albany for review. The bill for the Cornell Library landed on the desk of the chairman of the Literature Committee, whose purview was education. The committee's chairman, Sen. Andrew Dickson White, was impressed with Cornell's generosity and his vision in creating a library for the citizens of Tompkins County. He was less pleased to learn, after asking about the Ithaca philanthropist, that Cornell proposed splitting the Morrill Land

Grant funds between the People's College of Havana and the Agricultural College in Ovid.

In 1862 Andrew Dickson White was a young man of thirty. He had been born in Homer, and then his prosperous family moved to Syracuse, where he grew up. His passion was for books; that he would attend college was never in question. His father's choice was Hobart College in Geneva, but there, Andrew railed against what he considered inferior instruction and excessive reliance on religiosity as prescribed by the Episcopal Church. He also disapproved of his fellow students, who were more rambunctious than studious. Young Andrew, with the aid of his mother, wheedled his way from Geneva to New Haven.

Yale College proved only marginally better than Hobart, however, and upon graduation White headed for Europe—first Paris, then to Germany, where new ideas about education had aroused considerable excitement. White was in his element. When he completed his postgraduate studies, he returned to New Haven, where the college offered him a teaching position. He had heard of a western experimental college, however, and thinking Yale no place for innovation, went to Ann Arbor in 1860 to teach history at the University of Michigan. This experience, on top of his European travels and study, suited him well. He lectured on modern European history, attracted a student following, and developed innovative ideas about higher education.

White mused about what a great university might aspire to be, envisioning "distinguished professors in every field, with libraries as rich as the Bodleian, halls as lordly as that of Christ Church or of Trinity, chapels as inspiring as that of King's, towers as dignified as those of Magdalen and Merton, quadrangles as beautiful as those of Jesus and St. John's." White would place this model institution in central New York, where it would become a "university worthy of the commonwealth and of the nation." This dream, he acknowledged, "became a sort of obsession." He thought of his university with "professors in the great modern literatures—above all, in our own; there should also be a professor of modern history and a lecturer on architecture." White insisted that "my university should be under control of no single religious organization; it should be free from all sectarian or party trammels; in electing its trustees and professors no questions should be asked as to their belief or their attachment to this or that sect or party."

In 1862 Andrew Dickson White's father died, and he returned to Syracuse to take over the family business and care for his mother. Now wealthy in his own right, White was desirous of creating a great work for himself. He was also newly elected to the New York State Senate. Writing to abolitionist and philanthropist

Gerrit Smith, White outlined ideas that echo his early dreams of a great university and prefigure his later thinking about education. He wanted to create a university that would "welcome all, regardless of color or sex," a school that would provide an education for the public good rather than for commercial gain, and would encourage scientific exploration. It would be nonsectarian and would focus on living languages and literature. "My soul is in this," he acknowledged.

White's ideas were revolutionary; his university was unlike any institution in existence in the United States in 1862. He envisioned a school where the "current of mercantile morality wh[ich] has so long swept through this land" would be countered; where the "current of military passion" would be restrained and tempered; a place that would be an "asylum for Science—where truth shall be sought for the truth's sake, where it shall not be the main purpose of the Faculty to stretch or cut science exactly to fit 'Revealed Religion.'" It would be a center for the "new Literature—not graceful and indifferent to wrong but earnest;—nerved and armed to battle for the right." White's university would offer instruction in moral philosophy, history and political economy "unwarped to suit present abuses in Politics and Religion"; its legal training would ensure that "Legality shall not crush Humanity." It would be a place "around which liberally minded men of learning,—men scattered throughout the land—comparatively purposeless and powerless,—could cluster,—making this institution a center from wh[ich] ideas and men shall go forth to bless the nation during the ages."

Gerrit Smith, while interested, did not offer aid. White, estimating that on his own he had only enough money to endow the library, returned to the business at hand in Syracuse and Albany. His ideas, however, would soon reappear to great effect when he considered what New York might do with the funds from the Morrill Land Grant Act—and when he encountered Ezra Cornell in the state Senate.

In his *Autobiography,* White recalled the older man's dilemma. Cornell had told him that he had "about half a million dollars more than my family will need." He asked White, "what is the best thing I can do with it for the State?"

"In our country," White responded, "the charities appeal to everybody. Any one can understand the importance of them." Education, however, presented a different case. In his opinion, "the best thing you can do with [your fortune] is to establish or strengthen some institution for higher instruction." He said that the needs of a large and great institution were greater than what the state would be able to fund; "that such a college or university worthy of the State would require far more in the way of faculty and equipment than most men supposed; that the time had come when scientific and technical education must be provided for in such an institution; and that education in history and literature should be the bloom of the whole growth."

What seems inevitable to us today, because we know the outcome, was then far from certain. For a moment in time, these three forces were still not united in purpose, nor had they even met the formidable obstacles they would have to overcome. And the People's College, with the blessing of the state legislators, had time on its side.

———

When the state designated the People's College in Havana as New York's land grant university, the school's wealthy and influential sponsor was State Sen. Charles Cook. Once the state's conditions were met, the remainder of the land scrip would be turned over to him. Fate intervened, however, and Cook was felled by a stroke. Plans for his college hung suspended; months and then years passed. Then in 1865, the time granted by the legislature was about to run out.

Second in the running for the Morrill Land Grant funds was the New York State Agricultural College in Ovid, enthusiastically supported by State Senator Folger and the State Agricultural Society, on whose board of trustees Ezra Cornell served. The trustees had erected a stone building overlooking Seneca Lake in anticipation of the return of students and faculty from the war. In Albany, each time Cornell or Folger attempted to enter a bill suggesting that the land grant monies be split between the Havana and Ovid schools, Senator White stepped in to block the effort. Still, Cornell took the idea to the Agricultural Society meeting in Rochester in February 1864, and with the college floundering, Ezra Cornell suggested that if the trustees could obtain half of the Morrill grant, he would donate enough money to make up the entire sum. There must have been a moment of stunned silence in the room, followed by murmurs of astonishment and appreciation. The Agricultural College appeared close to becoming a reality. In Albany, however, when Cornell proposed that the land grant be split between the two schools, White blocked his bill.

Consider Andrew White, listening to Cornell's generous proposal but refusing even under those fortunate conditions to allow a division of the land grant money. On no account, he said, should the funds be divided, for the needs of higher education in the State of New York required concentration. There had been a scattering of resources, he argued, and there were already more than twenty colleges in the state. Yet not one of them, he insisted, was "doing anything which could justly be called university work."

White, in his own words, "persisted in my refusal to sanction any bill dividing the fund, declared myself now more opposed to such a division than ever; but promised that if Mr. Cornell and his friends would ask for the *whole* grant—keeping it together, and adding his three hundred thousand dollars, as proposed—I would support such a bill with all my might." Senator Folger, in whose Seneca County district the Agricultural College was located, saw his plum about to slip away. He would have to be appeased.

In Albany, White and Cornell conferred. White must have suggested Syracuse as a suitable location, but Cornell did not have fond memories of that city, where as a young man he been robbed not once but twice. Later, Ezra Cornell countered with his own proposal. If you will locate the college at Ithaca, he said, "I will give you for that object a farm of three hundred acres of first quality land, desirably located, overlooking the village of Ithaca and Cayuga Lake, and within ten minutes' walk of the Cornell Library, the churches, the railroad station, and steamboat landing." He promised to erect suitable buildings for the use of the college and to give an additional sum of money—"on condition," he added, "that the legislature will endow the college with at least thirty thousand dollars" a year, thereby placing the

Andrew Dickson White,
albumen print photo-
graph, ca. 1865.

Ezra Cornell, albumen
print photograph,
ca. 1865.

college upon a "firm and substantial basis, which shall be a guarantee of its future prosperity and usefulness, and give the farmers' sons of New York an institution worthy of the Empire State."

But nothing happened, for the legislature had given the People's College an additional three months to meet the state's requirements. Then, proving that the course of history is often shaped by serendipity, Dr. Sylvester Willard, long an advocate of compassionate care for the insane, arrived in Albany to plead their cause. Mid-speech, Willard died. Young Senator White thereupon demanded that a memorial to Willard in the form of a hospital for the insane be located in Seneca County, giving Senator Folger solace and making him an ally. He then suggested that the Morrill land grant scrip be allocated to a new university, to be sited on Ezra Cornell's farm in Ithaca.

Speaking to the Senate in March 1865, White insisted that his bill to charter the land grant university in Ithaca would be "the most important of the session. . . . I know of none which so demands earnestness in thought and promptness in action." The university bill, he pointed out, privileged no single person but promoted the highest interests of the state. It was a bill not for the present only, but for all time, as it would meet the "wants of our children and of our children's children. From our action on this bill shall go forth influences to help or hurt what is best in this state for centuries." There was more. The university would "bring modern science to bear upon those two great sources of State wealth—Agriculture and the Mechanic Arts"; it would "energize our noble system of public instruction," which was at the heart of the undertaking. Finally, White played his trump card: the university bill needed no tax monies. "Not a dollar is asked from the treasury," he pointed out, for "the fund already exists, and on a scale commensurate with the great interest it is to serve. Thanks to the wise policy of the government of the United States, you have a gift of lands worth a million; thanks to the patriotism of one"—Ezra Cornell—"you are offered half a million more." The question, he posed to the senators, was "shall we accept these gifts?" How could they not?

It was in this Senate speech that White proposed to honor Sylvester Willard, noting that the buildings standing ready in Ovid could be appropriately used, for "the state to-day needs a place for the blind asylum, and the asylum for the incurably insane." Placing one or both of these on the old Agricultural College property would save the state "tens of thousands of dollars" in building costs and would, more importantly, "save the reputation of the state for humanity." This Senate, White pointed out, had "resounded for two years with complaints against the blind asylum in its present position, and Willard's report shows that the condition of the incurably insane in the alms houses of our state would disgrace Dahomey." Could the senators act less nobly, he asked, "than those who have gone before us?"

White later wrote that there were three points he had endeavored to impress upon the Senate. The first was that "as regards primary education, the policy of the State should be diffusion of resources," while it should be, "as regards university education, concentration of resources." The second was that the existing sectarian colleges could not do the work required to qualify for the Morrill funds, and the third, that "any institution for high education in the State must form an integral part of the whole system of public instruction." And here was the nucleus of White's plan, for he saw the university integrated and having a "living connection" with the state public school system, and suggested that state scholarships be created, one for each of the 128 Assembly districts, to be awarded to the best scholars in the public schools, entitling the holders to free instruction for four years. The university and the schools would be "bound closely together by the constant and living tie of five hundred and twelve students."

George S. Batchellor, an Albany official sitting in the Senate that day, was impressed by Ezra Cornell and by the young senator "who during those early struggles stood courageously by the side of his elder colleague, displaying at all times . . . skill and energy." It was White, insisted Batchellor, who "did all the literary work, who directed all the legislation." And so it must have been.

Yet it was not easy: barbs came from a number of sources, and it soon became necessary for Ezra Cornell to defend himself and the new university he was endowing. The founder of the People's College, Charles Cook, his lawyer speaking on his behalf, grumbled more than others. They complained that what was being planned for Ithaca was an elite university. Cornell was shocked. He laid out his lineage as the son of mechanics and farmers, noting that these were the occupations and status even of his sisters' husbands! "I have no relation," he explained, "of any degree within my knowledge who is or has been a lawyer, physician, Minister of the Gospel, merchant, politician, office holder, gentleman loafer or common idler." Indeed, he went on, "None who have been drunkards or recipients of charity. All have procured an honest and compleat support for their families by *productive labor,* none but myself have acquired anything like a fortune, and mine is placed at the disposal of the industrial classes." Who, Cornell asked, could be more thoroughly identified with the industrial, laboring, and productive classes than I? Further, he declared, "I find the only two institutions in the state which were organized on the basis of educating the industrial classes, failures, from the want of adequate means, and from other causes, which in my judgment render it unwise to attempt to rear the desired edifice on their foundation."

Never has a man had such trouble trying to give away a fortune. With some weariness, Ezra Cornell wrote to his eldest son Alonzo in February 1865 that the "College matter looks more hopeful, but I shall not go into fits to induce the state to accept 500,000 of my money."

The name of the university was another issue. White simply states that Cornell had urged "Ithaca." The suggestion of Cornell University, said White, "was mine. He at first doubted the policy of it; but, on my insisting that it was in accordance with time-honored American usage, as shown by the names of Harvard, Yale, Dartmouth, Amherst, Bowdoin, Brown, Williams, and the like, he yielded."

***

On April 27, 1865, the legislature passed "An Act to establish the Cornell University, and to appropriate to it the income of the sale of public lands granted to this State by Congress." The act's first three sections created the university, called for a board of trustees, and located the campus on Ezra Cornell's Ithaca farm.

The fourth section established the educational aims of the university: it would be responsible for teaching branches of learning related to agriculture and the mechanical arts, including military tactics, "in order to promote the liberal and practical education of the industrial classes in the several pursuits and professions in life." Other branches of science and knowledge "may be embraced in the plan of instruction and investigation pertaining to the university as the trustees may deem useful and proper." This is crucial to remember because deviations from the prescribed curriculum are justified by this section: thus journalism, forestry, music, and other unconventional courses of study were added to the offerings as years went by, and later domestic science, hotel administration, and labor relations. In addition, the charter states that "persons of every religious denomination, or of no religious denomination, shall be equally eligible to all offices and appointments."

The fifth section of the charter defined Cornell University as an educational institution with limited holdings "not to exceed three millions of dollars in the aggregate." This provision would later come back to haunt the young institution. At the time, however, three million was the sum mentioned in the charter of other universities, and who then could have envisioned any school having or receiving or even needing more?

The sixth section dealt with revenue from the Morrill Land Grant Act, appropriating it to Cornell University but stipulating that it was necessary for Ezra Cornell

Of all these recent munificent gifts, the most princely is that of Ezra Cornell, a citizen of Ithaca, who has offered to the State of New York more than half a million dollars, and about two hundred acres of land, to aid in the establishment of a university. Such generosity in the lifetime of the giver is almost unexampled. It surpasses the bequests of Astor and Smithson, and if it falls below the endowment of Girard, the terms of the gift are wiser and more liberal. . . .

The new university we presume will not be fettered by precedents, but will mark out for itself a new path, enlightened by the past but adapted to the present. In such a course there are great dangers, but also great advantages. The question is yet to be determined whether, in a higher seminary, the study of natural science, of modern languages, of history, and of political philosophy, may not lead to high intellectual culture, particularly fitted for American life.

The question often arises whether the city or the country is the place for the university. Experience shows that learning flourishes alike in the mart and in the field. In a metropolis like New York or Philadelphia or Boston, libraries and scientific collections, and art and eloquence abound. A country town like Ithaca can offer no such attractions. But quiet hours of study and reflection, simple modes of life, the wholesome and refreshing influences of good scenery, and moderate expenses, seem to be more than a balance for the advantages of a city.

. . . Let first-rate teachers be first secured. Let no expense be spared to secure the highest educational ability which the country will afford. Then, as the scholars assemble, as the courses and plans of the university are developed, let such buildings go up as will best provide for the wants which have been created.

—The Nation, July 13, 1865, 44–45

to first deposit, free and without restriction, five hundred thousand dollars to which he and his heirs maintained no expectation of repayment. Here, too, was mentioned the sum of twenty-five thousand dollars, which Ezra Cornell was to pay to the Genesee College of Lima, New York, as part of the horse-trading involved in getting the charter through the legislature. The seventh provision of the charter spelled out what Cornell University needed to do to become New York's land grant institution, listing the buildings, fixtures, and arrangements to be made within two years and that an inspection by the state's regents should be expected. These were substantially the same provisions that the People's College had been expected to meet.

Financial considerations were addressed in the eighth provision, and in the ninth, the charter stipulated that the university was to be open at the lowest rates to students without distinction of "rank, class, previous occupation or locality," and that it was to accept one student per state Assembly district free of tuition, awarded for superior ability.

The tenth provision confirmed that there would be payments from the state; the eleventh that the charter when approved was to be "deemed the law, and shall prevail" whenever there might be a conflict in the various laws that pertain to the university. In the twelfth, the legislature gave itself authority to "at any time alter, or repeal this act," and the last provided that the "act shall take effect immediately." Yet this charter would only go into effect provided the People's College did not fulfill its obligations as the Morrill land grant designee, for the three months' extension had not yet expired.

But they were confident, and two days later, at Geological Hall in Albany, the Board of Trustees held its first meeting. Present were Governor Reuben E. Fenton, William Kelly, Horace Greeley, Josiah B. Williams, George W. Schuyler, J. Meredith Read, Francis Miles Finch, William Andrus, Victor M. Rice, and Ezra Cornell. Of this group, Williams, Schuyler, Finch, and Andrus were Ithaca men, along with Cornell himself. Kelly was appointed chairman, and Rice, secretary. Ezra Cornell, still stinging from the charge of elitism, described the trustees as being "three mechanics,—three farmers—one manufacturer—one merchant—one lawyer, one engineer—and one literary gentleman." That was Horace Greeley, the New York City editor and friend of reform. There were, in addition, trustees representing the state government, the common schools, the State Agricultural Society, the County of Tompkins through its public librarian—and the Cornell family. "Can the industrial classes of the State select a board of trustees more likely to protect and foster its interests than the one here selected? I think not," Cornell wrote.

The first business of this newly convened board was to accept the land scrip and elect seven additional trustees. It then set in motion the new university. Cornell was to manage the land scrip to create the financial foundation of the university. White would build the superstructure; he was designated chairman of the committee to design the university, but he was not yet its president. They were poised to begin.

For the next three months the Cornell trustees waited for the People's College's time to expire. When the extension ended on July 27, Ezra Cornell deposited a bond for five hundred thousand dollars with the New York State Comptroller. In addition, as Morris Bishop noted, Cornell dipped his pen into gall and paid Genesee College twenty-five thousand dollars to establish, at that school, a professorship of Agriculture "and for no other purpose whatsoever." For his part, Ezra Cornell noted that he had "just Endowed the Cornell University with the sum of $500,000, and paid to the Genesee College at Lima my $25,000 for the privilege of endowing the University as above. Such is the influence of corrupt Legislation." The university did not have to suffer the effects of corruption long, however, for sixteen months later, in March 1867, with buildings beginning to rise on East Hill, the state legislature passed "An Act to refund to the Cornell University the amount paid by Ezra Cornell to the Genesee College at Lima."

To his wife Mary Ann, Ezra Cornell wrote that the "destiny of the Cornell University was fixed, and that its ultimate endowment would be ample for the vast field of labor it embraces, and if properly organized for the development of truth, industry, and frugality it will become a power in the land which will control and mold the future of this great state." The man who had spent most of his adult life in straitened circumstances, who had been deeply in debt with little hope of gain, knew at that moment that he was doing a great and good thing.

———

There was much to do before opening day. The campus needed to be laid out, buildings designed and erected, contracts let, supplies located, courses decided upon, and men found to teach them. First, however, it was Andrew Dickson White's task to design a university. Although this was something he had long considered, it was one thing to contemplate an ideal university on paper and quite another to erect a real one with buildings, a faculty, and students.

From the start, White's vision of the university was broad; his thinking expanded well beyond the requirements of the Morrill Land Grant Act. As Ezra Cornell wrote, "the enterprise expands from an Agricultural College to a university of the first magnitude-such as we have to go to Europe now to find." George S. Batchellor, hoping to see White receive due credit for his monumental efforts in creating the university, wrote in the 1880s that White's "pen traced the present motto as the language of Ezra Cornell." Morris Bishop was more blunt: "White liked to improve, for publication, the utterances of his rude companions." Probably, Bishop suggests, "Cornell actually said something like: 'I'd like to start a school where anybody can study anything he's a mind to.'" But Ezra Cornell, ever the democrat and a graceful writer himself, most probably wrote "I would found a university where any person can find instruction in any study," while White, despite his desire that the university provide a broad education, is unlikely to have said such an impractical thing. Rather than "any person," his expectation was that students would be scholars.

On October 21, 1866, White published the *Report of the Committee on Organization,* a distillation of his ideas about the new university. It contains an explanation of what courses would be offered, how the faculty would be recruited, and the means by which the university would be governed.

The faculty would be divided into colleges, or what we would today call departments. There were colleges of agriculture, chemistry and physics, history and political science, languages, literature and philosophy, mathematics and engineering, mechanical arts, natural science, and military science. It is a wonder that so much was to be attempted at the outset and that on this list were subjects not routinely taught elsewhere in 1868. From that original list of courses emerged the modern university that we know. Not seamlessly, of course, for at the time some subjects could not have been envisioned, and others (such as journalism and pharmacy) were attempted but soon abandoned as being too vocational or not of sufficient interest to students. Nevertheless, White's initial plan established a broad path for the university to follow. In the years after 1868, a course would be offered and appear in the annual register because a professor chose to teach it, or because of students' demands for instruction in a particular subject, or because funds were available. In addition, some of the early book collections purchased by Ezra Cornell, often at White's urging, developed as areas of specialization for which the university became known. White, for his part, clearly recognized the interdisciplinary nature of academic work and called on each professor to fulfill more than the duties of a single department. His earlier educational experiences prompted him to be sure that Cornell offered a broad range of subjects as well as teaching methods. He wrote of university professors in Europe who lectured "to large bodies of attentive students on the most interesting and instructive periods of human history, [which] aroused in me a new current of ideas. Why not help the beginnings of this system in the United States?" He complained that he had "long deplored the rhetorical fustian and oratorical tall-talk which so greatly afflict our country, and which had been, to a considerable extent, cultivated in our colleges and universities." He wanted something better—a faculty that would teach with "clean, clear, straightforward statement and illustration." For this, he hoped to locate "clear-headed, clear-voiced, earnest, and honest" men.

To this resident faculty he planned to add nonresident professors—admirable men, known both as scholars and as lecturers. Men of such stature, of course, were beyond the means of the new school to attract on a permanent basis, but some might be persuaded to visit. "I was influenced," he said, "by the desire to prevent the atmosphere of the university becoming simply and purely that of a scientific and technical school. Highly as I prized the scientific spirit and technical training, I felt that the frame of mind engendered by them should be modified by an acquaintance with the best literature as literature."

In hindsight, Andrew Dickson White's progression from state senator to university president appears preordained. Quite likely his appointment was in Ezra Cornell's mind the entire time, but he kept his thoughts to himself while White recommended one able scholar after another to take the helm of the new university. It seems clear, however, that White wanted the position, and there was no question that he would accept when it was offered. Later he wrote that "although my formal election to the university presidency did not take place until 1867, the duties implied by that office had already been discharged by me during two years." There is a discrepancy here, for the university dates White's presidency to 1866. Both dates are actually correct. White was elected president of the faculty, meaning of the university, at the meeting of the Board of Trustees on November 21, 1866, after which he was referred to in the minutes as President White. Although he dated his official start as president to January 1867, he stressed that he had acted as president even without the title since 1865, when the Cornell Charter passed the Senate in Albany.

White's ideas were bold and innovative, drawing attacks on the school that came quickly and from many quarters. Ezra Cornell, too, prompted criticism for his acts of generosity, which few could believe was without some hidden motive for personal gain. The rumble of discontent concerning the disposition of the land grant scrip could be heard from one end of the state to the other. In October 1868, as the university celebrated its opening, there came from the Rochester *Daily Union and Advertiser* a long and particularly nasty salvo. It was inconceivable to many, carped the newspaper, that a man with so much money would fail to secure a goodly portion of it for himself and his family: he must be up to no good. Regarding the legislation to finance the Cornell endowment, the writer complained, "These amendments are intended to cover up and perpetuate by their incorporation into the organic law one of the most stupendous jobs ever 'put up' against the rights of the agricultural and mechanical population of the state." The funds rightfully belong to the people of the state, hectored the newspaper, but they had been "wrested from them and put into the hands and management of Ezra Cornell, the founder of the Cornell University, by legislation as rotten as the worst that ever disgraced the State." Harsh words indeed.

The attack went on: Cornell had bought off the railroad interest to gain support for the university; the university charter contained a provision that the eldest male descendant of Ezra Cornell be a trustee "no matter what may be his moral character or the quality of his intellect"; and so forth. The crux of the complaint was that such a man as Cornell could hardly be interested in the idea of the university but was using it to gain control of "twenty-five or thirty millions of dollars in the future management of these lands."

Ezra Cornell responded patiently, answering each charge and attempting to be reasonable, though by the end his tolerance was clearly running thin. "This whole transaction is so plain and simple in its nature," he insisted, "that it surprises me to find it misunderstood by anybody." To the amazement of many, and the open admiration of quite a few, Cornell weathered the slings and arrows that came his way with greater calm than might have been expected.

Other critics acidly observed that the president of Cornell University was not required to be a member of the clergy, and that the university itself would not be allied with a sect or denomination. Oxford and Cambridge, on which America's colonial colleges had been patterned, were affiliated with the Church of England, and professors and students alike were expected to be communicants; nonconformists were thereby excluded, as they were from most public offices throughout the realm. From the very start, colleges and universities in the colonies and then in the United States had—with the exception of the University of Pennsylvania—a denominational affiliation, to attract those of a particular faith and to produce preachers for its churches. Cornell University, however, boldly asserted that among its special characteristics, as advertised in its annual register, was its nonsectarian character. Although the university's principal aim was to "promote Christian civilization," it had been established by a government that recognized no distinction in religious belief, and by citizens who held many different views. The State of New York operated under the same standard; its own public school system was open to boys and girls without prejudice or preference to any denominational affiliation. It would be false, insisted university officials, to "seek or promote any creed or to exclude any." The Cornell charter ensured that no trustee, professor or student would be accepted or rejected on account of any religious or political opinions that he may or may not hold.

While recruiting professors for Cornell, White encountered a candidate from Harvard who had glowing testimonials. An eminent bishop, however, "felt it his duty to warn me that the young man was a Unitarian." This incensed White, who wrote to the bishop that "the only question with me was as to the moral and intellectual qualifications of the candidate; and that if these were superior to those of other candidates, I would nominate him to the trustees even if he were a Buddhist."

THE COMMITTEE TO WHICH WAS REFERRED THE PROPOSAL OF CERTAIN GENTLEMEN IN THE CITY OF NEW YORK TO BUILD AND ENDOW A THEOLOGICAL SEMINARY IN THE VILLAGE OF ITHACA TO BE CONNECTED WITH THE CORNELL UNIVERSITY

REPORT

That Theology as usually understood, is human philosophy applied to revealed religion, and that this philosophy has never yet been so fully perfected as to account for all the phenomena of man's spiritual history or to be consistent with itself.

All history and all experience shows that the promulgators and adherents of religious philosophies have never yet been able to hold and propagate their opinions with the same spirit of amity and good will which characterizes the adherents of other branches of philosophy, but on the contrary its tendency has been to engender strife without [illeg.] the purity of heart or the beauty of daily life and conversation, which revealed religion without the philosophy, has contributed so many striking examples of.

. . . Since there is no generally opposed system of Theology extant, if an institution for teaching it should be established, it must necessarily be devoted to some Sectarian guidance, Your Committee earnestly recommend to the Board to avoid what they consider a very great evil and rigidly confine the religious teaching of the University to that which is imparted through its chair of Christian Ethics.

Your committee therefore recommend that the board should respectfully decline the proposals that have been made to them for the foundation of a Theological Seminary in connection with the University.

—Minutes of the Board of Trustees meeting, 1866

In response, the bishop questioned whether "laymen had any right to teach at all, since the command to teach was given to the apostles and their successors, and seemed therefore confined to those who had received holy orders."

The charges concerning Cornell University's nonsectarian nature persisted. The attacks "on our unchristian character are venomous," noted White. In 1869, Willard Fiske, Cornell's first librarian and White's boyhood friend, advised him not to "bother answering the clerics. They will, like editors, wilt." The press sputtered in outrage that at Cornell even atheists could become professors, that President White was not a member of a church, and that the university was peopled with nonbelievers.

In response, President White issued a pamphlet entitled *The Cornell University: What It Is and What It Is Not,* in which he wrote, "any institution under denominational control inevitably tends to make allegiance to its own form of belief a leading qualification. It may become a tolerably good denominational college, like the hundreds already keeping down the standard of American education, but it can become nothing more." So common were the complaints about Cornell that the "cry of 'infidel' is ceasing to scare, the claim of 'sound learning' and 'safe' instruction is ceasing to allure . . . As to 'sound' learning and 'safe' instruction, it has well-nigh killed the great majority of colleges which have boasted it."Amid all the commotion, Andrew Dickson White worked on the organization of the university and created his ideal institution on the foundation stipulated by the regulations of the Morrill Land Grant Act. Ezra Cornell, meanwhile, kept up with his business interests, including the progress of Western Union, a proposed railroad from Elmira to Ithaca, and a telegraph line out of Philadelphia. And he engaged in extensive correspondence, exchanging letters with family and friends and answering letters from strangers—many requesting money, some seeking information about the university. He also supervised the agents locating the federal land in the forests of Wisconsin and oversaw the construction of university buildings. The first campus plan featured a fifteen-acre square, with South University (now Morrill Hall) placed on the western edge of the hillside to house students and to hold the library, president's office, and classrooms.

To make clear to the public what Cornell University was all about, and to attract prospective students, Cornell sent a letter to the *New York Tribune* explaining "how a poor boy can pay for his education" by working his way through school. There was employment available in the machine shop, advised Cornell, where there were lathes, a twenty-five-horsepower engine, and many other pieces of equipment for working with iron and wood. The "erection of additional buildings required for the University will furnish employment for years to come to students in need of it." There would also be employment in improving and beautifying the farm and grounds on which the university was sited. "It will be a constant aim of the trustees and faculty," wrote Cornell, "to make the school attractive and to afford students the means for self-support and independence, while receiving all the advantages of the University." He added that there were already some students who had come to Ithaca to work until classes opened, earning money for their expenses. "I will assure the boys," he wrote, "that if they will perform one-fourth as much labor as I did at their ages, or as I do now at 60 years of age, they will find no difficulty in paying their expenses while prosecuting their studies at Ithaca." Working one's way through college has become part of American mythology, but at the time this exciting prospect attracted the attention of many ambitious young men.

For the moment, however, little in Ithaca was ready for them.

———

The inauguration was to have been in 1867, but the buildings were not ready, and the state granted the university an extension. One year later, while construction continued on campus, Cornell University opened. On October 6, 1868, young men who had passed the entrance examinations, given in a variety of subjects, gathered at the Cornell Library. Of those who had tried for admission, 412 were found academically qualified, while several with credit awarded for previous college work registered in the upper classes. The inauguration ceremony on October 7 was scheduled for ten A.M., but far earlier than that, students, townspeople, officials, and the curious began to arrive at the Cornell Library on Tioga Street to take seats. The hall had been decorated in red and white, and at the sides of the steps were urns filled with masses of ferns and moss. The citizens of Ithaca, reported the *Ithaca Journal,* had decided even before a class had met that the university was a grand success. The university, every townsperson knew, promised as much for the economic health of the community as it did for the incoming students. Ithaca might finally have an institution that would provide a secure economic base.

Ithaca at this time, however, had little to boast about. Mary White, the president's wife, "detested Ithaca" and had "urged her husband to try for a professorship at Yale." Although others decreed Ithaca picturesque and extolled its natural beauty, the English historian Goldwin Smith later found the waterfalls a crashing bore and hoped he would never be taken to see another. In the early days of the nineteenth century, Ithaca had been a collection of buildings at the headwaters of Cayuga Lake, a terminus for goods shipped down the lake. The Depression of 1837 highlighted Ithaca's isolation from major eastern markets, as had the Erie Canal when it opened in 1825. At mid-century, Ithaca still lacked a sound economic underpinning. When the university opened in 1868, the streets in Ithaca were hard-packed dirt, as they would remain well into the 1880s; there were no sidewalks and the commercial section was clustered on Owego Street. The Clinton House was the grandest building in town. Ithaca's population numbered not quite eight thousand, and there were just over thirty thousand residents in the county. Ithaca had sixteen churches, a private academy, a large grammar school on North Albany Street, and the Cornell Library. There were farms within the village limits and on the land ringing the flats at the head of Cayuga Lake. Ithaca received the designation of a city only in 1888.

Early view of Cornell as seen from Ithaca,
with the Village Hall and the Cornell Library
in foreground, ca. 1870.

A student writing in *The Cornell Era* in 1881 speculated that "very probably the gently-sloping infantile mountain, which we are compelled to ascend five or six times a week," had induced the founders to settle the university in Ithaca. Or it might have been the "gorges scattered about in the most prodigal manner." Theaters were probably not a reason, though their "boards are occasionally graced by the presence of some great theatrical or musical star. But the appointments of this popular place of entertainment are not exactly what one would call first-class." There was, concluded one writer, "coasting." The popular winter sport of sledding down the steep streets "divides the chances of being killed or of not being killed in so delightfully even a manner, that it cannot fail to be a source of great pleasure to many."

There have been times when Ithaca was thought too rural to be home to a great university, times when Ithaca was regarded as a bucolic retreat for undisturbed study and research, and times when the scenery was extolled as compensation for low faculty salaries. Ithaca has been called both the most centrally isolated place on the East Coast and a well-connected regional hub; picturesque and antiquated; parochial and enlightened. In every era, however, Ithaca would grow because of the university's presence.

On October 7, 1868, Ezra Cornell was sixty-one years old. The newspaper noted that the "ravages of his late illness were painfully apparent, but his voice was steady" as he spoke at the inauguration "in a quiet and simple manner" to describe the object of the university. That within one decade he had created a public library and endowed a university was most certainly amazing to the people of Ithaca, and surely it must have been something of a surprise to Cornell himself. In his talk that day, Cornell stressed the ongoing nature of a university. He cautioned the crowd against any feeling of disappointment at what they saw, citing a visitor who had come to Ithaca expecting "to find a finished institution." Nothing was completed, he noted, and at no time thereafter could Cornell University ever be considered finished. "Such, my friends," he continued, "is not the entertainment we invited you to. We did not expect to have a 'single thing finished,' we did not desire it, and we have not directed our energies to that end. It is the commencement that we have now in hand."

It was the commencement of a new "institution of learning" that Cornell heralded, a school that would "mature in the future to a great degree of usefulness, which will place at the disposal of the industrial and productive classes of society the best facilities for the acquirement of practical knowledge and mental culture, on such terms as the limited means of the most humble can command." Cornell directed the audience's attention to the future: "I hope we have laid the foundation of an institution which shall combine practical with liberal education, which

South University (now Morrill) and North University (now White) halls, ca. 1869.

shall fit the youth of our country for the professions, the farms, the mines, the manufactories, for the investigations of science, and for mastering all the practical questions of life with success and honor."

"I believe that we have made the beginning," he said, "of an Institution which will prove highly beneficial to the poor young men and the poor young women of our country. This is one thing which we have not finished, but in the course of time we hope to reach such a state of perfection as will enable any one by honest efforts and earnest labor to secure a thorough, practical, scientific or classical education. The individual is better, society is better, and the state is better, for the culture of the citizen; therefore we desire to extend the means for the culture of all."

Certain words reverberate from the commencement to the present: useful, beneficial, poor young men and women, practical, scientific. Although Harvard was and continues to be a meritocracy, Cornell has always leaned toward democracy. Even today, when it is classed among the elite universities of the nation— an Ivy League school—it is a democratic meritocracy in so many ways, from the students to the faculty. And in his emphasis on the unfinished and the future, it is clear that Ezra Cornell understood that a thriving institution would always be in the process of becoming.

Ezra Cornell believed that this new education would serve agriculture by pairing it with science, thereby proving the usefulness of the new science taught at the university. "The veterinarian will shield" the farmer, said Cornell, "against many of the losses. . . . The entomologist must arm him for more successful warfare in defence of his growing crops. . . . we find ample opportunity for the applications of science in aid of the toiling millions." The farmer too, had a part to play in this interchange because the improvement of his life and knowledge would benefit "the knowledge and power of the mechanic."

In closing, Cornell linked the university to moral goals and to national needs "for the culture of all men of every calling, of every aim; which shall make men more truthful, more honest, more virtuous, more noble, more manly; which shall give them higher purposes, and more lofty aims, qualifying them to serve their fellow men better, preparing them to serve society better, training them to be more useful in their relations to the state, and to better comprehend their higher and holier relations to their families and their God." At this point Cornell defended the school's nonsectarianism. "It shall be our aim," he said, "and our constant effort to make true Christian men, without dwarfing or paring them down to fit the narrow gauge of any sect." The nonsectarian designation established the university's link to the public schools of New York, and its commitment to educate the graduates of those schools, whose students were of both sexes and of every—and even no—religious faith. Cornell attempted to define the expansiveness of knowledge: this will be "an institution where any person can find instruction in any study." He then commended "our cause" to the "scrutiny and the judgment of the American people."

Andrew Dickson White followed Ezra Cornell at the lectern that day. He too had been ill, but this was surely his moment. He discussed the underlying ideas on which the university was built, beginning with the two "Eliminated Ideas." Cornell University would not tolerate pedants—those who paraded learning or who were unimaginative and "unduly emphasized minutiae in the presentation or use of knowledge." Nor would the work of the university be directed by or be conducted on behalf of "Philistines"—those guided by crass and material rather than artistic and intellectual values.

Let us take a brief look at what President White had in mind. The foundation ideas he spoke about on that October day in 1868 mirror in many ways what he had written so passionately to Gerrit Smith earlier in the decade. He insisted on a close union between liberal and practical education and on their equal status; he confirmed the nonsectarian nature of the university, including the charter's stipulation that a "majority of the Trustees shall never be of any one religious sect or of no religious sect," and that "no professor, officer or student shall ever be accepted or rejected on account of any religious or political views." Further, White reaffirmed Ezra Cornell's motto and said that the university would represent a living union with the state school system and a "concentration of revenues for advanced education," recognizing that such a vast undertaking required firm financial support.

White then explicated a set of "Formative Ideas": that at Cornell University there would be an "equality between different courses of study" and compatibility between study and labor, thereby incorporating Ezra Cornell's plan by which poor boys could attend the university. And there would be emphasis upon scientific study, for at Cornell the accepted truths of the past would always be challenged.

White's "Governmental Ideas" ensured that the Board of Trustees would not perpetuate itself and that the students would be self-governing—they would arrange and manage their own housing and dining while at the university. This feature of the new school was intended to relieve the administration and faculty of oversight of the students' private lives and to scatter the students among the householders of Ithaca, whose positive influence, White believed, would ensure better behavior than that of students massed into dormitories. Students were to be treated as adults capable of managing their own domestic arrangements.

There were two "Permeating or Crowning Ideas": that obtaining an education required effort, and that its ends were noble—education was to have an importance and bearing on society.

How thrilling it must have been to be in Ithaca on that first day. Everyone was filled with hope and expectation; all things, at that moment, seemed possible. This, crowed the *Ithaca Journal,* was the fullest and most perfect exposition ever given of the fundamental ideas on which the university rested. It was a most "scholarly and logical defense of great principles, a fervent plea for true Christian culture, and training untrammelled by the fetters of narrow minded sectarianism and bigotry."

White closed his long oration by addressing the founder of the university: "You have been accused, sir, of creating a monument to yourself—would to God more men would erect such monuments to themselves!" Even while explaining the new institution to the assembled crowd, White was conscious of the difficulties ahead and the snubs to be endured. In his printed copy of the Order of Exercises, White noted acidly that "the governor, bowing to Methodist & Baptist & other sectarian enemies of the University," had sent the lieutenant governor to represent the state so that he might avoid criticism from those quarters by being present. White

Cornerstone of McGraw Hall, "laid with all
ceremony by the Grand Lodge of Masons of
the State of New York," 1869.

**John McGraw,
albumen print
photograph,
ca. 1865.**

fully realized the political and religious tensions with which the new university would have to cope.

That afternoon, stores in Ithaca closed in honor of the inaugural festivities. Throngs of people made their way to the campus to witness the presentation of the chimes by Jennie McGraw. Hung in a wooden scaffold, they would later be placed in the tower of McGraw Hall and in the 1890s be moved once again, to McGraw Tower, where they hang today. Although the wind on that October day of commencement was so high that many could not hear the addresses, the bells wafted their music over all.

Louis Agassiz, a noted professor at Harvard and White's adviser during the time he was organizing the university and collecting faculty, spoke of Cornell's uniqueness. His audience was celebrating an "institution of learning such as never existed before," said Agassiz, looking out over the hillside where all was under way and nothing finished. He then voiced a comment often heard about Cornell: "I trust this University will do something more. It starts on a firm basis; it starts with a prosperity which the world has not contemplated before." Agassiz believed the new university presented an opportunity for teachers unlike any other: "They break soil on a fresh ground. There is no proscription here. No absolute authority imposes appointed textbooks on the student or on any special department of learning. The teacher will come before his class with his own thoughts, with what he brings in his own head rather than in a stereotyped print. The students will select their studies and attend the instruction of the man of their choice." The students, too, would not be like students elsewhere but would be examples to others. "We appeal to them," he shouted over the wind, "to show themselves worthy of this confidence, and thus help in emancipating their fellow students throughout the world. The students of this University are in a position to do this." Agassiz predicted that Ezra Cornell would be remembered as "one of the greatest benefactors, not only of America, but of humanity" and heralded the university as inaugurating "a new era" of public education.

And there it was: the challenge that the community of people who formed the university would launch a new era of education in the United States. It was the signal that at the university on East Hill, the classes offered would be well taught, everything would be thoroughly debated, and all would be welcome. The students took Agassiz's words to heart and named their first literary magazine, launched that fall, *The Cornell Era.*

Everyone recognized that the university was a great and important undertaking. At the close of the exercises, Henry Sage, a wealthy businessman who lived in Ithaca, turned to his friend John McGraw, a man from Dryden who had made a fortune in the timber industry, and remarked, "John, we are scoundrels to stand doing nothing while those men are killing themselves to establish this university." McGraw would give the means to erect McGraw Hall. Later, when the time was right, Sage would add his own contributions.

Despite worry and problems, buildings still unfinished, and preparations somewhat haphazard, students made their way to Ithaca, some by boat down the lake, others on the train from Owego, still others by wagon or carriage or on foot. They were eager to be part of this new experimental enterprise, to help usher in the Cornell era. They, like those who followed them, would meet many challenges; the first was the climb up East Hill.

Gleams her beacon bright

The inaugural ceremonies on October 7, 1868, set a tone of high optimism for the educational experiment taking place in Ithaca. Now it was the responsibility of President Andrew Dickson White to see that his Plan of Organization was carried out. What needed attention first? How many ideas could be implemented at one time? There was the fear of doing too little, the danger of attempting too much.

White had described his plan on opening day, asserting that a university could not be great and important without a library, equipment for scientific experimentation, places in which to teach, laboratories to support classroom lessons and basic research, and perhaps most important of all, teachers. He hired seventeen professors, four assistant professors, and five instructors, for a total faculty of twenty-six.

Students and faculty crammed into Cascadilla Hall, a gray stone building at the edge of the gorge. Cascadilla had been built as a water cure hospital, but having more faith in the idea of a university, its trustees, including Ezra Cornell, had closed it down and deeded it to the university. North and South University (today White and Morrill halls) were nearly complete; McGraw Hall, to be located between them, was still being designed. These first buildings were perched on the rim of the hill, overlooking Ezra Cornell's home above the village. Connecting the academic buildings and Cascadilla were rough paths that became dusty when the weather was dry, muddy after rain. What was to become the campus was still rough pasture. The farm for the agricultural school lacked sheds and even livestock. Where were the laboratories and scientific equipment? "A preparatory pandemonium," *The Cornell Era* called it.

Nevertheless, the work of the university commenced. Some lectures were held in the village at the Cornell Library, admission usually by ticket; the students quickly learned that they needed to arrive early when a nonresident lecturer was scheduled because townspeople vied for seats. There must have been a general sense of improvisation. Many of White's faculty were young and inexperienced, and all had to teach with few resources. But the disadvantages of being at a new and unformed university on the outskirts of an unprepossessing village were outweighed by the advantages of participating in an exciting educational experiment. To these teachers, White added his nonresident faculty—men willing to visit, deliver lectures, and inspire students and faculty. In White's scheme, these professors

Cascadilla Hall, ca. 1868.

were necessary to stir up the campus, infuse it with life and ideas, and prevent provincialism.

In a series of twenty lectures that drew large crowds, Louis Agassiz came from Harvard to give students "higher insight into various problems of natural science and stimulated among many a zeal for special investigation"—White's first mention of research. James Russell Lowell lectured on early literature and George Curtis on literature more recent, exciting the interest, White reported with satisfaction, "among students of a more literary turn." Theodore Dwight's lectures on the U.S. Constitution and Bayard Taylor's on German literature, White thought, "awakened a large number of active minds to the beauties of these fields." James Hall arrived to lecture on geology and John Stanton Gould spoke about mechanics as applied to agriculture. It was the arrival of historian Goldwin Smith from Oxford, however, that most pleased White, because Smith settled in Ithaca and stayed for three years, "exercising, both in his lecture-room and out of it, a great influence upon the whole life of the university."

White set things in motion as if spinning a dozen tops at one time. He ordered plaster casts of classical statuary for student inspection and acquired collections of fossils and shells for research. He proposed the addition of a department of architecture with a four-year course of study, unlike anything else in the United States, and donated to the university his own library of one thousand books about architecture—a collection that some considered the best in the country.

Most important, he oversaw the collection of books for the library. It was the library that White considered the core of the university. He identified collections of books for Ezra Cornell to buy, and when school opened, there were approximately twenty-five thousand volumes, many still boxed and waiting for stacks to house them. White purchased some books in Europe, others in this country: collections on agriculture, the mechanical arts, chemistry, engineering, the natural sciences, physiology, and veterinary surgery. To these he added his own personal library of four thousand volumes on history and English, French, German, and Italian litera-ture. He acquired the Anthon Library, nearly seven thousand books collected by a

Andrew Dickson White (president, 1866–1885), albumen print photograph, 1885.

Henry W. Sage, engraving, ca. 1870.

First Cornell
crew team to row
at the Intercollegiate
Races at Saratoga,
1873.

Columbia College professor of classics. When twenty-five hundred books on Oriental languages, literature, and philology amassed by Franz Bopp of the University of Berlin became available, White had to have that collection, too. In 1869 Goldwin Smith donated thirty-five hundred books, chiefly historical works. There were, in addition, some twenty-five hundred volumes of the Patent Office of Great Britain, important for the student of technology. Other special collections included the Agricultural Library, purchased by Ezra Cornell in 1868, and books and pamphlets concerning slavery and antislavery, gathered by the Reverend Samuel J. May of Syracuse. In 1872 White purchased the Jared Sparks Library, possibly the most important privately owned collection of American history in the country: "six thousand printed volumes, illustrating American history more fully, probably, than any other similar collection"—volumes that had long been "the envy of scholars." White envisioned these books supporting the work of the faculty and leading scholars to new endeavors. He regarded the range of what could be taught as limitless and he wanted it all, echoing the motto ascribed to The Founder.

Thus it was that the Cornell library could support research, almost from the start. And unlike libraries elsewhere, it was open nine hours a day. Even as he worried about its location in South University with students' coal stoves overhead, White yearned for its continuing expansion.

The students, for their part, attended classes and improvised what we call student life. In October 1868, within a month of the inaugural ceremonies, students issued the first edition of *The Cornell Era,* which took its name from Agassiz's remarks on opening day. From the first issue, the *Era* covered the state of affairs on the hill—reporting items about faculty and students, pointing out critical needs such as sidewalks, expressing a preference perhaps for two semesters rather than the trimester division with which the university began. The *Era* also noted that the library was still "not in suitable condition," lacking shelves, and many books and some basic references needed by students were still in crates. The student editors cheered what was innovative at Cornell and pointed out what they thought the curriculum lacked. Cornell's distinctiveness was especially appealing to them. There were courses offered at Cornell, even in its infancy, that were not given at any other university in the United States, a writer in the *Era* commented in February 1869. The *Era* also quoted another school's newspaper: "We do not believe that any other college or University in this country offers a system of education so perfectly adapted to the wants of our times, as the one which has been established by the Trustees of Cornell University." The responsibility for making the most of the curriculum, observed the *Era*, depends "upon the students now frequenting Cornell as upon any other set of men."

The students formed associations modeled on student life at other schools and created new clubs and organizations appropriate for Cornell. They started the Cornell Christian Association. By April 1869 there were six fraternities or secret societies. By 1872 the university had its school song, "Far Above Cayuga's Waters," written by two members of the class of 1874, Archibald Croswell Weeks and Wilmot Moses Smith. By 1873 Cornell had a natural history society and chemical, agricultural, and engineering clubs, plus four literary societies, the Irving, the Philanlatheian, the Adelphi, and the Curtis. For recreation, the students played baseball, they visited the lake, they explored the countryside. They established routes from the village up East Hill—for many the easiest path to the top of the hill was the Bone Yard Cut, which snaked through the City Cemetery.

The *Era* and the *Cornell University Register* also trace the diversity of the students, seen as a sign of Cornell's early cosmopolitanism. In 1869 the 563 students

CORNELL UNIVERSITY

. . . .

The majority of the students are sons of poor and struggling parents, men who know what time and money are worth. The trustees have done far more for students of small means than was ever dreamed of when the institution was organized. The books show an expenditure for students' labor on farm grounds, buildings, and in shops, printing-office, laboratory, etc., of over \$32,000. The number of free scholarships is 512. The dormitory system is gradually going out of favor, as the students prefer lodgings and board in the town, where each one can adapt his expenses to his means.

The university is still in its infancy. As years pass on, it will develop a still more liberal, comprehensive, and thorough basis of instruction, and become one of the chief fountains of popular intelligence and morality; and down to remotest times the name of its generous founder will never be spoken among men save with gratitude and honor.

—HARPER'S WEEKLY, June 21, 1873, 530

Felix Adler,
albumen print
photograph,
ca. 1874.

included two from England, two from Haiti, several from Canada, and one Karl Shallowitz, who had been born in Prague and subsequently moved to Ithaca; he later left college to set up a popular student drinking establishment in Ithaca. The *Era* announced that a "mulatto presented himself for examination last week, but we infer from various reports that he failed to satisfy our Faculty that he knew enough to enter." There was no bar against African Americans, or any others—the charter read "person" when it referred to students—but academic qualifications had to be met by examination. In 1870, the 609 students included a most exotic freshman, Kanaye Nagasawa of Kagoshima, Japan.

Goldwin Smith observed that Cornell University had been "emancipated from the old mediaeval system of Faculties, and other trammels imposed on study." The students marveled at the lecture system at Cornell. No other university in the United States, they boasted, provides instruction in the Scandinavian tongues; in 1873 they hailed the future meteorological station on campus set up by Estevan Fuertes, professor of civil engineering; in 1875 they applauded a new approach to the study of American history, which was to be taught "not by textbooks or by a series of lectures but by individual research." In 1880 a course in money, banking, and finance was introduced. In summer 1876, Burt Green Wilder, who taught comparative zoology, ran a school of zoology, prefiguring the tradition of summer use of the campus (it would be almost twenty years before Summer School began). Students noted, too, that in 1876 two current Cornell students with special expertise were tapped to offer courses: John Henry Comstock became an assistant professor in entomology when no one else was found who could teach the course, and W. R. Dudley was named assistant professor of botany and arboriculture.

In 1874, when a group of New York City Jews offered a nonresident professorship in Hebrew and Oriental literature and history, White welcomed Felix Adler to campus. His association with Cornell lasted two years, and while at Cornell he was popular with students, who called him the Young Eagle. Adler's appearance on campus caused some comment from Cornell's critics, but an *Era* writer asked rather smugly, "How long has it been that a Professor in an American college could take up the Hebrew Bible, speak of it, discuss it, explain it, as a purely human production? In how many American colleges can such a thing be done now?" The answer, of course, was very few. That sense of being at a place so daring, so innovative, delighted the students, who constantly commented on the uniqueness of their education.

Speaking to the New York State Agricultural Society in 1869, White asked, "what shall this new education be?" His answer: a Cornell education stressed the power of observation and the power of practical reasoning, with a thorough grounding in the sciences and the arts. Charles Frederick Hartt, professor of geology, embodied this ideal blend of scholar and empiricist. In 1870, Hartt took nine students to Brazil to study the Amazon Basin because, he said, the true way to teach geology and natural history "is not simply to lecture to the student or to drill him with a text-book" but to let the student do the work himself. "He must go into the field and collect and observe. In the laboratory he must patiently study the raw material he has gathered together, working to a large degree independent of books, observing minutely everything for himself, as if no one else had worked before him, and then compare his own results with the investigations of others." Hartt died on his second journey up the Brazilian Amazon, in 1878. Thereafter, students and faculty often went off on expeditions, although not always to places quite so distant or dangerous.

As the curriculum grew and the students expanded in number and diversity of background, the question of women arose. From the start, Andrew Dickson White and Ezra Cornell had wanted to include women. An exchange of letters between Cornell and Henry Wells, one of the founders of the Wells Fargo Express Company, is revealing. Wells had spoken frequently about the education of women and had even talked of establishing a seminary for girls in honor of his mother. Cornell asked Wells to consider locating his school for women in Ithaca.

Wells replied bluntly that *his* institution would be "one of higher standard than those referred to in your letter." Wells intended to "prepare young ladies to be Wives and Mothers. To educate the rising generation who are to take our places & influence & direct the destinies of a great nation." His purpose was to "educate American girls to fulfill the duties & take the position that a kind Providence has assigned to the *better half* of our race in this broad land, & woman then can fulfill her mission without going to the polls or entering the arena of politics." He hoped for "a higher standard of moral and intellectual culture than has yet been obtained by the ordinary village and town institutions to which you," he wrote pointedly, "allude." The school for women that Ezra Cornell envisioned would never do. The seminary created by Henry Wells is today Wells College, in Aurora, halfway up Cayuga Lake.

Ezra Cornell thought that education for women should be practical—aimed at giving them equal opportunities with male students. When Vassar College opened in 1866, Cornell enrolled his daughter Mary Emily. The following year he wrote to his granddaughter Eunice, inviting her to visit the university growing on East Hill, where he hoped "you and your brothers and your cousins and a great many more children will go to school when they get large enough and will learn a great many things that will be useful to them and make them wise and good women and men." He added, "I want to have girls educated in the University as well as boys, so that they may have the same opportunity to become wise and useful to society that the boys have." Cornell advised Eunice to "keep this letter until you grow up to be a woman and want to go to a good school where you can have a good opportunity to learn, so you can show it [to] the President and Faculty of the University to let them know that it is the wish of your Grand Pa, that girls as well as boys should be educated at Cornell University."

The education of women, White knew, was an even bolder departure from current educational ideas than any of the other innovations he was promoting for the new university. Some years before, the Reverend Samuel May of Syracuse had advised White that "the training of women in all respects [should] be as thorough" and as "profound as that of men." May went further: "Indeed, if the education of either sex should be the more complete, it is that of the female, for to them more than the other is committed the instruction of children." But May would not have women's education watered down; he continued, "I would have both sexes educated equally well—educated together. God made man dual and he cannot be singular in anything, without detriment to some part of his character." May believed that denying women the advantages of education crippled their powers of self-support and was the "source of some of the direst evils, that debase and afflict mankind."

White believed that the presence of women in the classroom had a positive influence on all students. His own mother was well educated by the standards of the time. She wrote to him, "I am not so sure about your other ideas, but as to the admission of women you are right." At the academy she had attended, she recalled, "the young men and young women learned to respect each other, not merely for physical, but for intellectual and moral qualities; so there came a healthful emulation in study, the men becoming more manly and the women more womanly; and never, so far as I have heard did any of the evil consequences follow which some of your opponents are prophesying."

But to press so many new ideas forward at the same time, White wrote, would "certainly have cost us the support of the more conservative men in the legislature." He worked diligently to "keep out of the charter anything which could

Class of 1875, albumen print photograph.

embarrass us regarding the question in the future, steadily avoiding in every clause relating to students the word 'man,' and as steadily using the word 'person.'" Thus Cornell and White quietly laid the groundwork for coeducation, "he favoring it in general terms," noted White, "and I developing sundry arguments calculated to prepare the way for future action upon it."

Their careful words at the opening ceremonies, however, did not go unnoticed. Later in the day, Henry Sage, a businessman who had earned his fortune in timber, had approached White and said, "I believe you are right in regard to admitting women, but you are evidently carrying as many innovations just now as public opinion will bear; when you are ready to move in the matter, let me know." Why would Sage support the education of women? His father had died when Henry was young, leaving him the sole support of his mother and sisters, and perhaps this situation impressed upon Sage a woman's need to have the means to support herself. Whatever his reasons, unlike White's intellectual arguments, they were certain to be practical.

Many people—and especially women—wrote to Cornell or White asking when women might matriculate. The replies show that both men were eager to bring women to the university, and as early as 1870 there was an opportunity. Jennie Spencer, who had scored highest in the state Regents' examination in Cortland County, presented herself at Cornell to take the entrance examinations. Spencer is a ghost who haunts the university's past: we know she came to Ithaca, yet traces of her are faint, and her name is not in the registrar's book of enrolled students. Stories reverberate about her decision not to remain, and many reasons for her departure have been invented. It was the wicked winter, they said, that forced her to abandon her studies; the terrain was too perilous. A few local women did attend classes as early as Cornell's second year, but none were officially registered students and the records only hint at their presence. About Jennie Spencer, however, we know more because the *Era* printed a short report in September 1870 announcing that "Mrs. Jennie Spencer" had passed "creditably, receiving in several [tests] the highest marks." She did not remain past that first week, however; "not finding convenient accommodations," she concluded to postpone her attendance at Cornell. "She leaves with the highest opinion of the University," cooed the editor, always ready to pay a compliment, "and her ladylike appearance has won for her the high respect of all."

To understand why women were not accepted initially, we have to remember the times. Even though one of the planks that Elizabeth Cady Stanton had written into the *Declaration of Sentiments* adopted at the 1848 Seneca Falls Convention called for educational opportunities for women, most people believed that women in the mid-nineteenth century functioned best in the domestic sphere. Higher education was seen as unnecessary for women, and many, even medical doctors, believed it would harm them physically. Although the founders were in favor of educating women, they delayed admitting women for the very practical reason that women students would be subject to criticism and ridicule for attending a coeducational university and their presence would surely give Cornell's many critics even more fuel. Families, too, had to feel secure that their daughters would receive the same supervision and protection that they would have been given at home. Might all this have been done in 1868? Possibly.

But recall Henry Sage's words to White: "you are evidently carrying as many innovations just now as public opinion will bear." All around, the idea of university education for women was being hotly debated—and generally dismissed as inappropriate, harmful to them, and not at all good for male students. Most men and many women regarded coeducation with skepticism. Higher education would sap a woman's strength and cause madness, or divert blood and energy to the brain, starving the uterus and rendering her unfit to bear children. It would create the sort of woman who could never marry, which was then the only socially acceptable path for America's daughters. Nevertheless, for his own reasons, Sage offered to endow a female college when the university was ready to admit women.

In June 1871, encouraged by Ezra Cornell, President White, and Henry Sage, the trustees created a committee to consider the admission of women to the university. Sage and White visited Oberlin and other colleges to observe coeducation in practice; they wrote to people who had an informed opinion on the subject. In January 1872, White published his *Report to the Board of Trustees of Cornell University in Behalf of a Majority of the Committee on Mr. Sage's Proposal to Endow a College for Women*. His justification for moving forward had little to do with idealism, however; rather, he linked coeducation to Cornell's responsibility to educate the students of the state's public school system, which enrolled both boys and girls. He pointed out the use of the word *persons* in the Cornell charter and argued that the persons who entered Cornell should be the same persons who were being educated in New York's public schools and academies—that is, "persons of both sexes." He saw no way to refuse women an education at Cornell. In April 1872, the trustees voted to permit no distinction by gender, "the only aim being to secure the 'best scholar,' as the law requires." Later that April, the university admitted its first female student, Sophie P. Fleming of Ithaca, who had competed with four other local women for the appointment as State Student. Two more women matriculated

Mr. Sage himself once told me that early in his boyhood, as far back as he could remember, he had been possessed by a longing to help women, and that as he had come to value education more and more he had come to believe it all important for women; but that not until after his gift to Sage College had he met more than one woman who believed in women's higher education. He told me that he had happened to be away from home when the newspapers announced that the University had accepted his gift and established co-education at Cornell and that on his return his wife, who was afterward to approve so fully of this action, said as she greeted him: "You have meant to do women a great good, but you have ignorantly done them an incalculable injury."

. . . He asked for women's education as a condition of race progress. "The efficient force of the human race," he said, "will be multiplied in proportion as woman by culture and education is fitted for new and broader spheres of action. . . . He exorcised with a word—the only word there is to say—the fantastically lying spirit which declares that education will transform educated women into educated men. . . . Will she be less woman," he asked, "with riper development of all her faculties? As wife and mother, as sister, companion, and friend, will she be less true to faith and duty? Is man made dwarf or giant by increase of moral and intellectual power?" . . . And finally Mr. Sage urged, in words that to-day set every generous soul aflame, the necessity of fitting women for self-support; he instanced the surplus of women in many of the older civilized countries of Europe . . . and he emphasized the fact that these women could not hope to marry and must in the immediate future either starve or work . . .

There should be no restriction upon a woman's right to sustain herself in any honest calling; and she should, as much as man, be fitted by education to use the faculties God has given her where they will avail her the most.

—M. Carey Thomas, in MEMORIAL EXERCISES IN HONOR OF HENRY WILLIAMS SAGE (Ithaca, 1898)

in fall 1872, and one, Emma Eastman, who had studied at Vassar, graduated in June 1873.

Other women followed. In fall 1873, sixteen women enrolled at Cornell, one in a postgraduate course. The trustees agreed that "women are to be hereafter admitted on the same conditions as young men, except that they must be at least eighteen years of age." Men were allowed to matriculate earlier.

The reaction of male students to aspiring women was generally favorable, although for a time everyone stumbled over what to call them: the term *coed* came into use only slowly and was at first not complimentary. Now and then, some puffed-up young man or group of fraternity brothers would question the suitability of women to be Cornell students, or the suitability of Cornell for women. College boys will be college boys, and jokes of all sorts were made. Should not Sage College, asked one, be called the *Collège des Sages-femmes?* And complaints were vented: "when all the women get to be students in Cornell University, and doctors and lawyers and ministers and brokers, who is to do the child-bearing?" But "J.P." wrote in 1870 that even though he was not an "admirer of 'male woman,'" he supported the idea of women at the university. "Be it ours," commented the *Era,* "to 'break the latest chain' and inaugurate a really new era." And then there was this prescient statement: "the admission of females into our University dates the most important era of its existence. It is a step which directly concerns ourselves, which is pregnant with consequences that will ultimately affect the entire country and to a great extent revolutionize our social system."

Henry Sage's gift to the university was a building called Sage College, a place where women students lived and dined; its gymnasium was for their exercise, but it also had classrooms where men and women pursued botanical studies. Susan Linn Sage spoke at the groundbreaking ceremony. Speaking of her husband's donation and the university's desire to educate young women, she is supposed to have said to the men assembled, "you have meant to do women a great good, but you have ignorantly done them an incalculable injury." And she might have said just that and meant it, for Mrs. Sage was a mature woman in 1872, and her world had placed women in a domestic role. She probably feared that educated women would be unlikely to marry and enjoy what she would have considered to be a normal life. Her sentiment would have been well understood and widely shared by both men and women of the day.

Memorabilia, including a letter from Ezra Cornell, were placed in the cornerstone of Sage College. As he deposited his envelope, Cornell was said to have remarked that his letter, addressed to "the coming man and woman," would identify what he considered the greatest danger to the university. Morris Bishop in his *History of Cornell* and other writers speculated that since the letter was deposited in the Sage College cornerstone, the threat envisioned was coeducation. Not until 1997 was his letter made public. That fall Sage College—a once-handsome but increasingly shabby building—became the S. C. Johnson Graduate School of Management, and during the renovations that dismantled the old interior and placed a new building within the 1873 shell, the cornerstone was opened and the box removed. The letter Ezra Cornell wrote on May 15, 1873, surprised everyone.

Sage College and Sage Chapel as seen
from McGraw Hall, ca. 1875.

It was not, after all, coeducation that Ezra Cornell feared, but sectarianism. The university's lack of a denominational affiliation worried many people, and the fact that its president was an educator and intellectual rather than a minister invited an ongoing and grinding chorus of criticism. The faculty didn't escape comment, either, and were said to "neglect no opportunity to manifest their opposition to Christianity and its most sacred beliefs," according to one critic who had heard of a lecture on religious enthusiasm at which the professor "took occasion to say some very bitter words against revivals of religion." Cornell was called a "sink hole of corruption and a hot-bed of sin, from which few students come uncontaminated." Another detractor warned that Cornell students were a "crowd of dissolute roughs and murder is of frequent occurrence among them." In 1881 came a complaint about atheism at Cornell; in 1882, the cry was "infidel Cornell." In 1883 the *Era* complained that "it is positively tiresome to read the incessant tirades against Cornell University appearing in various papers, sectarian, secular and collegiate. Infidelity, atheism—wickedness in general, are laid at our door without the slightest cause." Coeducation simply added another contentious issue, along with the lack of dormitories, which implied a lack of proper supervision for the men, and the freedom granted them to monitor their own behavior and select their own courses of concentration.

Perhaps just as threatening to those of a more settled way of thinking was that Cornell was open to students of all economic classes. Yet the cost of a Cornell education, though modest, would have been an obstacle for students with limited means. Expenses included fees of $10 per trimester for instruction, plus $5.46 per week for room, board, lights, and fuel in a university building (or $4 to $6 a week for a room in a boarding house or with a family in town). Adding $10 to $25 worth of textbooks and stationery, a year at Cornell might cost as much as $275—a considerable barrier to higher education for most people of the day.

The manual labor program was Ezra Cornell's way of enabling poor students to attend the university. There was work on the university farm, in the carpenter

. . . .

Ithaca, New York
May 15ᵗʰ, 1873

To the coming man & woman

On the occasion of laying the cornerstone of the Sage College for women of Cornell University, I desire to say that the principle danger, and I say almost the only danger I see in the future to be encountered by the friends of education, and by all lovers of true liberty is that which may arise from sectarian strife.

From these halls, sectarianism must be forever excluded, all students must be left free to worship God, as their conscience shall dictate, and all persons of any creed, or all creeds must find free, and easy access, and a hearty and equal welcome to the educational facilities possessed by the Cornell University.

Coeducation of the sexes, and entire freedom from sectarian or political preferences, is the only proper and safe way, for providing an education that shall meet the wants of the future, and carry out the founders idea of an Institution where "any person can find instruction in any study." I herewith commit this great trust to your care.

Ezra Cornell

—Letter in the cornerstone of Sage College for Women

The campus, looking north, with
(from left) faculty houses, Morrill
Hall with McGraw Hall tower behind
it, Sage Chapel, and Sage College,
ca. 1875.

The first university library, in McGraw Hall, ca. 1875.

shop, as janitors in the buildings, waiting tables at Cascadilla Hall, as assistants in the library, as pressmen in the printing office, and as accountants and copyists in the business and other offices. Some students found work in construction and some cut stone for Cornell's house on University Avenue. Such work, insisted Cornell, did not "prevent them from reciting as well as the rest," and much was made in various press clippings about students in the labor program who also did well academically. Nevertheless, the work available to students sometimes sapped their energy, they were not always qualified for the tasks that needed to be performed, and the pay—ten cents an hour—was hardly enough to cover even modest room and board, much less tuition. Although manual labor was the founder's pet, it was controversial and ultimately proved impractical. Despite efforts to provide suitable work, after Cornell's death in 1874, the program gradually faded away. Students who needed to work found campus jobs at fraternities, in the library, and by waiting tables but the university ceased to promote the idea of manual labor. Cornell women in need of funds to finance their education often lived with a faculty or local family, providing childcare and performing some housework in exchange for room and board.

Even six years after opening, the financing of the university remained a subject of debate in the press. Was Ezra Cornell really aggrandizing himself, laying up for his family funds that should be applied to education? There were so many questions about the university that in January 1874 the New York State Senate conducted an investigation. Although this inquiry targeted financial questions, some senators expanded the session to other issues. "I see a statement in the treasurer's report of a chapel contribution of $30,000 to build a chapel," said one (unnamed) senator. "I would like to know how you intend to use that chapel?" Andrew Dickson White explained that the money for the chapel came from Henry Sage, who had hoped the structure might be identified with his denominational affiliation. That, said White, would not be permitted under the terms of the university's charter, which clearly stated that Cornell would be nonsectarian:

> *White:* . . . the gentleman offering the endowment agreed that eminent clergymen might be selected from various denominations to preach from time to time.
>
> *Senator:* Let me understand what you mean by "various"; do you mean from all denominations?
>
> *White:* From all denominations, yes.
>
> *Senator:* From all religious denominations?
>
> *White:* From all religious denominations . . .
>
> *Senator:* Each man to be at liberty to conduct the services according to his own method?
>
> *White:* Yes, sir.
>
> *Senator:* You would include in that, I suppose, Jews, as well as Christians?
>
> *White:* That would certainly be in accordance with the spirit of our charter. We have several Jewish students in our institution, and among them some of our very best students, and I would never sanction any thing which would infringe on their privileges, deprive them of their rights, or tend to degrade them in any manner.

The university did not act cautiously, and its motives sometimes appeared suspect to a public on the lookout for scandal. Nor did the students always act in such a way as to improve the public's opinion of the school or its students. In 1873 students founded the Cornell Young Men's Heathen Association, giving fodder to the religious press. Felix Adler's appointment inspired additional comments. Vice-President Russel noted in a letter to White that "the sullen murmur of the evangelicals is like the noise of many flies. I hear of excitement and of hobnobbing, of lamentations of the righteous and prophecies of the carrying away of the children into captivity on the hill." It was not only Felix Adler, noted the vice-president, but the "demoniac host of professors generally" and the vice-president in particular who "fall under the condemnation of the just made perfect"—that is, the religious critics of the university.

In 1874, at the age of sixty-seven, Ezra Cornell died. He was mourned by the university community, by people around the state, and by the citizens of Ithaca. There are many memorial statements from that occasion; one that was little noticed subsequently appeared in *The Cornell Era*. Although it was unsigned, who but Andrew Dickson White could have written it? Who else could have known so much about the founder or described him with such bitter eloquence?

During high times and low, as academic ideals met the hard edge of reality, the university weathered its first ten years. The anniversary was celebrated with festivities, a concert, and a gathering of alumni. University enrollment that year was 529 undergraduates and 30 graduate students. The faculty numbered 49. The scope of instruction had expanded to twelve programs, and the campus had seven major buildings and six laboratories, drafting rooms, a general and an experimental farm, and the university press—the first university press in the nation, established in 1869. The library housed forty thousand books, a staggering number for any academic institution at the time, but especially for one so young. There were museums devoted to agriculture, architecture, botany, geology and paleontology, and mineralogy, plus a museum of fine arts. Military science flourished; the cadets practiced with rifles instead of the broom handles they had used at the beginning. There was a special laboratory for creating technical models, and there were collections for the study of zoology and physiology. Alumni associations were active, the largest in New York City. In speaking before that group in 1883, White had commented that Cornell, "while adhering to what she has found best in the old, has never feared to adopt that which she has found good in the new." He insisted that this was the Cornell tradition. The alumni, for their part, took seriously their position as guardians of the university; many stayed in close contact with the campus, and several served on the Board of Trustees.

Yet the New York City alumni, led by John DeWitt Warner, charged the trustees with neglect, the faculty with desertion, the president with autocracy, and the students with degeneracy. Gone were the strong-minded scholars of years past, which these alumni believed themselves to have been. Their attacks on Cornell were virulent enough to appear in the New York City press; they were bothersome enough, in addition, for White to appear before the students to refute them. White called the leading critic a hothead, and supporters quickly pointed out that Warner had always been difficult, even as a student. Fellow alumni, alarmed at Cornell's growing notoriety, voted in a replacement for Warner as alumni trustee. But that did not silence him, nor did it answer the critics' concerns about the university, and in fact, the charges were not entirely false. Enrollment at Cornell had dropped significantly; professors had been lured away by better paying positions elsewhere, sometimes at other universities, often to industry. The president's actions were sometimes arbitrary; the local trustees had been lax in their oversight, and trustees far from Ithaca had been somewhat indifferent.

The changes made in response to the alumni outburst tend to confirm the validity of some of their complaints. Faculty, for instance, were given more voice in hiring decisions, and more careful review of proposals to institute new programs— or to jettison old ones—was promised. Warner's contention that White had too often been absent from the university and too involved in diplomatic and political matters, was valid: the president summered in Europe and had taken a leave of absence in 1879 to assume diplomatic responsibilities in Berlin. To manage in his stead White appointed William C. Russel, not the easiest of men, as vice-president and acting president. Yet White nonetheless insisted on approving all decisions, thereby constraining his deputy's ability to act. Russel had weakened his own position by clashing with Henry Sage, a powerful presence on the Board of Trustees by virtue of his residence in Ithaca and the money he had given the university. Russel soon became anathema to the trustees, faculty, and even the students. In 1881, the trustees asked Russel to resign. When he refused to respond to their request, they ordered his resignation and forced him out. With the acting president out of the picture and Andrew White in Europe, Henry Sage, as head of the trustees, filled the vacuum.

Much of the internal machinations escaped the public eye, and during this era, the university had some influential supporters. James A. Garfield wrote in the *Albany Argus,* "I think Andrew D. White has been doing the most commendable, rewarding, and agreeable work at Cornell of any man of his time; at least that is

· ·

A stature somewhat above the average; a form slender and rigid; a thin face of the well known puritan type, with lips which expressed, in their compression, an unwonted firmness of character; a slow, steady, stiff gait; a demeanor of unusual gravity, but which was sometimes a little too brusque to be dignified; a sharp eye, with a straightforward look in it; a voice tending a little to shrillness and harshness, but in its more quiet modulations not unpleasant; an utterance slow and precise, as if every word was carefully, if not painfully thought out—such was the founder of Cornell University as he walked among us during the first six years of the Institution's history. In whatever community, or in the midst of whatever surroundings his lot had been cast, he would have been a man of mark. A stranger, meeting him in a crowded railway car, would straightway see that he was not a mere individual of the ordinary human type; that he possessed strong characteristics which made him noticeably different from other men. He had a good memory and a quick eye, and was, as far as his culture permitted, a close and careful observer of men and things. On every topic and event in the whole range of his observations he had a settled opinion; and although this opinion may have differed from that reached by men of higher education, it was generally unchangeable by any argument however powerful, or by any proof however plain. In his judgment of men he was equally inflexible; having once formed his estimate of a person he rarely altered it, his confidence and his antipathy being alike unbounded. Like many another man of stolid aspect, he not infrequently showed an unexpected sense of humor; and when this appreciation of the humorous did not take a too sarcastic turn, it lighted up his grim countenance with a noticeable and agreeable smile. But his most predominant trait, overtopping all others, was his complete self-abnegation. He was utterly and intensely unselfish; no human being, with similar qualifications in other aspects, could be more thoroughly uninfluenced by any considerations of his own comfort, his own aggrandizement, or his own fame. He was generous alike of his time, his labor and his wealth, and no thought of his own interest ever limited the flow of this generosity.

Three very natural sentiments appear to have influenced him in the establishment of the University. The first was a consciousness of his own early defects which he felt in spite of his obstinate expression of his opinions—and his sad experience of the few educational facilities which were accessible to him in his younger years. The second was his strong local feeling, his wish to benefit, in some marked way, the place of his residence. The third was his desire to do good, upon a scale as large as his means, to his fellow men. He seems to have had a tolerably positive idea, in outline at least, of the kind of an institution which he meant to found. It was to be a sort of school of refuge, with the penal features left out. All those whose poverty, or whose early lack of opportunities had prevented their obtaining an education elsewhere, were to be taken in at his new school, were to earn their livelihood by manual labor, and were to be taught a little of everything in the way of human knowledge, and especially of that species of knowledge which is vaguely termed practical. This was, of course, in no wise a university, for of the highest scholarship, which a university is intended both to produce and to maintain, he had little conception. He looked upon scholars as men who were generally harmless, and might occasionally even become useful men who studied one particular branch of a subject so devotedly that they knew almost nothing about anything else. That the University developed into something quite different from his ideas at the outset, was owing partly to the force of circumstances, partly to the nature of things.

Though he clung, with all the persistence and generosity of his nature, to his pet manual labor scheme, he could not avoid seeing that it had failed, and he tacitly acquiesced in the failure—at least until he could evolve some new project which should remedy the evils of the old one. But how great so ever may have been his defects—and they were those which he shared with the majority of his countrymen in this pioneer age and this pioneer land—his good qualities outnumbered and excused them all. His name has now become a part of the past; it will retreat, as the years go on, more and more into those recesses of history, where the fame of those who loved their fellow men is kept modestly enshrined. To us, who knew him, he is still the living man with a few frailties and a hundred virtues. To those who come after us he will be merely the unknown founder of the University—one of the unfamiliar heroes of an earlier age. To the world in general, that light, kindled partly by history, partly by tradition, which burns steadily but not too brilliantly, and which lights up the names of John Harvard and Elihu Yale, will forever shed its radiance on the name of EZRA CORNELL.

—Unsigned, THE CORNELL ERA,
January 8, 1875

Campus panorama, looking north from Sage College tower, with (clockwise from left) Sage Chapel, Morrill Hall, Mc-Graw Hall, White Hall, West Sibley Hall, wooden laboratory building, and faculty house, ca. 1880.

the work which I regard as the most honorable and enviable." Despite such compliments, White was probably eager to move on: he had lived and breathed Cornell for twenty years, and Ithaca had remained a small and rather provincial town. Overseeing a university with its day-to-day struggles had proved less interesting than planning it; dealing with real students and faculty was more onerous than envisioning their idealized selves.

White announced his resignation in 1885 and in his final *President's Report* set out a general policy for the university, stating what he had learned during his years in higher education, what he had observed elsewhere, and what he had learned at Cornell. It is, in many ways, a response to the alumni criticisms; it also sets clear directions for the future. The report represents what Andrew White did best: conceptualizing new goals for higher education. In his farewell speech White stated that the real object of Cornell "is to send forth true men and women; if it can do this, all our labor and expense, all our care and sympathy, will not have been in

vain." But to White the routine had become a thankless task, and he lamented that he had neglected his family.

After leaving Cornell, White maintained his house on campus, to which he returned from time to time. Near the end of his life, White was more continually in residence, a campus presence, offering advice even when unasked. Carl Becker, who had arrived at Cornell in 1917 to teach history, recalled being taken by historian George Lincoln Burr, once Andrew White's secretary, to visit White in his study in what today is the living room in the Society for the Humanities. Becker wrote:

> He received us with unstudied courtesy and an air of pleased anticipation, as if we were both old and valued friends, the two men in the world whom he most wanted just then to see. He began talking before we were fairly in the room, and kept on talking for an hour and a half, not so much to us or with us as for us and for himself, and for the pure joy of practicing the

The President's House, built in 1876 for Andrew Dickson White by William Henry Miller '72, now the A.D. White House, home to the Society for the Humanities.

CHAPTER TWO

art, as if cultivated conversation were God's best gift to men. He spoke of the good fortune of Cornell in inducing me to join its faculty, and of my good fortune in being associated with his friend George Burr whose learning and wisdom he had himself found of unfailing assistance; spoke of the new book he was then reading, and of other new books he had recently read by authors unknown to him, and asked us what we thought of them, and then, before we could start anything, told us what *he* thought of them; spoke of the war and the Fourteen Points and of Bismarck whom he had known and liked, but now thought in some sense responsible, with his blood and iron, for the war; spoke of early Cornell days and difficulties, and of Ezra Cornell, a remarkable and lovable man, and of the realization of his early dreams for the university, and of its future prospects, which would always be good so long as the most eminent scholars could be got to come to it; spoke of many other things besides—a copious flow of narrative and commentary, of incidents and anecdotes and judgments light and serious, moving on, without haste, without rest, like a prairie river in spring, gently irresistible, swelling up and around and over all obstacles, all conversational reticences and awkwardnesses, filling all silences, carrying us and himself serenely along on the broad surface of his knowledge and experiences recalled.

We said, and needed to say, and had a chance to say, very little.

Sibley machine shops, College of Mechanical Engineering, ca. 1885.

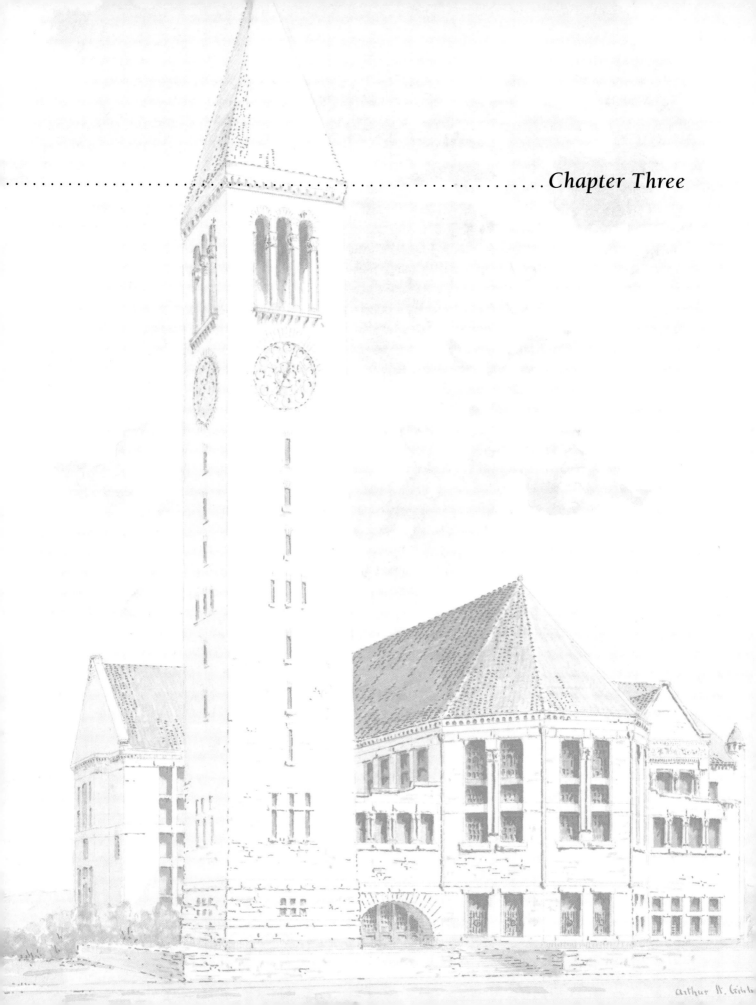

Chapter Three

AGAINST THE ARCH OF HEAVEN

When Andrew Dickson White tendered his resignation on June 17, 1885, he turned over to the trustees the task of finding a new president by the fall term. He had a candidate in mind, however, urging on them Charles Kendall Adams, who had studied history with White at the University of Michigan. Adams was very much White's opposite. He was deliberate where White sparkled; he was from an impoverished family and had enjoyed none of the privileges of wealth. His lectures at Cornell the previous year had been "not so popular in their style as the lectures of the non-resident professors are usually to be expected," and after one or two sessions, attendance had fallen off. Although the faculty and students were indifferent and many of the trustees cool, Adams's candidacy had the support of both White and Henry Sage, who had begun to play an increasingly powerful role at the university. That was enough to ensure his selection.

Enrollment at Cornell was on the upswing after what Morris Bishop called "the doubtful years." When the university opened in 1868–69, the students numbered 412, several of them seniors getting credit for previous academic work. Their number increased to 561 by 1875–76 but plummeted to an alarming low of 384 in 1881–82 and over the next four years gained only slightly. Then a rebound began; in 1884–85, enrollment reached 575 students and rose steadily thereafter. Adams could not claim credit for the improvement, but he and the university benefited from it. And after a year as president, the students warmed to Adams, whom they regarded as less rigid than White. The *Era* crowed: "Now behold a dawn of better things."

In describing the students, Adams noted approvingly that Cornell was, in his opinion, and in a "very broad sense a Christian institution," but he added, nothing is allowed that "would in letter or in spirit violate the provision in its charter against denominationalism." There was no required attendance at chapel, weekdays or Sunday. "We have," he added, "a number of Jews and a good many Roman Catholics—there are 15 in the present freshman class." The greatest number of students, reported Adams, were Presbyterians but there were also Methodists, Congregationalists, and Episcopalians. "Out of the 400 freshmen," he stated, "180 are members of some church." Which meant, of course, that 220 listed no religious preference at all.

Charles Kendall Adams (president, 1885–1892), albumen print photograph, ca. 1890.

The students' interests were as varied as their religious affiliations. The most popular major at Cornell was mechanical engineering; agriculture accounted for only fifty-six degree candidates during Cornell's first thirty-one years. These figures do not account for the number of students who came to Cornell and left before taking a degree, a relatively common pattern that makes counting majors and relying on matriculation figures a less than reliable way of assessing the university's strengths and gauging student preferences. Degrees were not of great importance at the time, and anyone who attended college—even for a semester or a year—could claim an affiliation that in many cases served almost as well as a degree.

In 1885 the faculty numbered 56; by the time Adams left Cornell in 1893, there were 142 on the faculty, but again, the figures do not tell the whole story because the majority were instructors, some hired to teach only one course. There were 27 full professors in 1885 and 34 in 1893, a less impressive increase. By 1893 there was an 11.9-to-1 student-faculty ratio.

Trends in student enrollment invariably prompt questions about student performance. From opening day forward, faculty and trustees had been anxious about the academic qualifications of incoming students: should even more be required of them? Yet every time enrollment dipped, the question changed: are Cornell's high standards discouraging applicants? A related concern involved cost: might rising tuition drive enrollment down? Tuition had increased from the original ten dollars per semester to one hundred dollars a year in 1900. The trustees wrestled with these problems as they tried to balance academic standards, costs, and the university's books.

In his inaugural address in November 1885, Adams defined his educational philosophy and identified some simple rules that he believed students should follow. He urged students to develop both mind and character and to cultivate good manners. Cornell's aim, he stated, was to prepare students for active careers. He supported courses in the liberal arts, believing that they had practical applications for life. When James Russell Lowell commented that "a university is a place where nothing useful is taught," Adams asked whether Cornell was any less a university

because so many "useful things are taught here." Speaking to the students, he cautioned that "at times you may not know what to do,—a professor is the happiest when a student comes to him with open mind to ask his advice." He invited students to "come as often as you have the impulse, as often as you need help." To the applause of the students in his audience, Adams said, "Professors are made for students, and not students for professors." Adams also raised the question of dormitories, initiating what would become an almost annual discussion about the university's responsibility to house its students and the students' right to expect university housing. Unlike White, for whom student self-regulation was a conviction, Adams believed that the prosperity of the university depended "largely upon the extent of the accommodations that can be afforded to students at a reasonable price."

Adams also attempted to address the alumni's numerous complaints about the university. He increased faculty salaries, raising the salary of a full professor to three thousand dollars a year. To allow time for research, he instituted a sabbatical system

Students and faculty on the Arts Quad near the site of East Sibley Hall, ca. 1890.

TO MAKE A MAN SELF-GOVERNING

· ·

PRESIDENT ADAMS, in his address, expressed himself as much pleased with the large freedom accorded our students; that, as long as this is not abused, he is in favor of giving them every reasonable liberty. Sometimes we have thought that even here at Cornell the student body was bound with too many restrictions; but in the main we feel compelled to admit that these have been necessary ones. With President Adams, the ERA believes that students should be made as nearly self-governing as is compatible with the best good of the University. To make a man self-governing is to increase his reliance and self-respect, which become great factors in the development of character. Some rules are necessary to provide systematic routine work; but let these be good and as few as may be. Let the student feel himself something more than a child, let him feel that he possesses volition, let him fully sense his responsibilities—that it is his to make or to mar, then he will feel that he had a mission to fulfill and will be likely to act in conformity therewith. . . . We ourselves, have little of which to complain; we feel sure that Cornell will never depart from her liberal principles; nay more, we hope to see her grow more liberal as time advances.

—THE CORNELL ERA, October 9, 1885

that gave faculty members a year's leave with pay after six years of service, and even more crucially, he reduced the teaching load so that the faculty could spend more time aiding students and pursuing their research interests. He also set aside modest funds to ease retirements, but since there were few retirements in the offing, the amount made little difference.

For some, however, those important reforms were not enough, nor did those who disparaged Adams give him much credit for what he managed to do. The disgruntled alumni invited the new president to attend their sixth annual banquet at Delmonico's restaurant in New York City. Some of these men, Adams knew, had opposed his appointment as president because he was White's hand-picked successor. The banquet was a potentially awkward occasion. Yet with an agility his Ithaca enemies would not have thought possible, Adams disarmed the alumni with wit. Their invitation had come as a surprise, he admitted, akin to what an African chief might feel when required to undergo an experimental ordeal before assuming high office. He might be "dipped into a river of hungry and open-mouthed crocodiles," but facing crocodiles, Adams said slyly, would be "paying a pretty large price for an office, even in New York." He had taken precautions at table, he told them. He had not eaten or drunk anything until after the alumni president had tasted *his* food and wine. "If I am to die as a result of this indiscretion, I shall at least have the satisfaction of seeing him die first."

In these years under Adams, the university grew visibly stronger. In 1886 Adams negotiated the purchase of 4,060 volumes of British and American legal reports and textbooks. The trustees allocated thirty-three hundred dollars for the volumes and thirty-seven dollars for the cases that housed them. With a law library installed on the upper floor of McGraw Hall, a department of law quickly followed. In fall 1887 the College of Law

opened with a faculty of three, augmented by half a dozen practicing lawyers of some reputation who delivered lectures during the term. Adams admitted that "we opened it with some hesitation, there being so many law schools already in existence. We should have been satisfied if there had been twenty-five students," but instead, the opening class numbered fifty-four. Rather than lumping students into one program, which was the usual practice, the school offered a graduated series of courses leading to the state bar exam. A dozen of the entering students qualified for the senior class, and all but two were college graduates. Lawyers already in practice were welcome to attend, and a moot court was organized to give students practice in investigation and preparation for trial of cases.

With equal optimism, a School of Pharmacy opened in 1887. Over time, however, it proved untenable because programs offered elsewhere cost far less in tuition and could be completed in weeks or months. Adams explained that he had not intended Cornell's pharmacy program to compete with the "city schools in the mere training of druggists' clerks"; rather, he had hoped to educate students to

Franklin (now Tjaden) Hall and West Sibley Hall, College of Engineering, with faculty houses along East Avenue, ca. 1888.

enter the work of manufacturing chemists and pharmacists. Nevertheless, Pharmacy closed in 1890, having graduated only one student.

Andrew White gave his historical library to the university, and in recognition of its value and of White's unique service, the trustees created the School of History and Political Science. In 1881, Moses Coit Tyler arrived from the University of Michigan to become the first professor of American history in the United States. Tyler introduced new teaching methods that became popular with the students, who thought weekly quizzes far preferable to a single examination at the end of the semester. In his American history seminary, as he termed it, Tyler also exposed students to historical research. But in 1889 Adams hoped to appoint a rising young scholar named Woodrow Wilson to become dean of the School of History and Political Science. In promoting Wilson, Adams managed to offend the faculty, who had just won from the trustees the right to approve those who would join it. Nursing their grudge against Adams for attempting to usurp their privilege, faculty members refused to appoint Wilson, though he did appear at Cornell to give a lecture. Tyler, in turn, believing himself the best candidate for the position—something Adams should have had the wisdom to see, especially since they had been colleagues in Ann Arbor—was offended by the president's lack of support. As a result, Tyler broke with Adams.

Other programs proceeded more smoothly. Adams strengthened connections between the teaching of agriculture and farmers by promoting the creation of agricultural experiment stations. He approved the use of college buildings for a summer school, beginning in 1893. He fostered the creation of a department of electrical engineering, the first in the nation, and in 1886 opened the first college bookstore. He also approved the expansion of mechanical engineering into a four-year program and in 1890 created the College of Civil Engineering. Alumni associations were active in several states, and the Cornell Athletic Association, a private organization that supported the university's athletic program, became a recognized entity.

Under Adams, in 1886 a chair in the Science and Art of Teaching was established, to foster the instruction of teachers and to strengthen the university's connection with the state's public schools. The trustees, in announcing this innovation, thought it desirable that Cornell "exert a wholesome and an elevating influence" upon the state school system. Many Cornell students, both men and women, Adams observed, came to Ithaca with the "desire to fit themselves for a career of teacher."

Henry Sage, chairman of the Board of Trustees, endowed the Susan Linn Sage School of Ethics in memory of his wife. For this purpose, he donated two hundred thousand dollars, of which twenty thousand was to be used to build and maintain a house for the professor of ethics "to be forever a perquisite of the chair"—so long as that person was agreeable to Sage. After a wide search, Sage selected Jacob Gould Schurman, a professor of philosophy at Dalhousie College, in Halifax, Nova Scotia, as the first incumbent. The professor of teaching became part of the Sage School, and over the next few years Schurman and Sage made several fine appointments, creating a coherent program that became a model for other universities.

Schurman's appearance on campus, however, signaled a beginning of the end for Adams, who had no reason to know that he had a rival in his faculty. From the start, Schurman was wildly popular with students. Professors and trustees openly admired him. Each misstep by Adams made Schurman all the more attractive, especially to Henry Sage. One stumble occurred in 1886.

On June 16 Adams asked the trustees to pass a resolution to award two honorary degrees at commencement, scheduled for the following day. Adams had all in readiness, and at such a late hour and with two eminently significant individuals present for the ceremony, the trustees could hardly protest. One degree was to honor Andrew Dickson White for his service to Cornell—and who could oppose that? The other was for David Starr Jordan, Cornell's most famous alumnus, who had become president of Indiana University and would go on to the presidency at Leland Stanford Junior University. The trustees voted approval and Adams presented the degrees. White, however, had long been opposed to honorary degrees, which he considered meaningless, and the Cornell faculty had voted that previous January against giving them. Even the students disliked honorary degrees or any degree that indicated a distinction in a Cornell diploma, fearing that some Cornell degrees would then be valued less—or more—than others. This democratic ethos permeated the campus. Disquiet grew, and many Cornellians recoiled at this trampling of "tradition." Alumni collected more than five hundred signatures, including that of honoree David Starr Jordan, on a petition requesting that Cornell adhere to its former policy of granting no honorary degrees. Jordan even wrote that he would much rather "give up the honor than have Cornell depart from the honored custom of giving no degrees not earned." What Adams had intended as a graceful and fitting gesture became a bone of contention on and off campus.

Adams might have blundered at commencement, and he might have veered from White's ideas about student housing, but he concurred with White and others who wished that a medical college be joined to the university. There had been an attempt when the university opened to add a medical school, and another even more feeble gesture in 1884 by some New York City doctors who hoped to raise

University museums in McGraw Hall, ca. 1889.

money for a school in New York City to be associated with Cornell. That, too, had come to naught. In 1891 things seemed more hopeful as Adams entered into discussions with the head of Bellevue Hospital Medical College about a union with Cornell. The negotiations reached a stage of particularity that included an agreement stating that there would be no teaching in medicine that was sectarian, but another stipulating that "women shall not be admitted as students of the Medical College, without the express approval of the Medical College as well as trustees of the university." The first statement adhered to Cornell's firm policy of nonsectarianism; the second hardly followed the Cornell tradition. The justification for excluding women was that New York City already had a fine medical college for women, run by Elizabeth and Emily Blackwell. The more likely reason for the ban was that the "presence of a woman in the lecture room and in the dissecting room would seriously disturb the good order and discipline of the class." If this bar against women did not sit well with the Cornell trustees, neither did the uncertain financing that was to support the merger. Nothing came of the medical school at this time.

Women on the Ithaca campus, however, took premedical courses under Burt Green Wilder and were free to follow whatever other academic interests they had. Nevertheless they chafed because the university regulated their personal lives. The freedom enjoyed by the first "lady scholars" faded away, for once Sage College opened, the trustees—that is, mainly Henry Sage—required that all women at Cornell live in the college unless they had family in Ithaca. The reason was financial, for empty places meant that the building's high costs could not be met. Having donated the money for Sage College, Henry Sage expected to dictate how it was used. At his urging, the trustees hired a "Lady Principal" to oversee the women of Sage College. They passed regulations, too, requiring that women be in by ten at night. As an *Era* writer scorned, "doubtless many anxious parents have kept their daughters away from Cornell, fearing some harm from the freedom here allowed." The *Era* also commented that the women at Cornell had "too much purpose in being here, and are too womanly," to need boarding house rules.

The men had no such regulations and lived with local families or in fraternities or in boarding houses in Ithaca. In many cases, the rooms available to students were small and inadequately heated—or sometimes not heated at all. The boarding conditions for men grew ever more troublesome, and after a time, eating houses on East Hill came to be called "dogs."

All during the 1880s an unpleasant legal issue ran like an undercurrent, causing constant anxiety until finally it burst forth in a spate of ill will. Although its origins can be traced to the years of White's presidency, it did not conclude until after the turn of the century. The story has all the classic Dickensian elements: love and lawyers, money and misunderstandings and motives, but it is also about friendship—the one thing that survived.

When Cornell opened, John McGraw donated money to build McGraw Hall, and his daughter Jennie gave the funds for the university's chimes. When John McGraw, a widower, died in 1877, Jennie inherited his fortune. In 1880, she hired an architect to build a mansion on the edge of campus overlooking Fall Creek Gorge. While the house was under construction, Jennie, age thirty-seven and suffering from consumption, set sail for Europe. Willard Fiske, the university librarian and a forty-eight-year-old bachelor scholar, soon followed. He courted her, and they decided to marry in Berlin, where White, his friend, was head of the U.S. Legation and where Douglass Boardman, Tompkins County judge and, later,

first director of the Cornell Law School, was visiting. Fiske borrowed money from White to buy a wedding ring and was advised by Boardman to sign a prenuptial agreement stating that he had no interest in his bride's money. After the wedding, the couple set out for Egypt, where Jennie's health worsened. The couple cut their honeymoon short and on a doctor's advice made their way back to Ithaca.

Jennie died three days after reaching home and was buried in Sage Chapel. There was some mystery about the location of Jennie's will, but when found and opened, it revealed that Jennie had left nearly two million dollars to the university, some to be used for a hospital, and more than a million and a half for a grand university library. In addition, significant sums of money were set aside for her uncle, Thomas, and for her husband, Willard.

The drama hinges on two points. First, Jennie's will, drawn up by Judge Boardman while in Berlin, was invalid under New York State law, which stipulated that no spouse could receive less than one-half of a partner's estate—something Boardman certainly knew. Second, Cornell University, as a New York State charitable organization, could not hold more than three million dollars in funds—the figure written into the university's charter for no better reason than that was the sum named in Harvard's charter, and who could have envisioned more money than that? Jennie's bequest, however, would bump the university's holdings above that limit. To avert the loss of this money, White and Boardman, by then both back in Ithaca, quietly went to Albany and urged the New York State Legislature to amend the university charter.

Willard Fiske knew of neither legal point, and he certainly knew nothing of the trip to Albany. He moved into Jennie's house, held dinner parties and long literary discussions, and earned a local reputation as something less than a grieving widower. There was gossip about his motives in marrying Jenny, and there were snubs. Fiske finally decided to set off for Italy, but before he departed, a lawyer informed him of the change in the university charter and his legal rights as Jennie's widower. Fiske was stung: his dear friend White, he believed, had acted deviously to secure the money, and Boardman, perhaps believing that Jennie would not live long enough to reach Ithaca, had forced on him a prenuptial agreement that was invalid in the state. Thus the McGraw-Fiske case

Jennie McGraw Fiske, ca. 1880.

Willard Fiske, ca. 1880.

began its long, complex journey through the courts. It seemed at times to have a life of its own as each court invalidated the ruling of its predecessor until the U.S. Supreme Court made a final judgment in 1890, finding against the university and for Willard Fiske and Jennie's uncle as sole benefactors.

The outcome was as tragicomic as the machinations that led to it. The university lost both the new library and the hospital that Jennie's money would have built. Thomas McGraw and his family were delighted, of course, and eventually sold the mansion to house a fraternity. Willard Fiske bought a villa in Florence, where he installed his mother and spent his time writing and collecting books and rare objects of art. Henry Sage, enraged, built the university a hospital and then donated the money for the University Library (now Uris Library), where he had inscribed at the front door:

THE GOOD SHE TRIED TO DO SHALL STAND AS IF 'TWERE DONE
GOD FINISHES THE WORK BY NOBLE SOULS BEGUN.
IN LOVING MEMORY OF JENNIE MCGRAW FISKE WHOSE PURPOSE TO
FOUND A GREAT LIBRARY FOR CORNELL UNIVERSITY HAS BEEN DEFEATED
THIS HOUSE IS BUILT AND ENDOWED BY HER FRIEND
HENRY W. SAGE
1891

Some have wickedly pointed out that it was not God but Henry Sage who finished Jennie's work—and that Sage's tablet blurred the distinction between the two.

Yet the friendship between White and Fiske endured. The two men visited each other when White was in Europe and corresponded with great affection over the years. There was, however, more drama to come, because when Willard Fiske died in 1904, he left the university half a million dollars and his collections of Dante, Petrarch, and Icelandic books—all treasures of which the university is justifiably proud. Fiske's only request was that his body be placed in the mausoleum in Sage Chapel with that of his wife. This so inflamed the Sage clan, whose father had built the chapel and who had rescued the university when the expected funds from Jennie's estate had "gotten away," that Henry's sons withdrew their support from Cornell.

In the end, the university received more than it could have anticipated: Sage infirmary, the vast University Library, and important book collections of immeasurable value. Today, Willard and Jennie lie together in Sage Chapel near Ezra and Mary Ann Cornell and their eldest son Alonzo, former governor of the state; Andrew Dickson White and his first wife Mary; and John McGraw. They were joined in 1949 by Cornell's fifth president, Edmund Ezra Day.

Everything the university wanted to do depended upon the funds available. When appraising the university's financial situation, the trustees acknowledged that Ezra Cornell had given them sound advice when he cautioned against selling the Wisconsin pinelands acquired with the Morrill land grant scrip. Cornell had insisted that the timber on the land be cut and sold, and the land held until the price rose. When the trustees finally sold the Wisconsin land in the 1890s, the university received four dollars an acre, bringing in a significant amount of money then crucially needed for Cornell's new period of expansion.

A great many things improved during the later 1880s and early 1890s, though few people were willing to give Adams credit for any of it. Adams's expansion of the Cornell campus and programs, however, increased the work of the president's

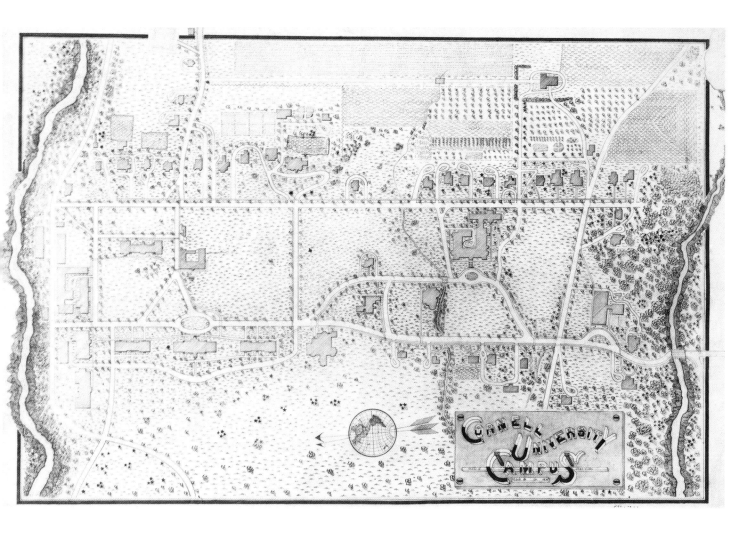

Cornell campus plan, 1890.

USEFUL AND PROPER DEPARTMENTS

. . . .

The nature of our obligations, therefore, may be reduced to this formula: The "Land Script Fund," amounting to $594,000, must be used in strict accordance with the provisions of the National grant; the Cornell Endowment Fund may be used for the establishment and support of any departments of the University that may be deemed useful and proper by the Trustees. It must not be forgotten, of course, that within the category of such interests are to be included the technical as well as the non-technical departments. In these fundamental laws and early agreements is to be found the ample justification of the founding of any department of the University that seems to promise to be useful to the people of the State and the Nation.

—Charles Kendall Adams, Annual Report of the President of Cornell University, 1885–86

office, and in 1889 he gave notice that he would no longer offer his course in history. Cornell's enrollment was growing, too. In 1893 students numbered 1,801, of whom 225 were women and 287 were graduate students; 1,003 were from New York State, and of them, 175 were from Tompkins County. Foreign students came predominantly from Canada (49); there were 5 from Asia, 8 from Europe, 9 from Central America, and 2 from South America.

All that Adams accomplished was not enough to improve his relations with the trustees. He even fell out with his few remaining friends on the faculty. Moses Coit Tyler spoke of Adams's "tactless rule" and noted in his diary, "I feel real pity for this poor old pachyderm of a president, persistently reiterating the same old blunders and plunging forever into the quagmire deeper and deeper." Then in spring 1892, Jacob Gould Schurman was invited to visit California, where he gave a series of lectures that so impressed his audiences he was offered the presidency of the University of California.

Henry Sage did not want to lose Schurman to Berkeley, and he was increasingly dissatisfied with Adams. Acting on his own as chairman of the trustees, he went to Adams's house in the middle of the day and, according to Morris Bishop, told him that he should resign, thereby "spoiling both his career and his lunch." Adams submitted his resignation, citing "seemingly irreconcilable differences of opinion in regard to matters of administrative importance." He hoped that the university would be "even more prosperous than it has been during the seven years of my administration." Sage took this letter to a meeting of the Board of Trustees, which accepted it and immediately voted to invite Jacob Gould Schurman to become the university's third president.

Charles Kendall Adams's tenure at Cornell was difficult, but having to follow in Andrew White's footsteps would have challenged anyone. Adams blundered by seeking to reverse White's policies regarding honorary degrees. His judgment about candidates for the faculty was generally sound, even if the faculty chose to ignore his advice and resented what it considered the president's meddling. He presided under rules that had not constrained his predecessor: unlike White, he needed to

consult departments before making faculty appointments, and he could not fire
faculty members at will. In 1889 the death of his wife struck a blow just as he was
haggling with faculty members he had long considered friends. His second wife,
the widow of Alfred S. Barnes (who had donated the funds to build Barnes Hall for
the Cornell Christian Association), was accustomed to living in a large city; she
probably found Ithaca small and unprepossessing, possibly even boring. Given the
awkward situation of his being at odds with both the faculty and the head of the
Board of Trustees, his new wife might have thought that Adams deserved better.
And that is how it turned out, for upon leaving Cornell, Adams became the very
successful and popular president of the University of Wisconsin.

**Football team,
1890.**

Chapter Four

THE TUNEFUL CHORUS BLENDING

When Jacob Gould Schurman became Cornell's third president in 1892, he enjoyed the enthusiastic support of the Board of Trustees and the students who had observed and applauded his courses, his public lectures, and his campus activities. Under Schurman, Cornell matured. He presided over the growth of the university's facilities, the development of its departments and colleges, the creation of new schools, the institution of a governing system of faculty committees, and the expansion of its student population. He stressed the university's service to the state and, most particularly, the state's financial responsibility to the state colleges—the College of Veterinary Medicine, the College of Agriculture, and growing from that school, the Department (and later the College) of Home Economics. It was during this era that we also find the origins of the university's research mission.

Jacob Gould Schurman (president, 1892–1920), platinum print photograph, ca. 1910.

Cornell had begun as an unconventional institution; under Jacob Gould Schurman, who refined some of Andrew Dickson White's ideas, Cornell University became less radical, a more familiar place—a university thought to provide an ideal collegiate experience. Captured in silent movies made in Ithaca in 1911 and afterward, Cornell's buildings and setting were admired, its active student life documented and cheered, and its female students accepted, their place in the academy secure, at least at Cornell. The university's winning athletic teams brought fame and popularity. As the twentieth century came of age, Cornell stood for an American wholesomeness—what American college life, now popular and desirable, stood for.

Yet in 1910, Edwin Slosson, who studied America's institutions of higher education, would write, "we expect more of Cornell." Were Cornell to become tame and lose its radical nature, Slosson worried, the essential character that had set it apart from other, more traditional institutions would be lost. He wanted Cornell to maintain its traditions, by which he meant its originality, its daring nature. To innovate, suggested Slosson, was to be true to Cornell's origins. It saddened him to think that Cornell might "slow down."

WE EXPECT MORE OF CORNELL

. . . .

. . . we expect more of Cornell. Cornell, in
order to be conservative in the sense of being
true to its traditions, must be radical and
progressive, for that is the way it started. I
do not mean to say that Cornell compares
unfavorably with other universities in this
respect, but does it not compare unfavorably
with its former self? Is the university as conspicuous an educational innovator in any of
its departments as it was a generation ago? Yet
one would have to be very much of a conservative to maintain that educational innovation
is not now as much in order as it was then. I
realize and wish to make plain that Cornell is
in a vigorous and healthy condition, is growing
rapidly, is improving all the time, and developing in many new directions, but somehow I
get the impression that it is now in its forties
beginning to settle down, and I do not like to
have Cornell settle down.

—Edwin E. Slosson, Great American
Universities (New York, 1910)

Cornell's rough edges were wearing smooth in part
because at the turn of the century, what had been innovative was now accepted and even emulated. Cornell
was no longer quite so distinctive: at the older colleges,
the traditional curriculum was falling away, and other
educational institutions were slowly becoming more
like Cornell. President Eliot of Harvard insisted that a
modern university could emerge even from old institutions, not just at new schools like Cornell and Johns
Hopkins. What the new American university required,
however, was leadership and money—more money than
had ever before been envisioned for higher education.
Science had become important: research in all fields was
now expected, especially for graduate education.

Jacob Gould Schurman presided over this transformation. He had been a professor of philosophy at Cornell, and his former colleagues on the faculty expected
him to understand its needs, which in most cases he
did. As Schurman began his term, the trustees ruled
that the president needed to consult with faculty members in each department when determining that department's needs and the means used to supply them. No
longer would the president decide on his own what was
best for the university; growing specialization meant
that faculty members were in a better position to determine academic appointments and departmental con-
figurations. *Consult* is an ambiguous word, however. The reforms were intended
to inhibit arbitrary action by the president, which does not mean, of course, that
arbitrary action ceased altogether.

Schurman's prior experience on the faculty helped him understand the complexities of the evolving academic world. Yet the "spirit of the age," he feared,
was not favorable to the "notion of liberal culture." He worried about the chasm
between the "idealism of Athens and the industrialism of America" and wondered
how a university should respond. Youth sought gainful occupation, but this voca-
tionalism meant that "colleges of arts decline, while the scientific and technical
schools" become overcrowded. "Our faculties of liberal arts should uphold the
banner of disinterested truth, beauty, and humane culture," he wrote, lest the arts

"truckle or succumb to the spirit of the age." His recommendation in 1906 was that the arts fight for their rightful place in the curriculum. He failed, however to lay out a plan of action. Nor was he to know that near the end of the twentieth century this same problem would reappear, its outcome as murky then as it had been in Schurman's time.

In 1911 Schurman reflected on the relationship between the faculty and the trustees in determining the governance of the university, and which group better represented the institution. He observed that "the supremacy of the Faculty in all educational matters has been maintained for a score of years, and professorial tenure of office is permanent and secure." The right of "absolute freedom of thought and speech for all members of the Faculty has been vigorously asserted and constantly enjoyed." Nevertheless, he noted an uncomfortable tension in American universities, where the "president and trustees hold the reins of power and exercise supreme control while the professors are legally in the position of employees of the corporation." The university is an intellectual organization, he asserted, "comprising devotees of knowledge—some investigating, some communicating, some acquiring—but all dedicated to the intellectual life." The faculty *was* the university, yet it lacked representation. How might Cornell apply the principle of representative government? In 1916, the trustees invited four faculty members to join the board, but without voting rights. This approach became known nationally as the Cornell Idea. On several occasions the faculty requested full voting privileges and were flatly denied or advised that the time was not auspicious. Not until 1950 were the faculty on the Board of Trustees granted the right to vote. To aid in running the university, Schurman created several faculty committees—a committee on educational policy, an administrative board in charge of freshmen and sophomores, and a committee on academic records. These remained in place until the 1950s.

Other significant innovations during the last decade of the nineteenth century include the formal creation in 1893 of the summer school, which began with an enrollment of 115, of whom 85 were public school teachers, mostly from the New

Delta Gamma sorority sisters, ca. 1895.

There are certain peculiar features and dangers necessarily inherent in a people's university, which I should like to mention, with special reference to Cornell. The first is, that it is enormously expensive. It takes several millions of dollars to maintain our present organization. And did Cornell completely realize its ideal, I know not what additional millions would be required to provide for all the subjects of human knowledge and practice yet unrepresented in our curriculum. Even our inadequate approach to this ideal involves a fast increasing outlay, which taxes all our resources. But, besides the cost of equipment, Cornell makes heavy sacrifices, which only the few know of, to bring its facilities within the reach of all the people. Our fees are only from one-half to two-thirds of what is ordinarily exacted at other institutions of the same, or even of inferior rank. We offer free instruction to over five hundred students from the State of New York. And if other students are too poor to pay their tuition fees, we take their promises to pay, and give them an education. Now, with our present resources, this beneficence on the part of the university is necessarily limited. . . .

My second remark is that institutions so general in their scope are especially liable to be misunderstood. People with hobbies will complain that they are neglected. Thus Cornell has been accused of neglecting the so-called liberal arts, in her devotion to the mechanic arts. But the fact is, as we all know, Cornell stands up for all subjects alike. And it has steadily aimed, and at an enormous outlay, to make its departments of literature, language, philosophy, science, and the like, second to none in the country. And the recent unusual increase of students in these subjects shows that at last our efforts have been appreciated. From the same illiberal spirit that has declared us without culture, because we endeavored to supply all the means of culture, our university was formerly branded as godless, apparently because its ideas was to study all the works of God . . . was due to that clause in the charter which makes Cornell forever undenominational. But time and a mutual understanding have shown that a secular university is not irreligious, because it is not sectarian . . .

—Jacob Gould Schurman, Founder's Day
address, January 11, 1888 (Ithaca, 1888)

Main reading room,
University Library,
1903.

York educational system. In addition, a summer session entirely devoted to law attracted 170 students. These special programs hired and administered their own faculty and kept separate books, which enabled the president and trustees to evaluate their results. In 1893 the law school cost $19,431 to operate. Schurman found it the easiest segment of the university to discuss because it "is a self-contained department." It is not surprising, then, that by 1896, the trustees had reorganized the university into distinct units, each with its own director and separate accounting, recognizing a Graduate Department and an Academic Department, which in 1903 became the College of Arts and Sciences.

The most significant change at this time involved New York State. Ezra Cornell had wanted his university to hire a "horse doctor" and had told White that of greatest importance was someone who could teach veterinary medicine. Professor James

Law had arrived in Ithaca in 1868 to fill this slot. By 1885 he was the unpaid state veterinarian, appointed to that position by Governor Hill, who valued his advice and wisdom. In 1893, Law excoriated the state for its failure to adequately fund instruction in veterinary medicine. Pointing to the danger and costs of epidemics and untrained doctors, he challenged the state to match the commitment of other states to protect their livestock and promote animal health. Within a year the state funded the New York State Veterinary College, and from 1894 on the state assumed full financial responsibility for the new college while granting its administration to the university's Board of Trustees, who appointed the director, hired the faculty, and determined the curriculum, salaries, and admissions. In 1904, the state created the New York State College of Agriculture under a similar arrangement.

Cornell was assuming its modern shape. In 1896 the Department of Architecture became a college. In 1919 Schurman remarked that the "educational ideal of Cornell University has been to combine the idealism of ancient Athens with the industrialism of modern America." That year, Schurman and the trustees combined the College of Civil Engineering with the Sibley College of Mechanical Engineering and Mechanical Arts to create a unified College of Engineering.

From Cornell's first year, the biology courses taught by Burt Green Wilder and others provided a firm scientific foundation for those who wanted to enter the medical profession. It was well recognized, however, that book learning alone did not make a physician. Since 1865 Cornell had been the object of flirtations by New York City hospitals seeking university affiliations, but as with many romances, the time and the circumstances were never quite right. In 1897 a merger of the University Medical College, Bellevue Hospital, and New York University came apart. A segment of the trustees, including Col. Oliver H. Payne, a wealthy benefactor of medical education, and some of the staff looked to Cornell. Payne gave money to "establish a medical department in New York City to be known and designated as the Cornell University Medical College." In 1898 the Cornell Medical College opened with 278 students, 26 of them women. They were housed in new facilities on 27th and 28th Streets. At the same time a two-year medical program began in Ithaca. Beginning in 1908 an undergraduate degree was required for admission to the medical college, and in 1913 the New York Hospital allocated to the medical college half its beds. Other affiliations were established, one in 1912 with the Russell Sage Institute of Pathology, and another in 1914 with the Memorial Hospital of New York.

With the university reorganized and invigorated, in 1894 Schurman gave the trustees a list of other urgent needs. He hoped to establish professorial chairs,

additional departments, and a fund for meritorious but indigent students, who were applying to Cornell in increasing numbers. President Schurman appreciated the fact that there were no warring factions at Cornell, as at other universities: Cornell was unique, he thought, for the "harmony and mutual good feeling and esteem, which are present among the several authorities—administrative and instructional."

There were exciting innovations, some stemming from the president, others from faculty who saw needs or opportunities. Isaac P. Roberts, director of the Department and then the College of Agriculture, and after him, Liberty Hyde Bailey built the program of extension as a way to disseminate the benefits of research to the state's working farmers. Research and extension have always been closely connected: extension workers in the College of Agriculture devised methods to

The Ithaca Trolley, seen from the portico of Boardman Hall, first home of the Cornell Law School, with University Library at left, 1895.

Liberty Hyde Bailey, dean of the College of Agriculture, ca. 1904.

improve agricultural yield, and then used the extension network to communicate their results to those who would most benefit. University researchers set off on lecture tours, speaking in church halls and granges, in community buildings and barns; they made presentations at state and county meetings of agricultural associations and at agricultural fairs; they wrote and distributed articles and pamphlets and taught courses, long and short, on campus and elsewhere. Three-day Farmers' Institutes had begun in 1886. When in 1908 Bailey expanded the program into Farmers' Week, later called Farm and Home Week, attendance was 800.

Extension courses and lecturers originally focused on the condition and needs of the state's farmers. To share the innovations from Ithaca's research labs more widely, the College of Agriculture received funding in 1898 to produce a farmers' reading course. In its first year, 4,600 farmers subscribed, and when they had completed that first course of study, they clamored for more, thereby extending the university's methods of teaching and also the categories of students.

Nature study followed the extension pattern. Intended to aid teachers in rural schools, the first *Nature Study Bulletin* was issued in 1898–99, along with leaflets detailing how to organize Junior Naturalist Clubs. Mary Rogers Miller and Anna Botsford Comstock pioneered in this work. The following year there were additional leaflets for teachers. In his annual report, Director Roberts wrote that Miller had lectured to numerous groups around the state and that Comstock was preparing literature to be distributed by the Extension Bureau. In 1905 another extension product appeared—the first issue of the *Junior Naturalist Monthly,* with Alice G. McCloskey its editor. Nature study became an important feature of the summer session curriculum as well, attracting public school teachers especially, who in turn passed along this new knowledge to their classes. Such innovations extended the teaching mission and student population associated with the university.

Agricultural extension connected more and more rural New Yorkers to the research conducted at Cornell and to the university faculty. Liberty Hyde Bailey lectured on campus and throughout the state, and he encouraged farmers in granges and extension courses to lobby the state for money for his program. It was Bailey who is credited with developing a "vision of rural progress that combined Darwinism and uplift, utilized science in gardening, and linked rural cultivation with rural culture." There was nothing small about Bailey's vision or narrow about who might qualify as an extension agent.

Under Roberts and Bailey, extension work followed a natural progression from a consideration of the needs of farmers, to life in rural areas, to the plight of rural schools, including both teachers and schoolchildren. In 1900 Melvil Dewey, the state librarian who was interested in many aspects of reform, called a meeting at Lake Placid to discuss domestic science and to consider ways this new subject might be brought to Cornell. The idea encountered resistance, and Schurman is said to have sputtered, "cooks on the faculty, never!" But it was supported by the New York State Legislature, which granted Cornell University ten thousand dollars to direct attention to the needs of farmers' wives. At the suggestion of Anna Comstock, Bailey hired Martha Van Rensselaer to adapt the extension approach to the needs of this new audience. In a letter addressed to rural women, Bailey asked what they needed to know, and what their working conditions were. Their answers poured in, with requests for information about all aspects of life, from making clothing, caring for children, and decorating homes to preserving and preparing food. Working on a simple kitchen table in the basement of Morrill Hall, Van Rensselaer wrote *Saving Steps,* the first of many pamphlets directed at improving the lives of rural women. She held daylong meetings called Women's Institutes, heard what farmwomen had to say, and received and replied to dozens of letters that illuminated the extent to which they suffered from exhaustion, ignorance, and isolation.

In his 1908 report to the president, Bailey extolled the New York State College of Agriculture not as "one definite curriculum leading to a profession or a single occupation" but instead as a college comprising "a great variety of subjects, all so organized as to form part of a liberal education in terms of country life." He extended agricultural education to agricultural chemistry, biological subjects, and even teacher training to prepare students to teach agricultural subjects to rural youngsters.

In 1907 Flora Rose joined Van Rensselaer in domestic science. In addition to their extension work, she and Van Rensselaer offered popular classes on campus centering on home topics and family life for students in the College of Agriculture. By 1909 this program had become a department and Bailey proposed to grant Van Rensselaer and Rose faculty status. Under the agenda heading WOMEN MEMBERS, on October 18, 1911, the faculty voted in the affirmative to allow women to join the faculty—but with caution and no obvious enthusiasm. "While

THE SCIENTIFIC SIDE OF
HOME MAKING

. . . .

[In 1900] I came to Cornell University, to the Department of Agriculture, which was not yet a college, to find out what a state department could offer to parallel the work being done for farmers to promote the interests of production. Public appropriations were secured for extension work with the idea of helping production. It was Dr. Liberty Hyde Bailey, then at the head of the extension work and teaching horticulture, who proposed that one of the best ways to help the farmer was to help the farmer's wife to make the farm home contribute to the best interests of farming. This has been the fundamental principle in agriculture and in home economics.

After an acquaintance had been gained with the farm women of the state and various plans of reaching the home were organized, we started work at Cornell which led to resident instruction. This was in the form of a short course in the winter (1902) for women on homemaking subjects. Later the trustees permitted a two hour course in homemaking to be introduced for credit.

In 1907 a department of home economics was organized in what had become the New York State College of Agriculture. Miss Flora Rose, who had been trained in the scientific side of home making, joined me at that time in this work. We were both appointed by the Trustees as heads of the Department with the supposition that in a short time the leadership would solve itself. We have continued for seventeen years as co-heads and with the assistance of a staff, which has increased from year to year, we have been able to build up a large department of home economics which has now been recognized as a professional school in the University . . .

—Martha Van Rensselaer

not favoring in general the appointment of women to professorships," read the resolution, the faculty would "interpose no objection to their appointment in the Department of Home Economics in the College of Agriculture."

As in Agriculture, research at other colleges at Cornell grew out of the needs of the school's constituencies, the interests of the faculty, and the availability of support. The earliest instances of federal government funding of research at Cornell occurred in 1899, when Cornell received a grant from the U.S. Deep Waterways Commission for an engineer to study the flow of waters over weirs. Subsequently, the U.S. Weather Bureau sent funds to establish a weather station at the university, which replaced the primitive facilities established by engineering professor Estevan Fuertes many years earlier.

Faculty of the
Department of
Home Economics,
with Flora Rose
and Martha Van
Rensselaer (first
row, center), 1914.

In 1909 Schurman addressed the condition of the graduate school, which he called the department of research. Research, insisted Schurman, would shape the future of the university. "It is by the enlargement of human knowledge that progress in civilisation and improvements in the life and condition of mankind are rendered possible," he told the trustees. "The scientific investigator who discovers new laws of nature does more for the relief, assistance, and uplifting of his fellow-men than all the politicians who deafen the world's ear with their panaceas." It would take money, Schurman was quick to point out, to support this mission. The age of research science was only beginning, Schurman said, and when the "realization comes—and come it certainly will, at Cornell and elsewhere—it will mark the final and culminating stage in the development of the university idea." At the current time, he noted, graduate schools produced teachers, and few universities heeded the "call to make explorations beyond the verge of existing knowledge." University research was hindered by the extent of teaching obligations and by a lack of funds. This, he said, would have to change.

Goldwin Smith (left) and Andrew Dickson White at the laying of the cornerstone of Goldwin Smith Hall, 1904.

In subsequent reports to the Board of Trustees and in reports from the deans to the president, calls for resources to support research become a dominant motif. Listen to the deans in 1911, for example: V. A. Moore, dean of the Veterinary College, needed "buildings for teaching medicine and a hospital for medical cases for both large and small animals." Liberty Hyde Bailey wrote of "congestion in the College of Agriculture," stating that "every department in the College feels the pressure for help and for space" and especially for a "business farm." In Civil Engineering, Lincoln Hall would have to "double in size to meet the need for recitation rooms, more and better lighted drafting rooms, larger laboratories with better equipment, and more space for the college library and reading room." Albert W. "Uncle Pete" Smith of the Sibley College of Mechanical Engineering saw a "pressing need for additional buildings for the accommodation of workshops and laboratories." The School of Education needed "a model and observation school."

How could the administration answer all those needs? Where would the money come from? There was some relief in 1912 as a result of Goldwin Smith's will. In it he left $800,000 to Cornell for the promotion of "liberal studies, languages, ancient and modern literature, philosophy, history and political science." He also left his brain to Burt Green Wilder's collection, but it did not pass through customs control at the border and spoiled there. Even so, the need for funds did not diminish; rather, this refrain sounded louder and louder throughout the twentieth century, reflecting the many changes in the educational mission of the university and the strain that research in its many forms continued to place on the university's resources.

Schurman noted in a report to the trustees that "the amazing growth and unparalleled success of Cornell University have brought on something like a crisis in its history." He pointed out that "the University has reached the point at which if it were a manufacturing corporation it would double its stock and duplicate its plant." In addition to the new pressures produced by a growing university, some long-standing problems remained. Schurman advised the board that faculty salaries were not competitive with the rewards possible in the world of business, and funds for retirement were totally inadequate. As Schurman saw the situation in 1901, "there is some danger of scholarship and science being starved out in America," and "serious danger of their falling into neglect, if not contempt. The office of professor needs to be dignified . . . by a salary correspondent to the intellectual eminence of the incumbent." Should not professors rank with capitalists and managers, "who now receive salaries many times greater than the professors"? The problem was not only salary, of course, but "every year Cornell University loses some successful professor because she has no endowment for pensions to which professors might look forward for their old age." Members of Cornell's original faculty, those who had joined the university in the 1860s, were just then announcing their own retirements, which only the most frugal could face with any confidence.

In this expanding and increasingly expensive academic world, Schurman and others reviewed the curriculum, still hoping to provide the broadest and most balanced education. The "modern engineer, if he is to be truly educated," Schurman wrote, "needs a training broader than physical science and technical study. He too, because he is a man, needs the culture of the humanities—that liberalizing and expansion of mind which comes from the study of literature, history, and philosophy." Also noticeable at this time was the growing importance of a college education. Robert H. Thurston, professor of engineering, saw the "college-man" as the appropriate leader of the work of the world, and he encouraged others to see the necessity of education in addressing the complex problems of the future. He wrote that he who would lead must have a combination of practical knowledge blended with the "hardly less valuable forms of culture" in order to cultivate the essential qualities of leadership.

SADLY CRAMPED FOR SPACE

Lastly, Sage Chapel has, thanks to the generosity of Mr. William H. Sage, been enlarged and beautifully decorated throughout. The north wall of the east transept has been removed and the transept extended to the northward, giving an additional floor space of thirty-two feet square for the organ and choir loft. New carved oak doors have been placed at the entrances and the pews have all been remodeled, both, together with the oak wainscoting, having been darkened to conform to the general color scheme of the walls and roof. The aisles and porches, also, have been laid with terraza and the open space in front of the apse has been filled with a large panel of mosaic showing Truth as represented in the True Vine; while the entire interior, including both walls and ceiling, has been embellished by an elaborate scheme of decoration, the motif of which is the olive vine, with branches, leaves, and fruit, which spreads over the panels of the roof, carrying in the midst of its foliage various ecclesiastical emblems, including the temple, the ship on the wave, the anchor, the lamp, the cross, and the interwoven triangles.

When all these new buildings, which represent almost $1,000,000, are completed, the University in certain departments will still remain sadly cramped for space.

—Jacob Gould Schurman, ANNUAL REPORT OF THE PRESIDENT OF CORNELL UNIVERSITY, 1903–04

A LIBERAL EDUCATION

. . . .

Those who fear the extinction of "the college" through the encroachments of the professional schools should study the situation at Cornell, where they will find much of interest and not a little of encouragement. Here, where the technical departments predominate more than elsewhere, humanistic studies, both in their ordinary and in their more recondite forms, have thriven from the beginning. At the present time the college of Arts and Science is growing more rapidly than the technical schools, and for the last few years has been the subject of special consideration by the president and faculty. In some institutions the early demise of the old college seems to be accepted as a foregone conclusion, and the quiet of the deathbed is disturbed by squabbles over its estate. In Cornell it is recognized that the difficulty with the college of arts is not the strength of its new competitors, but the lack of a clearly defined and generally accepted idea of its own purpose. As Professor Willcox put it: "The most vital need of college education throughout America is the formulation and application of some definition of a liberal education which will apply to the new conditions."

—Edwin E. Slosson, GREAT AMERICAN UNIVERSITIES (New York, 1910)

There were changes in the student experience as well. In 1894 the trimester was converted to a semester system, and student self-government expanded. In 1896 the Board of Trustees approved a more liberal system of course selection, with only drill and hygiene required for graduation. In addition, in 1899 Cornell joined a coalition of eastern universities in accepting a general college entrance examination to be given at various places in the Middle States and Maryland, as the Middle Atlantic States were then designated. As greater numbers of students were applying to college, selecting a class of students had become more difficult than in the days when all who could qualify were admitted.

Over the years, Cornell proctors for examinations were eliminated. In 1891–92 the university bought a mimeograph machine on which all examinations were to be duplicated, and students were required to use examination books. In the next years codes of conduct were discussed, adopted (1901), adjusted (1905), abandoned, then readopted after a flurry of cheating was exposed (1920), and finally quietly allowed to expire. Like so much else at Cornell, the honor system—what it was, and how it was to be administered—remained in a state of flux.

On St. Patrick's Day in 1901, led by Willard Straight, architecture students displayed their talents and class spirit by holding College of Architecture Day. Basing the celebration on St. Patrick's exploit of ridding Ireland of snakes and serpents, they constructed a dragon of wondrous proportions and paraded it around campus. The tradition became known as Dragon Day in the 1950s, and by then it was customary for the engineering students to impede the dragon's progress.

The student body took on a new aspect in the new century. Several Chinese students came to Cornell following the imposition of the Boxer Indemnities, which provided tuition for Chinese students in American colleges. A contingent of Indian students arrived too, numerous enough to form an association. The Cosmopolitan Club, founded in 1904, provided social activities for foreign students, and after 1911, it also provided housing.

African American students came to Cornell in the mid-1880s. In 1890 Cornell graduated its first black student, and blacks have been present on campus ever since, although their numbers were never large. Cornell's rural location and Ithaca's small African American population probably explain why more African American students were not attracted to the university, especially during the first half of the twentieth century. Given the times, these students encountered some racism—in 1900 some southern students threatened they might leave if blacks enrolled, and in 1907, when several black men tried out for the baseball team, a few worried they might qualify and expect to represent Cornell—but the university as an institution was expressly open to all qualified persons. The black men who came to Cornell lived off campus with local families or in the few boarding houses where they were welcome. In 1906 several black men formed Alpha Phi Alpha, a nonresidential fraternity that met first in the home of Edward Newton on North Albany Street, and also in rented rooms on East State Street.

African American women lived in Sage College, and we know some of them by name. Jane Datcher from Washington, D.C., graduated in 1890. Sarah and Nancy Brown were there in the last years of the nineteenth century.[1] In 1901 Jessie Fauset of Philadelphia arrived in Ithaca, directed here by M. Carey Thomas, who graduated from the university in 1877 and was at the time president of Bryn Mawr College. For four years Fauset lived in Sage College, and when she graduated in 1905, she had earned the respect and friendship of women students and faculty, in addition to a Phi Beta Kappa key. In 1907, however, a black woman was apparently excluded from living in Sage College, and in 1911, when two African American women arrived in Ithaca expecting to room in Sage, a petition signed by 269 women students asked that they be excluded. President Schurman responded by observing that "colored students have resided in Sage College in the past, and I see no good reason why that policy should be changed." He concluded sternly and in the tradition set by Andrew White and Ezra Cornell, stating "at Cornell all University doors must remain open to all students irrespective of race or color or creed or social standing or pecuniary condition." By the time Schurman's letter was written, however, the two women had left Ithaca.

Challenges to the university took many forms. In winter 1903 an outbreak of typhoid fever in Ithaca hospitalized 131 students. There were 82 deaths in Ithaca, including 13 students, and at least 16 others succumbed after leaving campus for

1. See Kammen, *Part & Apart: The African American Experience at Cornell, 1968 to 1945* (2008)

their homes. Although some people hastened to blame the university, the disease was traced to contamination of the water serving the City of Ithaca. Male students were particularly vulnerable because they lived in fraternities or boarding houses on East Hill; women living in Sage drank untainted water from Cornell's supply, and only one Cornell woman died from this outbreak. As the toll from the epidemic became known, Andrew Carnegie stepped forward to pay the expenses of those students who could not afford the extra burden caused by their unexpected medical bills. In 1907 a fire at the Chi Psi fraternity house killed three Ithaca firemen and four students. Both incidents revived discussions of the need for more university supervision of student housing and college-run dormitories where students could live close to the campus and in safety.

The extensive fraternity system relieved the university of some of the burden of providing housing, but many students continued to live off campus. "Cornell undergraduates," Kenneth Roberts '08 observed in the *Saturday Evening Post,* "can pretty well do as they please, go where they please in any manner that suits their convenience and pleasure." But they did not always enjoy healthful living situations. In 1910 Martha Van Rensselaer and Flora Rose raised questions about the unsanitary conditions in the boarding houses where students took meals. Much of the food served, they said, was unappetizing and decidedly unhealthful. The students followed up with investigations published in *The Cornell Era* that documented the awful conditions common in the boarding houses.

Another argument on behalf of building dormitories arose in 1907 when Lucian L. Nunn, who had made a fortune in the mines of Colorado, established Telluride House, which opened in 1910. The house provided room and board and more. It promoted itself as an intellectual community providing cultural enrichment to a select group of young men, who were to be freed of financial worry so that they could engage in the lofty life of the mind. Breaking with Andrew White's belief that students should board themselves, President Schurman broached the subject of dormitories and pointed to Telluride as a model. The debate was one-sided—Schurman usually got his way—but even after a decision had been made to construct dormitories at the base of Library Slope, funding had to be found. Baker Court and Founders Hall opened in 1916.

The new dormitories only partially solved the housing problem. Additional rooms were needed for the growing number of women seeking admission to the university, drawn especially to courses in the Department of Home Economics. Sage Annex housed women for whom there was no room in Sage College. In 1909 Schurman appointed Gertrude Shorb Martin adviser of women to coordinate and regulate the lives of women students, now that some women lived at Sage, some at the annex, and some in homes around Ithaca. Risley Hall opened in 1913, further dispersing Cornell's coeds around campus. Women participated in numerous activities on campus, and not just those at Sage College.

In 1910 Martin instituted a course of lectures to introduce Cornell women to the world beyond teaching—the career most of them considered the expected and perhaps inevitable outcome of their college education. Various speakers addressed the question, "What Shall the College Woman Do?" In her annual report the following year, Martin said she had spoken to alumnae around the country about opportunities for Cornell women, and the alumnae clubs in New York City, Buffalo, and Washington, D.C., had set up "vocation committees" to help graduating women find employment, thereby creating a women's network. Yet Martin found herself defending this work "against an imputation of Philistinism." She thought the criticism was based on one of two assumptions: that "the introduction of any vocational aim into college work is necessarily destructive of its 'culture' value"—reflecting what Schurman had told the trustees in 1906–07—and that "the effort to widen the vocational field for women is an effort to withdraw them from 'general culture' work," meaning those occupations, such as teaching or library science, generally approved for women. Martin believed that few women, even those registered in Arts and Sciences, came to Cornell without some vocational aim.

Questions and comments persisted about women at Cornell. From time to time, male students raised a protest, as did some individuals outside the university. In answering questions about what sort of women attended Cornell, Martha Van Rensselaer observed that it was difficult to make a "sweeping statement" about all Cornell female students, but "it would seem that the majority are attractive girls. There are not many who come to a co-educational university of this sort who do not know why they are here and who do not have very definite aims in life." As a result, she continued, "we have a lot of sincere young women who do much toward holding up the standard of scholarship." Van Rensselaer responded to the criticism that college women were somehow unfeminine or coarse by declaring, "I have never found a class of young women anywhere without finding a certain percentage among them who might be called common, and no doubt Cornell has its percentage; but I do not believe it has more than any other institution." The women at Cornell maintained good grades, she observed; they "make their own places, and if they have time for social affairs they have all they want." Had she a daughter to send to college, she added, "I should not hesitate to send her to Cornell."

My dear Mr. Mason:

. . . In Mechanical Engineering, in Civil Engineering, in Law, in Veterinary Medicine, there are not only no women on the faculties but in consequence of the nature of the subjects, no suggestions that women should ever become members of these faculties have been made. There remain the college of Agriculture and the College of Arts and Sciences. In the College of Agriculture the following women are members of the Faculty: Miss Rose, Professor, Miss Van Rensselaer, Professor; Mrs. Young, Miss Warner, Miss Hazard and Mrs. Comstock, Assistant Professors, all being in the Department of Home Economics . . .

You will see, therefore, that at Cornell University the struggle is narrowed to one college alone, the College of Arts and Sciences. Shall women be admitted to this faculty? This question has in the past been discussed in the Faculty, especially in connection with the proposal to admit the Adviser of Women and the sentiment was decidedly unfavorable to the new departure.

Even advocates of the admission of women to full faculty rights in our university would have to admit that some of the arguments which developed at that time were exceedingly weighty. I mention only two. One was that as women will receive lower pay than men, there was real danger that the Faculty might be "feminized" on grounds of economy. The other was, that the Cornell College of Arts and Sciences has to compete with other colleges of liberal arts in New York State and in this part of the country. These other colleges of liberal arts have men professors. It is believed by the faculty that young men would be much more apt to enter colleges of liberal arts in which the faculty was made up of men professors. Thus they argued that the introduction of women

President Schurman, on the other hand, found the issue of women at the university a difficult one. He was certainly in favor of educating women, and his own daughter was a Cornell student. He had agreed to hire Martha Van Rensselaer when the state offered money to fund work in domestic science. In 1911, however, Schurman tangled with women students over the issue of suffrage: most students were eager to participate in the political process, whereas Schurman seemed cautious about such a change.

Schurman expressed contradictory ideas about women on the faculty. In a letter written in 1914, he observed that of the many faculties at Cornell, women had been hired in the College of Agriculture but they had never even been considered —and in his mind most likely never would be—for Mechanical Engineering, Civil Engineering, Law, or Veterinary Medicine. But should women be admitted to the

in to the Cornell Faculty would tend to drive away men students from the College of Arts and Sciences.

Over against these and other weighty arguments stands the fundamental fact, however, that women in the history of civilization are coming more and more into possession of equal rights with men. My own belief is that no co-educational institution can adopt the theoretic position that women, if qualified as well as men for the work, shall hereafter be excluded from membership in the faculties of colleges which women students frequent, like our college of Arts and Sciences. And personally, I should be opposed to adopting any such programme.

I believe, too, there is a way in which the problem can be solved without inviting, and almost certainly avoiding, the disastrous result the members for the Faculty anticipate and deprecate. If, therefore, a woman were appointed an assistant professor or a full professor with a right to a seat in the Faculty, I would have her appointed in a department in which her work would not be prescribed for any class of students. I would not compel men to attend her course, nor for that matter would I compel women, but I would leave it open to all of them alike. The chances are that the great majority of her students would be women. But if she were an unusually able teacher and a master in her specialty, she would pretty certainly attract some men also. But it is not right in this matter to lay stress on the point of having men listeners to lectures by women. If the woman did her work well I should regard it as successful even if she failed to attract a single man student. . . .

—Jacob Gould Schurman to H. D. Mason, Tulsa, Oklahoma

faculty of the College of Arts and Sciences, where there were women students? Seeking to answer this question, he identified two dangers. The first was that if women taught in the College of Arts and Sciences, and if they were paid less than the men—which was his unquestioned assumption—the faculty might be "'feminized' on grounds of economy," which is what had happened in the nineteenth century to the occupation of primary and secondary school teaching. This would certainly not be good for the College.

The second danger, he cautioned, was that the College of Arts and Sciences competed with other liberal arts colleges where there were only male professors, and therefore women on the faculty at Cornell might drive away from Cornell those male students who would not want to be taught by a woman. Thus, for Schurman, the problem was not what was best for women at Cornell, or what was best for

Students in the Department of Plant Pathology, New York State College of Agriculture, ca. 1910.

the university itself, but how to maintain the application rate of competitive male students. What Schurman did not mention was that a woman had already taught in the College of Arts and Sciences. In 1897 Louise Sheffield Brownell had been appointed Warden of Sage College and Lecturer on English Literature. Schurman agreed that women had equal rights with men, and he believed that no coeducational institution could justify excluding qualified women from the faculty. He saw the logic of hiring women faculty members, or rather, the illogic of denying them such positions, but he was not eager to face the situation. These are arguments that we shall hear again.

During the twenty-eight years Jacob Gould Schurman served as president, rapidly expanding academic interests led to greater specialization, and Cornell extended its curriculum and modernized its physical plant to keep pace. Schurman's hand is evident everywhere, especially in his reports to the Board of Trustees, which are long and detailed. New courses appeared in the catalogue: psychology, music, hydraulic engineering, and railway mechanical engineering (1898–99); agronomy, animal husbandry, poultry husbandry, apiculture, ornithology, and plant pathology (1907); domestic science (1908); and aerial engineering (1910–11). Cornell enlarged its population and the diversity of its students, particularly of foreign students and women. Dormitories were built to house some students, and buildings erected to accommodate Cornell's ambitious research agenda. One of Schurman's goals, however, was not achieved during his tenure.

Ever mindful of the need to link the university to the state, and in particular to state funding, President Schurman sought to address the inadequate training of many teachers in New York's schools. Teacher training had begun at Cornell in 1886 as the Department of the Science and Art of Teaching, then moved in 1890 into the Sage School of Philosophy. There was also a two-year nature study course in the School of Agriculture for teachers, and education courses were also offered in the summer school. The Smith-Hughes Act in support of agricultural education, passed by the U.S. Congress in 1917, provided more funds for the teaching of education in the School of Agriculture. Only in 1926, however, after Schurman had left Cornell for a diplomatic career in China, were the various departments of education brought together into a Division of Education.

Cornell settled into the new century under the steady leadership of President Schurman. During this time, the university became an admired institution, its athletic teams earned Cornell popularity, it achieved recognition in the press and from the fledgling movies made in Ithaca. Much of the system of governance from this period remained until the 1950s. It was external events in the following years, however, rather than the actions of any one man that next shaped change on East Hill.

Braving time and storm

In April 1921 Fred Morelli refused to wear his freshman cap. His defiance so incensed his classmates that young Morelli was dunked into Beebe Lake. The next day, when he appeared again on campus without his beanie, he was accosted and left tied to a tree until rescued by Acting President Albert W. Smith. The incident itself is of less interest than Prof. George Lincoln Burr's reaction.

Burr, a historian, considered himself a mild man, little given to making much of student pranks. Indeed, in forty years at the university, he insisted, he had never once paid any notice to such things. He observed, however, that wearing a cap was enforced on all freshmen as if by rule. But whose rule? he asked. "The Freshmen had never concurred nor been consulted," he wrote, "and the enforcement was by a physical violence not only dangerous and illegal, but in violation of an express understanding with the Faculty committee on student affairs." Moreover, he said, it was the freshmen who had acted against their classmate, goaded into action by upperclassmen, and it appeared to all as if the "president, deans, and professors [were] in sympathy with the action." The students had reacted as a "shouting crowd." By what right was their demand made? Burr asked. His fear, eloquently expressed, was that what "lies before us [is] a regime of lynch law. Let us not mistake. Your liberties and mine will not long be more sacred to it than those of this student." He warned, "We too, must soon or late expect to share his fate." Had not David Starr Jordan just spoken on campus, he reminded the Cornell community, saying that in the beginning the "only tradition of which Cornell was proud was that she had no traditions"? His own resignation, he threatened, lay upon his desk, partially written. "If I may not remain a Cornellian, I must be free to be still a man." The acting president advised Morelli to go home and come back in the fall as a returning rather than as a first-year student, thereby defusing the situation.

Some traditions at Cornell emerged from its origins, and some appeared as the university was tested during its first half-century. The Cornell tradition of tolerance and freedom of expression—and freedom from the rule of force—would be

George Lincoln Burr, ca. 1910.

IN WHICH JANITORS APPLY MORAL
Unconscious Sweeper Believed He Could Wear Bull-Dog Suspenders
PANDELOONIUMS BREAK LOOSE

Furnace-men's indignation rose to the boiling point Wednesday morning when Givem Morhelli, an apprentice janitor, first class, again attempted to sweep the dandelions from the Quad, clad in Bull-Dog Suspenders. Twelve days before, a group of the big "J" men of the Janitors Beneficent Protective Assn., meeting at headquarters, Local 23, to originate ancient traditions, passed the following resolution; "Each and every apprentice janitor, first class, shall wear at all times, except on Sundays, official suspenders of the following description: President Suspenders of three and one-quarter-inch elastic of pure Para rubber: color, Carnelian with white edging. It is forbidden to wear nails for buttons, without special permission from the officials of Local 23." An unsigned letter from the Lloph Spinach, the master janitors' secret society, warned Morhelli that if he refused to be bound by the tradition of President Suspenders, he would get hurt. Accosted by walking delegates, Morhelli, being an "avowed anarchist", objected to having Presidents over him, and belligerently hooking his thumbs in the Bull-Dogs, declared in the tones of Martin Luther, "Here my trousers hang; they can do no otherwise, so help them Bull-Dog grips!" At this, infuriated members of the Janitors'

Union streamed from coal holes and cellar windows, and but for the timely intervention of Benign Providence, pandelooniums would have broken loose. Lifted up to the Morrill Sanctum Sanctorum, "although it is not definitely known what transpired, the consensus of opinions is" that Morhelli was presented with an autograph copy of WHAT THE MEN WILL WEAR. Prominent members of the union, statue dusters, stiff tenders, and walking "J" men, declared that the[re] are but two alternatives for Givem Morhelli: either he must uphold tradition and trousers with presidential Suspenders, or be expelled from the union.

The WEEKLY WASTE PAPER, official organ of the union, remembering that the faculty prohibition of Force applied only to breakfast food, praised the red-flanneled, virile spirit, and declared that the legitimate enforcement of the law must continue, reminding him that the last janitor to defy the union threw up the mop trying to toddle to the JENNY MCGRAW RAG. At an early hour this morning Morhelli had been unable to decide the proverbial question, "Why does a janitor wear red suspenders."

—THE CRITIC, II/3, April 26, 1921

tested again and again in the years to come. That tradition of tolerance would, in turn, test Cornell's next president, Livingston Farrand, who came to the university with a medical degree, knowledge of public health, and experience as president of the University of Colorado. Farrand was a genial man, adept at administration. His educational background was broad and his opinions firmly held. His sixteen-year term as president of Cornell spanned the aftermath of World War I, Prohibition, and the Great Depression. In contrast with Schurman's tenure, it was the times more than the president that left a deep imprint on the university.

Out of concern for making Cornell a "more human," more comfortable place, Willard D. Straight, '01, bequeathed money to build Willard Straight Hall, a student union building of stone and wood, decorated throughout with murals. In the Straight were dining rooms, meeting places, guest rooms, and a theater. The women had their own entrance and reception room; there was a barbershop for the men. Other additions to campus included the spacious Balch Hall, opened in 1929, and new dormitories for men designated the Memorial Halls, built in memory of those Cornellians who had lost their lives in the Great War. These buildings, which opened in 1931, included McFaddin, Lyon, Mennen, Boldt Tower, and Boldt Hall.

Livingston Farrand (president, 1921–1937) with George F. Baker, reviewing ROTC cadets, ca. 1923.

There were also extensions of the university's physical plant, with natural areas set aside to be kept always wild for students' investigation, the addition of the Arnot Forest in Newfield, and farms to be used for student experimentation. In 1923, the state placed control of the Experiment Station in Geneva under the College of Agriculture. In a significant move, in 1932 Farrand negotiated an agreement that state scholarship winners would receive a $200 remission on tuition rather than the previous waiver of all tuition. The state provided money for an expansion at the Veterinary School and a new building for Plant Science in 1931, for Warren Hall with its agricultural economics and farm management programs and rural social organizations in 1932, and for Martha Van Rensselaer Hall for

Construction of Willard Straight Hall, Cornell's
first student union, December 1924.

Home Economics in 1933. There were others additions on campus too, with some athletic improvements, a new heating plant, and in 1929 WHCU went on air, its call letters standing for "home of Cornell University."

Farrand reacted to the increasing burdens of his office by enlarging the administration. The Bureau of Admissions began in 1928. He added the position of provost in 1931, and that same year appointed a public information officer. The Department of Purchases, originally started in 1921, expanded in 1934 with the expectation that it would be able to save the university money in the difficult days of the Depression. Farrand also appointed a university publisher to take over the press, which had declined in visibility. In 1931, the Comstock Press, started by John H. Comstock and his wife Anna Botsford Comstock, became part of Cornell University Press.

The medical school entered a new phase, partly because of Farrand's interest, but primarily because of the concern shown it by Payne Whitney, heir of Oliver H. Payne, who had helped create the school in 1898. In his will, Whitney provided money for the Cornell Medical College and for the New York Hospital, cementing what had been a loose relationship into a close union resulting in a modern medical center. Other benefactors came forward and new facilities at 68th Street replaced the crowded older buildings downtown. Affiliations with the Manhattan Maternity Hospital and Dispensary, the Nursery and Children's Hospital bolstered the patient base and scope of the medical school.

In 1932 Cornell opened the School of Nursing in New York City, whose graduates received both a nursing diploma and a B.S. degree granted by the College of Home Economics. Despite the dire financial times, the Medical College flourished and its endowment increased. With medical facilities clustered in New York City and enrollment on campus declining, in 1938 the Ithaca division of the medical program, housed in Stimson Hall, closed down, having seen 1,515 students pass through.

New technologies, so welcome in the field of medicine, created problems on campus. In 1922 William H. Hammond, dean of the faculty, expressed a concern about automobiles. As long as a quarter of a century before, he noted, the faculty had worried about "the invasion of the quiet and beauty of the University's grounds" by the extension of the streetcar line beyond the Cascadilla Gorge, but the faculty's worries had been overcome by the "siren of convenience and physical comfort." Now, reported the dean, automobile traffic increased day by day. "The danger from motor vehicles speeding along the campus avenues and interference with lectures by the noise they create" caused the faculty to ask the Board of Trustees to curtail automobiles on campus. He pointed out that "the extraordinarily beautiful University grounds are appreciably injured by the denuded areas set aside for the parking of a constantly increasing number of automobiles used by professors, students, and guests." The trustees' response, at a meeting on November 3, 1923, was to prohibit all student cars from parking on campus during daylight hours and in 1931 to create a Motor Vehicle Bureau.

In this new era, students' behavior and appearance were unlike those of the past—"modern" was probably the word people used in describing them, or "fast." Rym Berry, director of athletics for the university and also its graceful scribe, commented, "This community has awakened to the realization that the young person of the present day no longer follows mid-Victorian standards of deportment." We have become aware, he wrote, "that the combined elements of totally undisciplined stags, jazz music, synthetic spirits, girls and powerless chaperones form an unstable compound." Moreover, "the gin man is almost as regular and faithful as the milkman."

Early in his administration, Farrand voiced several concerns that echo those heard during Schurman's presidency. Most particularly, he worried that the university suffered in competition with business and the better-paid professions when hiring and attempting to retain good faculty. No American university had successfully met the challenge of keeping good staff, Farrand noted, but a few had mitigated the problem by increasing faculty salaries. He could contemplate such an adjustment in 1922; ten years later, salaries still had not improved, but by then, raises were not even a possibility.

Nor was the Depression a good time for change. When faculty sitting on the Board of Trustees again requested the right to vote, the board responded that it was satisfied with faculty participation as it was. It would welcome faculty members with full rights, but the University Charter would have to be amended. This was not the appropriate time, cautioned the trustees, to discuss the issue with the state legislature, which would have to approve any change. So nothing was done.

But much was done to the curriculum. New courses appeared in music, the fine arts, drama, regional planning, chemical engineering, and administrative engineering. The College of Arts and Sciences required students to take six hours in each of seven groups of study to acquire an "acquaintance with the principal fields of learning." In addition, the semester was shortened to twelve weeks. The president worried, however, that within the set academic program, "the student of exceptional ability is necessarily penalized in his progress" by average students of less or ordinary ability. To address this, the College of Arts and Sciences adopted a plan

of "informal study" leading to a degree with honors and invited the fifty highest-ranking sophomores to participate. When this concept had been debated earlier in Cornell's history, students had protested the creation of special or distinctive degrees. The idea was no less controversial in 1924, for it appeared to negate Cornell's long history as a democratic institution where all students and all degrees were of equal worth. Despite reservations, however, the program went forward.

Was Cornell's education too practical? Dexter Kimball, dean of the College of Engineering, considered charges of "careerism" and reported that much thought had been given to the future of engineering education, especially after the various programs had been brought together, in 1919, into a College of Engineering. "On the one hand," he pointed out, "are the advocates of efficiency who think the

Statue of Ezra
Cornell by Hermon
Atkins MacNeil,
erected 1918, with
Sibley Hall in
background.

curriculum should be intensified and made more closely applicable to the practical field." The other viewpoint came from those who believed that the curriculum should be greatly liberalized and broadened, the technical work confined to fundamentals. Finding a way to produce highly valued engineering graduates was the challenge. Medicine and law, he recognized, had struck a balance by imposing "a certain degree of liberal training at the beginning of the course," but Kimball added, "there are good reasons for doubting whether this method applies to engineering." Rather he thought, "a careful selection of both technical and liberal studies" would be best, "considered from the standpoint of the student's future professional life." Such a course might be organized but it would take five years of study to achieve it. This should, reported Kimball, "answer most of the criticisms" of engineering careerism.

Still, in 1924 President Farrand voiced his own concern about extensive specialization, about degrees that some might call careerist, and about the costs to the university of providing this sort of education. One alumnus cautioned him against a "disposition to pass on mere information chiefly of a supposed immediate interest," lest such specific study fail to impart the "ability to attack new problems." Ten years later, as the Depression darkened, few people worried about careerism. In response to widespread unemployment, however, the university created a Bureau of Educational Service, expanded in 1933 into the Placement Bureau, to find graduates jobs.

The College of Law became a graduate program in 1925 and changed its name to the Cornell Law School. Its course offerings reflected the new times and the legal complications that attended America's growing involvement with the rest of the world. The faculty hoped to lay a "foundation of practical value for the lawyer whose practice may be of an international character. Social, commercial, and financial relations are becoming increasingly international." Internationalism in the law curriculum mirrored newly emerging international concerns in other sectors of the university and the nation. In 1932, the law school moved into its handsome quarters in Myron Taylor Hall.

Farrand was well aware of the university's relationship to the state, and of the state's responsibilities to its colleges. In 1925, the domestic science program at Cornell became the New York State College of Home Economics, the third statutory college at the university. In 1922, Farrand brokered an interesting new venture. When the American Association of Hotelmen offered to sponsor a course in hotel education, Farrand placed this new privately funded program within the New York State School of Home Economics. Howard Meek became the department's

very successful director, and soon Ells-
worth M. Statler, of the Statler Hotels,
would say, "Meek can have anything he
wants."

Cornell's broad scope fostered academic duplications. Farrand saw this
diversity as "one of the great assets
of Cornell" yet realized that its posed
organizational and financial problems.
"It is inevitable," he wrote, "that, with
the artificial lines set up for administrative efficiency, academic complications
should result." He consulted representatives of related fields and announced
that "marked progress is being made in
the coordination of courses in the biological sciences and in education and

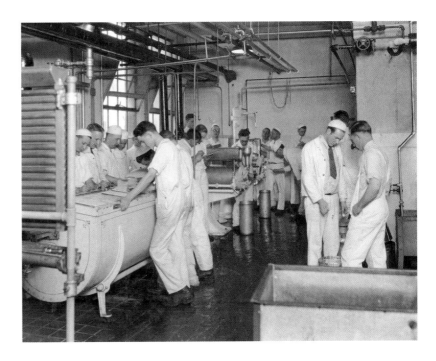

The dairy labora-
tory, College
of Agriculture,
ca. 1930.

consideration was being given to other subjects." This situation at Cornell has
always attracted administrative attention and tinkering, and while Farrand's integration of the biological sciences was a start, it would be fifty years before a Division of Biological Sciences would emerge. In the same interest of consolidation,
in 1926 the university approved a Division of Education to bring together courses
offered in the College of Arts and Sciences and those in the School of Agriculture.
To enhance this new program, the administration added a graduate department in
1931. The School of Education became autonomous in 1940.

Growth in enrollment during the 1920s caused President Farrand and the
Board of Trustees great concern and again raised the issue of the university's
responsibility regarding housing. The number of women admitted to the university was determined by the capacity of the women's dormitories, and Sage, Balch,
and Risley appeared sufficient for the time. But might the limited spaces for men in
the dormitories reduce applications to Cornell? In a long report, the administration
observed that students had to seek housing up and down East Hill and throughout
Ithaca, which was so small a city that suitable places were scarce. Rents in Ithaca
had increased, further curtailing students' opportunities for self-support and challenging Cornell's commitment to students without means.

In 1928 R. A. Emerson, dean of the Graduate School, voiced a related concern
about graduate students, whose numbers were also increasing. Graduate students

Construction of Balch Hall,
women's dormitory, ca. 1928.

CHAPTER FIVE

tended to be older, and many were married and had children: "of the 767 graduate students enrolled during the past academic year, 169 are married," noted Emerson, and many "had previously held positions in other universities or colleges and 32 per cent had had positions above the rank of instructor." Of the 98 graduate student families resident in Ithaca, 58 had children numbering 97 youngsters in all, 49 of them below five years of age. Yet most of these families lived in "apartments ranging from basements to third floors." Emerson called for action, either by the university or by businessmen in Ithaca. He thought there was an immediate need for fifty to perhaps a thousand inexpensive apartments for graduate student families. Nothing was done, and the problem was not addressed until after World War II.

Because of local high rents and other costs, Farrand worried that "there are every year in the University many students who by reason of scanty funds are forced to devote so much energy to outside remunerative work that not only does their academic standing suffer but in many cases their physical health is seriously impaired." The university offered loans to worthy students, and work to a few. Interestingly, funds for needy students from alumni and others had increased in a very encouraging way. "Nothing is more appealing, to the average right-minded individual," he observed, "than the case of a student struggling against odds for an education and this attitude prompts a considerable number of gifts to the University, restricted to that purpose."

The Cornell Era ceased publication in 1924, leaving the *Cornell Daily Sun* to become the university's as well as the community's morning newspaper. In 1930 the *Sun* marked its first half-century. In the commemorative issue, Farrand considered where Cornell was and where the university was heading. He wrote that "our educational system is still experimental and on trial." Cornell, he believed, "has come to occupy a unique position, partly due to her geographical location, partly to the nature of her foundation. She possesses the advantages of the older traditional institutions of which she is a protesting offshoot along with the vigor and democratic touch with the people which is the distinguishing mark of the great state institutions of the West." Cornell stands, he continued, "with a potential capacity for service, perhaps unequalled and needing but the material and human equipment to give it effective expression."

The *Cornell Daily Sun* became a potent vehicle for campus discussion. As Stanton Griffis '10 recalled, it also served as an advocate for reform. Students ran the paper, but everyone read it; students and faculty and alumni wrote letters to it, occasionally provoking notable exchanges. In 1926 "Five Unhappy and Bewildered

Freshmen" wrote to the *Sun* that they had begun to wonder "just what progress we could report to our parents." They had been at Cornell for almost an entire semester; they were taking courses, meeting people, talking to each other and to others, but they were suffering from a common confusion. They couldn't see why they were taking the courses they were enrolled in, they didn't comprehend any connection between their classes, they didn't understand where their courses were leading. "What's it all about?" they asked.

The question prompted a deluge of mail. Most writers offered advice, some scorned them for not accepting their situation, asking who were they to question what no one could answer? Carl Becker offered an eloquent response in which he called the freshmen wise for asking the question and confessed he didn't know what it was all about, either. Becker's answer was attacked by a senior who thought his answer "lacked substance beneath its very fine style." Did Becker expect the students to accept his own view, the writer asked? As a professor, he should have offered encouraging words. In rebuttal, Becker wrote that "college offers the student an opportunity (not so good an opportunity as we all wish) to enlarge his experience, extend his knowledge, to be initiated into many points of view, many philosophies of life." This was what Cornell stood for, and "no student should simply accept all the positions of all the professors, or that of any one professor." Instead, Becker pointed out, the student was here to work out an individual philosophy. "The college does not offer all these various and conflicting points of view in order to confuse the student. It offers them because they exist in modern thought, and the college necessarily reflects the conditions of modern thought." It was the student's job, wrote Becker, to sift through what was offered, and the student who managed to "work out any sort of philosophy of life during his four years has got the most a modern college can give him." The five freshmen probably remained in their state of bewilderment, not only at their academic predicament but also at the flurry of letters and opinions their question had elicited.

Even after fifty years, there was a sense of experimentation at Cornell—there was always trial and error. In 1928 the faculty recommended to the trustees that the daylight-saving experiment tried in spring and autumn 1928 "not be re-adopted in 1929." The impracticability of the plan was due principally to the confusion and inconvenience resulting from the use of two community times, standard time by the City of Ithaca and daylight-saving time at the University. Although the trustees expressed the hope that the faculty might work out some solution that would allow more daylight hours for recreation, they were not sympathetic to certain advantages the dual system afforded students, who could leave class at

. . . .

December 6, 1926

To the Editor of the CORNELL DAILY SUN:

I was interested in the letter of Five Bewildered Freshmen and in the discussion it gave rise to. The freshmen say they have been engaged in the intellectual life for more than two months and don't know what it's all about. This is bad, but who is to blame? Some say the students are to blame, and some say the professors. What is to be done about it? . . .

For my part, I don't blame anyone—not the freshmen, certainly. It's not especially the student's fault if he doesn't know what it's all about. If he did, he wouldn't need to come to college. That's why, I have always supposed, young people come to college—to get some notion, even if only a glimmering, of what it's about. They come to get "oriented." But why expect to be oriented in two months, or a year? The whole four years' college course is a course in orientation. It isn't a very satisfactory one, indeed. Four years isn't enough. Life itself is scarcely long enough to enable one to find out what it's all about.

Neither do I blame the professors—not particularly. Many people appear to think that professors possess some secret of knowledge and wisdom which would set the students right as to the meaning of things if they would only impart it. This, I do assure you, is an illusion. I could write you a letter on behalf of Five Bewildered Professors which would make the five bewildered freshmen appear cocksure by comparison. The professors are in the same boat. They don't know either what it's all about. They tried to find out when in college, and they have been trying ever since. Most of them, if they are wise, don't expect ever to find out, not really. But still they will, if they are wise, keep on trying. That is, indeed, just what the intellectual life is—a continuous adventure of the mind in which something is being discovered possessing whatever meaning the adventurer can find in it. . . .

The Five Bewildered Freshmen have got more out of their course than they know. It has made them ask a question—What is it all about? That is a pertinent question. I have been asking it for thirty-five years, and I am still as bewildered as they are.

—Carl Becker

two-thirty, hop on the trolley, and still make the two o'clock movie show in down-town Ithaca.

Two problems built up like roiling thunderclouds over both the nation and the university. Prohibition was one. The struggle to control and finally to suppress alcoholic consumption culminated in passage of the Eighteenth Amendment in December 1917. Prohibition, unfortunately, did not prove to be the panacea its advocates had promised. Instead, it generated widespread discontent and illegal activity—even by the otherwise law-abiding. President Farrand was frequently asked his opinion, and when he finally spoke out in 1926, his response caused pandemonium. In an open letter to the World League Against Alcoholism, he addressed the question "whether prohibition has increased or decreased the evils of the beverage liquor traffic among college and university students." His objections to Prohibition, he pointed out, were based not on the morality of the issue but, as he saw it, on the policy's long-term consequences. He believed that the evils of the liquor traffic among college and university students had increased rather than de-creased during Prohibition. Comparing 1926 with the situation ten years earlier, he wrote that drinking "is now of spirituous liquors whereas in the former period it was almost exclusively beer. In other words, habits are now being formed of far more dangerous significance than formerly." This might, he observed, touch a "smaller number of individual students" than in earlier times—an impressionistic opinion, he admitted, not one based upon absolute numbers—but it was dangerous because alcohol consumption was more likely to set a dangerous lifelong pattern. It was most probable, he warned, that this change was occurring not only in universi-ties but also in American communities. His judgment was that "even though it is possible there is less alcohol consumed today than before prohibition, the amount and method and extension of the traffic is so pernicious in its effects that the result must be designated a failure. I would therefore advocate a frank recogni-tion of a mistake and a change in the situation brought about by appropriate legis-lation." For this considered judgment, moderate and concerned, and aimed at the national as well as the college situation, Livingston Farrand received a barrage of hostile mail.

The other storm cloud over the university and the nation was financial. The consequences of the Great Depression for Cornell were dire. Each year during the 1930s, Livingston Farrand reported to the trustees the state of the enrollment and the detailed steps he, the administration, and the faculty were taking to reduce finan-cial stress on the institution. In 1931–32 he observed that "necessary retrenchment throughout the University has involved a sharp reduction in maintenance funds of departments and has left numerous vacancies unfilled." Some, he complained, were faculty positions of great importance to Cornell's mission. There had also been a reduction in the number of instructors and assistants and increased teaching loads for members of the faculty. The entire university staff recognized the necessities of the times and "is appreciative of the effort of the Board of Trustees to avoid a reduction in the salary scale."

News the following year was even less hopeful. Farrand reported that "after prolonged consideration, the Trustees decided that a general reduction of ten percent in the payment of all officers of the institution should be applied and such has been ordered." Faculty in the private colleges thought themselves lucky to retain their jobs. Their salaries were cut by ten percent; in the state schools faculty salaries were reduced by six percent with a twenty percent reduction of department funds. Farrand also noted, "while this step creates serious personal problems for a large number of individuals affected, the decision was received with a general recognition of its necessity. It is earnestly to be hoped that the previously inadequate scale of remuneration may be speedily restored and improved."

Enrollment dropped from 6,246 students in 1930–31 to 5,910 in 1934–35. The greatest losses were in the graduate program, engineering, veterinary medicine, and in the College of Arts and Sciences. While some students seemed unaffected by the national economic crisis, others had to find ways to remain in the university. The dean of women managed to help needy women with loans, a few outright gifts, and work, which most often took the form of housework for local families in exchange for room and board. As the Depression persisted, women students sought more remunerative work, but employment categories were specific to one sex or the other, and opportunities for women were limited. Some waited tables on campus, others answered phones. In 1931–32, 117 women received aid to remain in school. After that the sums available decreased; by 1934–35 the number of women enrolled at Cornell dropped by 26, and twenty-five percent of the female students required aid.

The situation encountered by Ruth Payton, an African American woman from Olean, New York, who had won a state scholarship to Cornell in 1927, was somewhat different. Her parents expected her to live in Sage College and were willing and able to pay the required fees, but for two years, according to a letter from her mother, Ruth was "forced on account of her being a colored student" to room on Cascadilla Street, seven blocks from the main trolley to the campus. Her mother wrote directly to President Farrand complaining that the dean of women had told Ruth it was "against the principles of the college to have colored girls in the

Campus panorama with (from left) Schoellkopf
Hall, Barton Hall, College of Veterinary Medicine
buildings, Stone Hall, Roberts Hall, East Roberts
(with Caldwell Hall to the rear), the greenhouses,
and Fernow Hall.

Dormitories." Why, she asked? Wasn't Cornell open to all? Farrand replied to Mrs. Payton—and also to M.J. Gilliam '01 of St. Louis, who had written on behalf of Pauline Davis, another African American student denied access to a room at Sage—that the university had "learned the folly of mixing the races" in Sage College, which had "caused more embarrassment than satisfaction" for the students involved. Yet Gilliam knew full well that when he was a student, Nancy and Sarah Brown—and possibly other African American women—had lived in Sage College without causing problems to anyone, black or white, as had Jessie Fauset '05, who had graduated with a Phi Beta Kappa key. In a clear and unfortunate break from the tradition established by Ezra Cornell and Andrew Dickson White, a principle strongly confirmed by Adams and Schurman, who had said the university was open to all, regardless of race, sex, or pecuniary condition, Farrand responded that he could not change a procedure established by the dean of women. Farrand disappoints: in reflecting the pervasive and rather casual racism of the day, he failed to follow established Cornell precedent.

It should be noted, however, that Cornell University never enacted the formulas that guided some other institutions, including Harvard, Yale, and Princeton, where quotas were established to restrict the number of students deemed undesirable. This is not say that there was no anti-Semitism at Cornell during this era: there were, as elsewhere in America, racist and anti-Semitic individuals, but there is no record of a university policy. In an informal note to Farrand, an alumnus wrote in 1934 that "you might be interested to know that any number of rumors have come to light in discussing with parents the possibility of Cornell for their children. These statements are in effect that we are being flooded with an unsatisfactory type of Jewish element." No response from Farrand exists, but when a faculty member cautioned Farrand about accepting too many Jewish students, Farrand, knowing that other eastern schools were restricting their number, responded that he was "aware of the problem" but could come up with no easy answer. Once more, his passive position was at variance with the principles on which Cornell had been founded. Livingston Farrand did become involved with several committees established to rescue Jewish scholars being hounded by Hitler in the years prior to the onset of war, but that activity had nothing to do with the policies of the university.

President Farrand can be credited with a staunch defense of Cornell's commitment to freedom of association. In 1936 State Sen. John J. McNaboe discovered two student clubs that appeared to him to be subversive. He was also alarmed by the publicity given a caravan of students who traveled to Pennsylvania to bring aid

Law school library in Boardman Hall
(used from 1892 to 1932), with librarian
E. E. Willever, ca. 1930.

to strikers there. He denounced Cornell in the press for allowing such groups to flourish on campus and charged that the university was a center of "revolutionary communistic activity." President Farrand is often quoted as having responded, "If we had no communists at Cornell, I would feel it my duty to import a few"—a statement that can be traced to no source other than tradition.

Communism, however, had become a national worry. In 1934 the state legislature passed the Ives Act, requiring all teachers in New York's public and private educational institutions to swear oaths of loyalty. This was not the first time the state had attempted to compel a profession of patriotism: a loyalty requirement had appeared in the Education Law of 1910, which was amended from time to time, and in 1921 the Lusk Acts had even established a special commission of inquiry into the political creeds of teachers, who could be dismissed if found subversive. It required the efforts of Justice Charles Evans Hughes, Gov. Alfred E. Smith, and others to bring about their repeal in 1923. The Ives Act of 1934, in the view of many on the Cornell faculty, was equally chilling. Under its provisions, all "teachers in tax-exempt institutions, whether public or private" were to take an oath of allegiance to state and national constitutions. University administrators were instructed to administer the oath and college officials were liable to fine and imprisonment if "any teacher failed to take the oath or to do his best work as a teacher." The faculty protested, insisting that allegiance could never be forced by legislation. Ours, they wrote, is a democracy that "rests on the free assent of the governed. Not only does it forbid special privilege, but it protects every class from special attack." When teachers are singled out for special legislation, "questioning their loyalty to the very traditions they devote their lives to inculcate in youth, a feeling of injustice is aroused." For what offense, the Cornell faculty asked, are we now put under oath? They then called for reconsideration of the Ives Act and its repeal.

Until 1935 the Cornell University Athletic Association, made up of alumni and other enthusiasts, funded Cornell's athletic teams. As economic hard times depleted the university's coffers, the administration transferred a number of athletic activities that were part of its physical education program onto the budget of the Athletic Association. At the same time, however, varsity sports teams were winning fewer games and inspiring fewer alumni contributions and only mild student interest. Soon, the strain became apparent. In 1935 the university assumed full responsibility for all college athletics, established the Department of Physical Education (changed in 1986 to the Department of Athletics and Physical Education), and named James Lynah '04 director. In addition, Farrand named a faculty Committee of Athletic Control. Lynah hired staff and set a new direction for

Cornell athletics. In 1937 he invited discussion among representatives of other eastern schools of the possibility of creating a separate athletic league. As he wrote to President Farrand, "there was much interest in such a league but it was the unanimous belief that the time was not ripe to launch it." The idea of a league "of their own" would resurface.

Another consequence of the Depression had a beneficial outcome at Cornell. In 1935 young men enrolled in the Civilian Conservation Corps arrived on campus to develop and improve the university arboretum. White had promoted the landscaping of the campus and placed the maintenance of the university grounds under the direction of the professor of botany. A. N. Prentiss proposed an arboretum in 1877, and although White had recommended it to the trustees, at the time other, more pressing needs received attention. In 1893 Schurman had directed that the specimen trees around Sage College be labeled with both their common and their scientific names. Prof. W. W. Rowlee oversaw the university grounds for more than thirty years, beginning in the mid-1890s, tending and adding to the collection of trees on campus and urging always that the university create a proper arboretum. But it was not until 1935, when the CCC boys arrived, that the Cornell arboretum came into being. By the time the workers left in 1941, Cornell had a facility to be proud of. The name was changed in 1944 to the Cornell Plantations.

From the very earliest years, ornithology was important at Cornell. In 1870–71, Greene Smith of Geneva, a nonresident lecturer, came to Ithaca to give talks about ornithology. He also donated to the university 362 mounted birds, some from Brazil. Prof. Burt Green Wilder and David Starr Jordan, while still an undergraduate, included ornithology in their course on systematic zoology and ecology. At the age of fifteen, Louis Agassiz Fuertes, son of Estevan Fuertes,

—AND PERHAPS CORNELL

. . . .

A college president from the Middle West made a fine speech in New York the other day, in praise of his institution and in scorn of the London SATURDAY REVIEW, which had referred to it as "a place of no particular intellectual pretensions." In the course of his philippic, he revealed that THE SATURDAY REVIEW had listed, as places of intellectual pretensions and as essentially American colleges, Harvard, Yale, Princeton, and perhaps Cornell.

. . . Should we complain because our Alma Mater has found no fixed and sure classification in the educational world? Why no, I should think not. Perhaps the amazing growth of the university from the seed planted by Ezra Cornell is due to characteristics implicit in the seed and developed by its isolation and independence. . . . As the qualities in the seed persist and fructify, it may be that foreign observers hunting the essentially American college will specify Cornell University. And perhaps Harvard, Yale, and Princeton.

—Morris Bishop, in Raymond F. Howes, ed., OUR CORNELL (Ithaca, 1939)

Arthur A. Allen (left) and James Tanner recording bird songs, with Elsa Allen driving the truck, ca. 1935.

professor of engineering, turned his artistic talent to painting birds, beginning in 1889 with a portrait of a passenger pigeon. To his untimely death in 1927, the younger Fuertes, though never a regular faculty member, was considered the "shining light of Cornell ornithology." The study of birds was incorporated in many courses, but Arthur A. Allen wrote the first Cornell thesis devoted solely to birds in 1909, and by 1933, of the thirty Ph.D.s in ornithology in the country, sixteen had been taken at Cornell. Bird study broadened in 1929 with the addition of bird sounds recorded by Cornellians, and many people still remember the popular program heard over Cornell radio called "Know Your Birds." The field was not limited to academic practitioners: amateurs were always part of the picture. When Lyman K. Stuart wanted to learn to photograph birds, he came to Cornell. When his efforts achieved first prize in a *Life* magazine contest, he bought Sapsucker Woods and built the first laboratory there, which came to be called Stuart

Laboratory. Ornithology moved to Sapsucker Woods in 1956 as a separate department and at first raised ninety percent of its operating funds from memberships and activities it sponsored. In 2003 the Laboratory of Ornithology moved into dramatic new headquarters.

Money was scarce all around campus but particularly at the library. Over and again, Livingston Farrand spoke about the needs of the main library (now Uris Library), which had been designed by William Henry Miller and opened in 1892. Always overflowing, it required continual adjustments to house the ever-growing collections. But this problem was not addressed until well after the Second World War, and even then, only slowly.

In 1937, in his final report to the Board of Trustees, Farrand observed that the "most important and significant aspect of the Cornell tradition and life and one which I earnestly trust will always be maintained" was the "delegation by the Trustees to the Faculty of responsibility for educational policies and academic procedure and, connected with it, the maintenance of that freedom of opinion, speech, and teaching which has always characterized this University." It was remarkable, Farrand commented, that this situation at Cornell "accounts for the vigorous and loyal atmosphere, not only on the campus but to a notable degree in the great body of alumni who have come under its influence." In the "confused world of the present," a world rapidly heading for war, these principles were under attack. Without adherence to them, he asserted, "no progress, economic, social or academic, is possible."

Chapter Six

WHERE'ER DUTY CALLS

In 1938 the last 160 acres of Ezra Cornell's endowment sold for $350. To Cornell's new president, Edmund Ezra Day, it was obvious that the cost of future initiatives would outstrip the university's ability to fund them. "Rufus," as he was known, wanted to improve the university's physical plant, expand the overcrowded library, relocate the College of Engineering, increase facilities for indoor athletics, start a business school, improve faculty salaries, support scientific research at the highest levels, and make Cornell preeminent in medicine. These were all worthy but expensive initiatives, and the question of how to pay for them became paramount. To address that issue, Day created a fund-raising committee and assigned the provost (a position first created in 1931) oversight of university development.

By 1940 some results were already evident on campus. An extension enlarged Sage Chapel by forty feet to the west, the arboretum grew into the Cornell Plantations, a golf course appeared north of campus, and new bells augmented the chimes. Sadly, to many, the Beebe Lake toboggan run was abandoned. New courses appeared in the catalogue: a nutrition program began in 1939, the Department of Sociology and Anthropology in 1940. Trustees voiced approval for the creation of the School of Education that same year, and courses in Slavic languages, funded by a grant from the Rockefeller Foundation, were offered beginning in 1941.

There were some ominous events, too. In 1940, in response to the worsening situation in Europe, all males over age 21 were required to register for the draft, and 1,682 Cornell men did. It was the rise of fascism in Europe that inspired an address that has come to define the essence of Cornell. On April 27, 1940, Carl Becker, the newly named university historian, delivered a lecture marking the seventy-fifth anniversary of the signing of the Cornell University charter. His essay on the value of freedom and the importance of universities, especially in trying times, defines

Edmund Ezra Day (president, 1937–1949), with Cornell's manuscript copy of the Gettysburg Address in Lincoln's hand, given by Marguerite Lilly Noyes in honor of her husband, Nicholas H. Noyes '06, ca. 1949.

In the process of acquiring a reputation Cornell acquired something better than a reputation, or rather acquired something which is the better part of its reputation. It acquired a character . . . universities are, after all, largely shaped by presidents and professors, and presidents and professors, especially if they are good ones, are fairly certain to be men of distinctive, not to say eccentric, minds and temperaments. A professor, as the German saying has it, is a man who thinks otherwise. Now an able and otherwise-thinking president, surrounded by able and otherwise-thinking professors, each resolutely thinking otherwise in his own manner, each astounded to find that the others, excellent fellows as he knows them in the main to be, so often refuse in matters of the highest import to be informed by knowledge or guided by reason—this is indeed always an arresting spectacle and may sometimes seem to be a futile performance. Yet it is not futile unless great universities are futile. For the essential quality of a great university derives from the corporate activities of such a community of other-wise-thinking men. By virtue of a divergence as well as of a community of interests, by the sharp impress of their minds and temperaments and eccentricities upon each other and upon their pupils, there is created a continuing tradition of ideas and attitudes and habitual responses that has a life of its own. It is this continuing tradition that gives to a university its corporate character or personality, that intangible but living and dynamic influence which is the richest and most durable gift any university can confer upon those who come to it for instruction and guidance.

Cornell has a character, a corporate personality, in this sense, an intellectual tradition by which it can be identified. The word which best symbolizes this tradition is freedom. . . .

—Carl Becker, THE CORNELL TRADITION: FREEDOM AND RESPONSIBILITY, 1940

Cornell and echoes across the remainder of the twentieth century, even finding resonance in our post-September 11, 2001, era.

In 1940, war was imminent, and even before the attack on the United States, war made its presence felt on campus. The College of Engineering added defense courses to the curriculum. In October 1941, President Day reported to the faculty that the oath of allegiance, required by the Education Law, would now be administered by the president or a member of the Board of Trustees and "must be taken by every person giving classroom instruction in the University." This time, there were no faculty reservations or comments.

A year later Americans were to refer to time as before or after Pearl Harbor, and President Day's elaborate plans for the university were put on hold. In his report to the Board of Trustees early in 1942, Day observed that "institutions of higher education have certain well-established functions in a free society such as ours. They cultivate the practice of the arts and the pursuit of truth. They support and facilitate the work of scholars, artists, and scientists. They provide liberal education." It was now evident, observed Day, that some crucial functions of the university were about to be eclipsed by war. "War, by its very nature," Day cautioned, is a "direct nullification of the basic purposes of higher education. In so far as war demands self-sacrifice and the recognition of supreme moral and spiritual values, it is, of course, in full accord with the aims of higher education soundly conceived. But in times of peace democratic education serves generally to promote humane and rational living." The university continued to function, its mission altered.

That first year of U.S. involvement in the war, Cornell's fall semester began with the same number of students as in 1941, but many more than previously were enrolled in engineering, and an accelerated program moved young men through their education to serve the nation's need. By the 1942–43 academic year, the campus resembled a military school. The activities that had constituted student life contracted, and women students occupied some campus positions previously restricted to men: women became editors-in-chief of the *Cornell Daily Sun* and *The Widow*, the campus humor magazine. In 1942 the Navy V-12 program brought to campus students who had been inducted, uniformed, and sent by the military for training. By war's end, 3,578 men had trained at Cornell for the U.S. Army, 14,896 for the Navy, and some 300 for the Marines: almost 19,000 in all.

The university offered special wartime instruction, and its facilities remained open throughout the year. There were special programs to meet military needs— courses in ordnance matériel inspection, electrical communication for the Signal Corps, and a diesel engine course for student officers of the U.S. Naval Reserve.

World War II commando training and physical education on campus, ca. 1942.

Olin Hall, completed in 1942, housed these initiatives. In addition, Cornell conducted secret war research. The School of Nutrition, started in 1941, attracted students whose skills were sought by the military to nourish troops and by civilians who faced shortages of basic ingredients and other constraints brought on by rationing. In a pioneering program at the School of Chemical Engineering, scientists explored the chemistry of food and nutrition.

While students at Cornell prepared to serve a nation at war, more than 195 faculty and staff with expertise in critical fields left Ithaca for duty in Washington and elsewhere. Those who remained on campus voted to postpone all considerations of tenure until peacetime. Graduate students took over much of the instruction and—for a time—the faculty in Arts and Sciences hired a few women to teach basic courses.

Although the war encouraged national unity of purpose, Cornell was still viewed suspiciously by some, and its academic innovations drew continued criticism. In 1944 President Day viewed the newest accusations as part of a pattern. He observed that "in 1868–69 (and, for that matter, quite a while afterward), Cornell was repeatedly attacked by unfriendly interests dominated either by fear of the then new broad and liberal philosophy of education in the young institution, or simply by jealousy." Now, he noted, the university was under fire again, and the attacks "bore a marked similarity to those of seventy-five years ago." The barbs focused on three aspects of the university's program: the Russian area studies and language curriculum of the Army Specialized Training Program, the civilian program of intensive study of contemporary Russian civilization, and a proposed series of lectures on civil liberties. Because of these activities on campus, one New York newspaper headline shouted, "CORNELL GOES BOLSHEVIST."

Americans' mistrust of things Russian deepened over the first half of the twentieth century. President Day spoke of the "spreading agitation with respect to communism, and the bearing that has on the whole problem of maintaining academic freedom." Day argued, however, not in terms of academic freedom but in regards to the political inclinations of professors. There could be no legitimate reason, he insisted, to retain a faculty member who avowed allegiance to communism. The heart of an educational institution was that "the Faculty should be composed of free, honest, competent, inquiring minds, undertaking to find and disseminate the truth," and no mind that was fettered to an ideology could also be free. What he hoped to determine was "a line behind which we can protect the essentials of academic freedom." He wanted Cornell to "define its position clearly, unmistakably and then fight through thick and thin to hold it." Cornell should defend the great American liberal tradition—which to Day meant keeping communists and communist sympathizers out of the classroom.

The planned civil liberties lectures that came under attack appear to be exactly what a university ought to offer. Scheduled for fall 1944, the series was to consist of five public lectures, two by members of the faculty, one by a scholar in political science associated with a major newspaper, one by the chairman of the Federal Communications Commission, and the last by the attorney general of the United States. The intent was to "throw light upon the adaptations of our traditional concepts of civil liberty in the light of the dislocations and complexities of modern urban industrialized society." Who could oppose such a topic? That these lectures would be given at Cornell and would explore a citizen's relationship to civil liberties, however, was enough to raise the eyebrows of the university's ever-vigilant critics. Morris Bishop in his *History of Cornell* suggests that even when the furor subsided, the general impression remained that the Cornell University was inculcating American youth with ideas that would turn them Red.

I would say that the University has been conspicuous in its continuing efforts to demonstrate the interrelations and the interactions of practical, social, and moral knowledge, understanding and competence. There has never been the disposition here to carve these areas of intelligence apart, to speak of practical intelligence on the one hand, of social intelligence on another, and of moral intelligence on still another, as if a man or woman did not, in very life, knot these varieties of intelligence together. The education program in this institution has always undertaken to deal with preparation for the job and preparation for life simultaneously and in the same broad curriculum. The idea of first taking a program to prepare for life and then, subsequently, taking a program to prepare to earn a living, has never found a place in the educational planning of this institution. These are varieties of intelligence, understanding and competence which have to be woven together in a single educational plan and a single educational opportunity. The pioneering of the institution has constantly embodied this notion of the fusing of these three areas of interest in learning.

. . . I would say that Cornell has stood all through the years for the strengthening of the forces of good will among men. There has been no rancor in the history of this institution internally. It has been repeatedly subjected to attack, in the early days to very vicious attacks as a Godless institution defying the established church. In that connection it is interesting to note that by common repute we have the most successful voluntary chapel on this campus that can be found in any institution in the country. It never had to go through the throes of moving from the compulsory to the voluntary. It has been voluntary from the outset, and every Sunday the chapel is filled with students—there, because they wish to be there. . . .

I would say that the University has concerned itself in its internal affairs and in its external influence with a constant effort to establish and maintain common justice. This is not an institution that is given to prejudice—not an institution lining up behind special interests. It is devoted to a service to the whole people that there be common justice among men.

. . . This institution has demonstrated faith in the disinterested pursuit of truth.

—Edmund E. Day, THE PIONEERING NATURE OF CORNELL (Ithaca, 1948)

Day later commented that he thought the university had "come through the recent attacks stronger than before." The trustees and faculty had shown courage in supporting the university's right "to give instruction in any study," and the "sense of being under fire created a sense of unity and independence of spirit that would have had warm approval from those early-day Cornellians who had to fight much the same sort of battle in their time." The lecture series and the Russian language program had been offered without devious purpose; but fascism was another matter. After the war, when asked whether the university would hire former German scientists who had aided the Nazi regime, President Day emphatically announced his opposition to "any scholars or scientists of foreign origin whose opinions exhibit sympathy for Fascist or Nazi ideals."

In 1949 President Day received a request from the House Un-American Activities Committee for reading lists from all courses at Cornell that touched on communism. Day regarded such investigations as witch hunts and acidly told the congressional representatives that he resented this intrusion in educational matters: "they could find out the reading lists," he retorted, "by matriculating at Cornell."

Transforming the university from wartime preparedness to peacetime after 1945 posed a great many questions. Could—and should—Cornell revert to its pre-war self? Would the student population remain the same? Would the same number of "legacy" students, those who parents and even grandparents had attended Cornell, be admitted as previously? How could Cornell finance the increasingly costly science programs demanded by its outstanding faculty? Some responses served to alter the character of Cornell—for the better, say most; not so, complain those who look back with longing at a smaller, more intimate, less bureaucratic institution. Still, student enrollment increased, and students' preferences for courses in history, philosophy, and government, in the physical sciences, and in engineering and architecture reflected the new times.

Faculty salaries, which had not changed during the war years, became an acute problem. After the war, faculty in the state colleges received a cost-of-living bonus. Lest the endowed faculty be left behind, the Board of Trustees voted to distribute a lump sum among all full-time endowed faculty whose annual salary was less than five thousand dollars. Any increase in salary was welcomed, but the improved scale did little to make Cornell more attractive in an ever-expanding and increasingly competitive academic market.

The needs of the library became even more urgent. When a Department of Regional History was added in 1942, funded by the Rockefeller Foundation, its collections were placed in Boardman Hall, then the home of the Department of

Cornell University faculty in front of Bailey Hall, 1949.

History. The main library, the building that Sage had given fifty years earlier, was full to overflowing and understaffed, its procedures age-old and in need of modernization. The library was open to readers 310 days a year, and circulation records document substantial use. Yet a librarian at another university sneered, "If you want to see how a great university has systematically killed its library, go look at Cornell." The problem was twofold: money had been tight and purchases of new materials had fallen off, yet at the same time, new materials continued to flow into the library, especially from the state, accumulating faster than they could be processed and made available. Taking action in 1946, President Day appointed Stephen McCarthy to be university librarian. McCarthy, a modern professional librarian, knew that before change could occur, the trustees and others needed to understand the extent of the problem and the critical role the library played at a modern research institution. He explained to the Board of Trustees the centrality of the library to the mission of the university and enumerated its urgent needs. He brought to the university several professional librarians, and aided by a council of advisers, laid plans for a modern research institution. That it would take a decade to triumph over limited budgets, lack of space, and competing ventures was probably not his expectation.

It would be misleading to assume that the institutional changes that attended the cessation of war occurred spontaneously.

Russian language class, 1943.

Much of what the university undertook after 1945 had been begun or thought about, and even designed, earlier. The end of the war merely set things in motion. Russian language and cultural studies had started during the war, joining a program in Chinese studies, supported in 1938 with a grant to hire a historian of China and enlarge the library holdings and faculty in these fields. The study of anthropology at Cornell was initiated before the war. The China initiative expanded into a Far Eastern Studies Program in 1945. With a Rockefeller Foundation grant in 1946, foreign language study was firmly established, and its faculty used some of the instructional techniques developed for the military during the war years. In 1951 Cornell received a Rockefeller Foundation grant to hire faculty for a Southeast Asia program. Cornell's area studies programs acquired national reputations, and concentrations in other world areas were contemplated, especially for Latin America and India.

Other ideas and plans that had been derailed by the war came to life. Serving *ex officio* on the Board of Trustees during the late 1930s and early 1940s, Irving M. Ives, speaker of the New York State Assembly, observed the nation's lack of scholarly interest in industry and labor. In 1942, he recommended that Cornell institute a new school to focus on these subjects. The trustees were hesitant: Could they plan for a new school in the middle of a war? Moreover, were these academic subjects? President Day, however, looking ahead to the war's end, gave his assent. Ives approached the New York State Assembly, which passed authorizing legislation on May 15, 1944, that Gov. Thomas E. Dewey signed into law. Within a year, in temporary wooden quarters on the lawn alongside Sage College, the New York State

Temporary housing for the New York State School of Industrial and Labor Relations, 1945.

School of Industrial and Labor Relations opened, with Ives its first dean. Eleven graduate students and 107 undergraduates enrolled. It was Cornell's fourth state-funded, or statutory, college.

The successful extension work at the College of Agriculture provided Ives and his colleagues with a model for taking their subject off campus to a broader audience. Agriculture's teaching and research presence on campus was supplemented by extension agents in every New York county. They created programs that included 4-H clubs and off-campus courses, lectures, and research. Industrial and Labor Relations followed suit. By 1948, only three years after opening, the new school offered extension classes in several locations around the state, given at times of the day and evening convenient for working people, and involving five thousand students.

Day also revived the proposal for a business school, first envisioned by Andrew White in 1865 as a school of commerce. Whether for lack of resources or lack of will, or because so much else was being undertaken at the time, nothing had come of the idea. President Livingston Farrand had also voiced interest in commerce as an academic endeavor, but creating a new school during the Depression had been inconceivable. When Day became president in 1937, he too thought business an important but neglected subject and had won the trustees' approval to proceed, but the war intervened. In 1946 the School of Business and Public Administration finally opened in Goldwin Smith Hall with forty-one students and a faculty of seven, offering a five-year program. In 1947 the school moved to McGraw Hall, where it remained until it moved in 1963 into its own building, Malott Hall. In 1954 the undergraduate business program was phased out and the name of the school changed to the Graduate School of Business and Public Administration. In 1983, it became the Graduate School of Management; in 1985, the named changed again to the Samuel Curtis Johnson Graduate School of Management. In summer 1998, having outgrown Malott Hall, the school moved into newly renovated Sage Hall.

The needs of the war set an education agenda in the United States, spurring new subjects, reviving some old ones, and significantly expanding the student population, this time by bringing to campus many who had never dreamed of attaining a college education. Some were the first of their families to attend college. The G.I. Bill opened the door to education for former members of the military, democratizing the American student body and challenging colleges and universities to absorb and educate greater numbers of students than ever before. Cornell expanded from 6,341 students in 1936–37 to 10,830 in 1947–48, with consequences felt throughout the university. The programs multiplied, and new efforts addressed some long-standing omissions. Day thought the changes meant that Cornell had "attained greatness in complexity and size as well as in pioneering. We now have fourteen separate faculties on two campuses," he wrote. But some thought the university too large and urged a return to some previous ideal. "Candidly," wrote Day, "I must say that that wish is not likely to be fulfilled." Since the war, college enrollments all over the country had increased enormously, at some places by seventy to seventy-five percent. The increase at Cornell represented a thirty-five percent growth. Cornell, explained Day, had responded to the national need while maintaining its traditional standards of instruction. The university in the future would not be the same institution that was engraved in the memories of its earlier graduates.

Graduates of the
New York State
College of Veter-
inary Medicine
with their families,
in front of Bailey
Hall, 1950.

Cornell had managed to maintain its standards despite the influx of students, and the academic performance of the G.I.s had proved commendable. The president's statistics showed that "veterans, if single, do slightly better than the ordinary civilian undergraduates; if married, they do still better; and their grades are even higher if they have children." Day did not speculate about the reasons, but we can: these students were older, more mature than the undergraduates who came to the university straight from high school, they had been at war, and they had family responsibilities, three factors that surely engendered seriousness of purpose and a disdain for traditional undergraduate mores.

Soon the wave of veterans receded. Their declining numbers could be seen as early as 1947–48, the same time that New York created its current state university system. To meet the needs of a growing public school population headed for college, and to keep more of those students in state, New York created a state university with junior colleges and four-year schools spread across the state, some in areas previously underserved. The costs at these schools were to be kept to a minimum. The College of Agriculture, the College of Home Economics, the New York College of Veterinary Medicine, and the School of Industrial and Labor Relations—the four statutory colleges, supported by the state but administered by Cornell—became part of this new entity. Henceforth the statutory programs at Cornell would be compared with those in the state university system in competition for financial support.

The postwar period also ushered in an era of intense scientific research on campus. This new emphasis demanded additional faculty, new facilities, and vast sums of money—much more, indeed, than any university or any one foundation could supply. In expanding the facilities and programs, Day called Cornell "fortunate to have here one of the most notable groups of nuclear physicists in American academic life." With the promise of university support, Hans Bethe, Nobel Laureate in physics, had returned to Cornell after service on the Manhattan Project at Los Alamos and brought with him outstanding colleagues. Rather ruefully, however, Day admitted that "the problem, from the point of view of administration, is not to control nuclear forces but to control nuclear physicists. They are in tremendous demand, and at a frightful premium. How we have managed to retain the men we have here I don't altogether know, except that they have extraordinary esprit de corps and apparently enjoy both being together and being at Cornell." Although the availability of federal dollars for this and other programs expanded research possibilities, periodic fluctuations in funding compromised continuity.

Expansion only exacerbated the need for updated research facilities, additional faculty, and more space. Faculty salaries were still not commensurate with faculty experience and dedication or with the salaries of professors at comparable schools, much less with industry pay scales.

In his report to the trustees in 1947–48, President Day reflected on what he called the paradox of leadership. He noted that even as Cornell celebrated its first fourscore years of "adventure and achievement," it was still a young institution. In academic processions, where university representatives march in order of institutional seniority, Cornell came near the end of the line. It was rather amazing, Day noted, that "so youthful an institution should have accomplished so much. It is almost incredible that a short three generations ago Cornell was little more than a collection of ideas in the minds and hearts of two great men." Both Cornell's "youthfulness and yet its leadership" stemmed from the founders and the revolution they had led from Ithaca's East Hill. Their ideals and policies, insisted

President Day, "differentiate the modern university from the previous church-dominated college. The revolt led by Cornell ultimately established a new pattern of higher education in America. Hence our University became a patriarch in its infancy." The question was, could Cornell continue to lead?

Presiding over an expanding university was a consuming business, as each segment of Cornell made its own demands known. Ailing, Edmund Ezra Day left the president's office in 1949, and the trustees named him university chancellor. He had overseen many changes. He had seen the establishment of the School of Chemical Engineering in 1937. He had closed down the Ithaca division of the medical school after forty years in operation, to concentrate the medical program in New York City. He had strengthened university administration and consolidated campus libraries under a single administrator. He had made efforts to stimulate alumni activities, tapping their resources when possible. He had instituted the Board of Athletic Policy. As president of the university, Day had brought to Cornell his own interests and vision but had also responded to changes from outside and the strengths and abilities of his faculty.

The university that emerged from the foundation ideas articulated in 1868 by Andrew Dickson White was reshaped in the era following World War II. What we consider modern Cornell stems from this period: for better or worse, Cornell became a large university, a more impersonal place, a multifaceted institution drawing support from many sources, offering a great array of subjects to an ever-expanding student population. Cornell now more nearly fulfilled the founders' vision.

The challenges ahead involved more than the need for growth, funds, and facilities. Peacetime had not ushered in an era of national contentment. Noting an "unmistakable drift toward Government in all our affairs," President Day saw that the only way to sustain a modern university was to contend for governmental monies that came with governmental restrictions. In his final report he warned the academic community to "be on guard against too much of it. We must retain private initiative and management." He emphasized the importance of independent institutions. "If this country ever loses its ways of freedom, its democratic tradition, its organization as a great self-governing nation, that will come about, if I am not mistaken, through no deliberate adverse decision on the part of the American people. It will come about, if it does, through a subtle corrosion of our social institutions." His warning echoes in tone, if not in substance, Ezra Cornell's 1873 letter "To the Coming man & woman"—a letter that Edmund Ezra Day never had a chance to read.

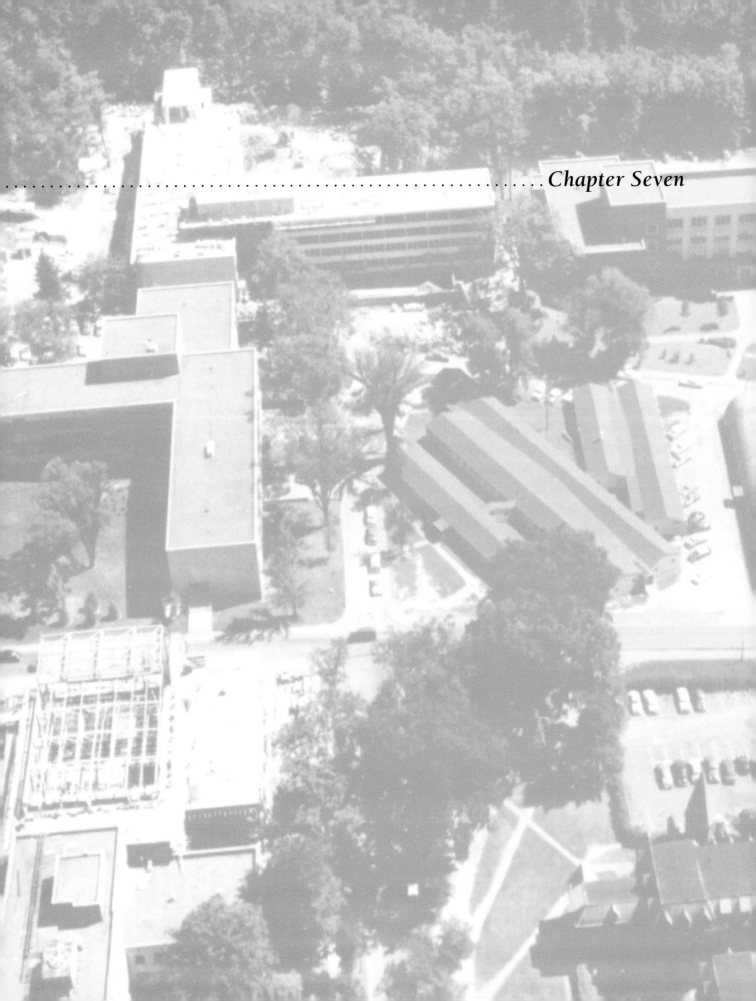

RISE HER STATELY WALLS

The two acting presidents who served Cornell after Edmund Ezra Day's departure in 1949 were not mere caretakers. Cornelis de Kiewiet, who had been professor of history and university provost, cautioned the trustees about the university's tendency to fragment into schools and departments and called on them and the next president to "restate the relationships between those fields of study, such as Agriculture and Sociology," that should work together. By the time he left his temporary position in January 1951 to become president of the University of Rochester, the trustees had named Deane Waldo Malott as the sixth president of Cornell. He would arrive in Ithaca during the summer. Until then, Theodore H. Wright, vice president for research, sat in the president's office for five months. He too, believed that an acting president should act—and give advice.

Wright took it as his mission to see that the university should tackle "teaching, research, and public service," in that order. During the war years, the university's teaching mission and research goals had been congruent with national defense needs, but in this new era "I would come all out for the view that our big job is teaching and that research or any other of the activities in which we engage are justified only to the extent that they contribute and make more effective the job we do in teaching the youth that come to this institution." He believed that Cornell students should "have a chance to gain a wealth of experience for later life," which study in the classroom alone would not give them. This reflects Cornell's early tradition of giving students practical experience along with classroom studies. "They will leave here with knowledge and a preparation that will permit them to go on to wisdom," he said. Wright suggested to the trustees that as "a matter of policy advising students is on a level with teaching and writing and research as a consideration in attaining promotion or salary adjustment."

Wright took advantage of his temporary office to voice additional concerns, acute at Cornell but to be found elsewhere, too. Faculty salaries, he cautioned, were "pitifully small." The faculty was also stretched thin, especially as the number of students increased. The administration of the university, he cautioned, also needed expansion and reorganization. As acting president, he had spent twenty percent of his time trying to reconcile difficulties the university faced from government inquiry and investigation regarding professors engaged in activities that, in some cases, seemed to "parallel the desires of the Soviet Union." Wright thought

Deane Waldo Malott (president, 1951–1963) examining portrait of Andrew Dickson White, ca. 1952.

this notoriety might frighten students and discourage applications. Any damage to the university's prestige, especially among "conservative or very patriotic people," would make it harder to raise money needed to increase the endowment, raise faculty salaries, build dormitories, and improve the library. He worried that taking action too quickly against faculty accused in congressional investigations would do more harm than good, especially when most allegations were unsupported by proof. Wright's fears proved prophetic.

Deane Waldo Malott arrived on campus in July, having been chancellor of the University of Kansas. He was quite possibly the right person to lead a university that needed to make contacts in the world of business and foundations, a man for whom raising funds to build the campus was an agreeable challenge. His start, however, was rocky. The national press pointed out that without any acknowledgment, his inaugural address drew heavily upon the work of another.

For his part, Malott focused on the Cornell's needs, observing that even though the university was not a business, was not efficient and "never will be," it should still be run in a businesslike manner. True to his inclinations, Malott oversaw a regularization of procedures, and he attempted to integrate various schools and departments into a more harmonious whole. He also instituted a more efficient structure in the central administration by reorganizing and centralizing several campus programs. The heads of the new art museum and the Laboratory of Ornithology would report directly to the president. So would the director of Cornell United Religious Work (CURW), which dated to 1929, when Rabbi Isadore Hoffman and Father T. J. Cronin expanded the Cornell University Christian Association into a larger and more representative organization. Malott also revived the Cornell University Press, which had become almost dormant during the Depression and war years. In 1950, the Department of Hotel Administration became the School of Hotel Administration within the College of Home Economics; it became a separate school in 1954.

Deane Malott accomplished more than many might have hoped or expected. We can look at the library as an instructive example of his leadership. The University Library had limped through the 1930s and 1940s with only modest funds. The building was crowded, library procedures antiquated. In 1937 Edmund Ezra Day, when listing his priorities, had named improvement of the library as the most crucial concern at the university, but his intentions had been thwarted by world events. The new university librarian hired a small professional staff and energetically called for a larger budget and better facilities. As acting president, de Kiewiet, a historian whose work depended upon library resources, surprisingly dismissed the library's problems, suggesting that books be placed in off-campus storage, and did not even mention the library in that year's fund-raising drive. In 1951, however, Acting President Wright focused attention on the University Archives as a place "where we can collect all the important historical material bearing on Cornell"—crucial because the university was already looking ahead to its centennial—and named Edith Fox, who became the forceful second director of the Regional History Collection and university archivist. With some fanfare, the university announced that Andrew D. White's diaries had been discovered; they and other important documents needed to be properly cared for.

Students learning cooking techniques, School of Hotel Administration, ca. 1954.

There was little to indicate that the business-oriented new president would understand the centrality of the library or develop the concern to do something about it. After touring the library facilities, however, Malott encouraged Stephen McCarthy, the university librarian, to plan for future improvements. In 1952 the opening of Mann Library, given by the state to serve the colleges of Agriculture and Home Economics, provided some relief for the problems caused by unprocessed materials and cramped space. McCarthy created a rare book room in the main library for the university's treasures, but these were only partial solutions: many volumes from the university's earliest collections remained vulnerable in the stacks. In 1955, Malott declared that a new library should be a university priority, and in 1957 trustee John M. Olin donated three million dollars to build a modern structure. Librarian and historian David Corson remembers that some decisions were unexpected. Air conditioning would add significantly to the building's cost; would it be included? Malott answered with his own question: "What is best for the books?" Olin Library was air-conditioned.

When Olin Library opened in 1961, librarians and scholars greeted the new research facility with delight. The next year the original library—Henry Sage's building—reopened as Uris Library in support of undergraduate education, and in October 1962 the two buildings were dedicated in a joyous ceremony. Deane Malott had understood the importance of the library to the teaching and research goals of faculty and students, and with the support of the trustees, he had provided the necessary leadership to build a modern facility. Protests over the razing of Boardman Hall—home first to the Law School and named for Judge Boardman, its first director, and later the home of history and government—to make room for Olin Library quickly died away. The placement of Jacques Lipschitz's *Song of the Vowels* in 1963 linked the two libraries visually, providing, as K. C. Parsons wrote, "the initial element for a sympathetic relation of all of the forms there."

Malott's conviction that Cornell needed to modernize campus facilities set his agenda and changed both the nature of the university presidency and the appearance of the campus. To find the money necessary to expand the faculty, renovate old structures, and construct new buildings, Malott created and strengthened contacts with foundations and businesses. This work frequently took him off campus, and he was less visible and less involved in the day-to-day administration of the university than his predecessors. But Malott knew that Cornell could grow into a modern university only with very substantial external funding, so he worked with the state legislature, served on company boards, and dealt with foundations and corporate executives and alumni likely to contribute. Through his efforts, the university received large donations, foundation grants, and government funding for new research and new buildings. Malott's vision was not unique. A 1951 article in *Collier's Magazine* pointed out that in the old days, educational institutions had been adequately supported by philanthropists. In this new postwar era, however, American business had a responsibility to step in and aid the growth of colleges and universities across the country—it was in the interest of business and in the interest of the country, now that the United States was involved with world events in ways unimagined earlier. Malott also strengthened the university's ties with alumni, who were increasingly considered primary assets, not just genial and

We must exercise constant care in the selection of the Cornell Faculty—care to see that we obtain the best possible teachers and the keep them from going to Harvard, or some other seaport. We must be watchful, too, that we do not become overly engrossed in research, as an end in itself, rather than as part and parcel of vigorous teaching; that our Faculty give constant attention to teaching methods, to modernization of curricula, to better counseling; also that we beware the pitfalls of overspecialization, with its influence toward proliferation of course offerings into education's never-ending minutiae. . . .

Cornell, fortuitous perhaps in its present complexity, has steadfastly refused to be lured into vast expansions. On the western fringe of the Ivy League and the eastern edge of the great state university macrocosms, we have been looked upon by both as slightly queer and unorthodox, and no one has ever been quite sure what did go on "Far Above Cayuga's Waters." Let us hold fast to that distinction. . . .

No institution of Cornell's rank could possibly maintain its stature without a vigorous and far-spread research program. At Cornell, research is an integral part of the stimulus of academic life . . . and the absence of "Verboten" signs is ample evidence of the free spirit of inquiry as we continue our policy of refusing secret research on the Ithaca campus, in the belief that exchange of ideas, of techniques, of procedure is part of the untrammeled spirit of the place.

—Deane W. Malott, address to the Cornell University Council, October 1, 1954

occasionally generous sons and daughters of their Alma Mater. In all this, Malott was remarkably successful.

The physical expansion of the university during Malott's presidency is startling. Cornell grew from its original configuration as flowers from tiny buds. Where there had been one building representing a college or school, clusters of buildings emerged. In this way, too, the academic mission of the university blossomed as research and intellectual interests grew into courses that became programs. More than thirty-two new buildings, valued at more than one hundred million dollars, were added to improve or extend Cornell's academic and research facilities. The College of Engineering, the School of Industrial and Labor Relations, and the College of Veterinary Medicine gained new campuses. In addition, the university removed the last of the faculty houses on campus streets, thereby freeing up space for university functions. Anabel Taylor Hall (1952) rose next to Myron Taylor Hall, home of the Law School (dedicated in 1932). Kimball and Thurston Halls opened in 1953, Phillips

The Engineering Quad, aerial view, 1957.

Hall in 1954, Riley-Robb Hall in 1956, Carpenter Hall in 1957, Grumman Hall and Noyes Lodge in 1958, Hollister Hall in 1959. Morrison Hall, Ives Hall, Mary Donlon Hall, and Hasbrouck Apartments for graduate students and their families all opened in 1961. Athletic facilities were enlarged to house an expanded program: Teagle Hall —the first campus building devoted to physical education—appeared in 1954, Lynah Rink in 1957, and Helen Newman Hall for women's physical education in 1963. During Malott's administration, plans were laid for Bard, Malott, and Hughes halls.

President Malott also oversaw the beginnings of the industrial research park near the airport, the Laboratory of Ornithology in Sapsucker Woods in 1956, and

the Gannett Medical Clinic in 1957. The Ionospheric Research Facility at Arecibo, Puerto Rico, also came into being with federal money, and on campus, the Andrew Dickson White House was transformed from the president's home into the university's art museum. Behind it, White's carriage house became the Big Red Barn in 1956 for gatherings of alumni and, later, students. To support increased research on campus, Malott and his team created the Cornell Research Foundation. In 1946 Cornell acquired the Cornell Aeronautical Laboratory (known as CAL), a self-supporting corporation that, despite Malott's assertion to the contrary, conducted secret research with no connection to the university's teaching mission. In the early 1960s many considered the laboratory important for providing an opportunity to advance research that "brought distinction to the university." That sentiment would change with growing opposition to the war in Vietnam.

In 1953, the Cornell Medical College in New York City joined with the New York Hospital to create the New York Hospital—Cornell Medical Center, offering increased opportunities for medical students and important medical research. But some proposed partnerships were declined. In 1953 a representative of the

The radio telescope at Arecibo, Puerto Rico, ca. 1963.

National Beauty and Barber Manufacturers Association offered to fund instruction at Cornell in cosmetology—without success.

With the enlargement of the physical plant came an expansion of the curriculum, the student body, and the faculty. As the number of people coming to campus increased, so did the number of automobiles. Efforts to deal with parking problems included building new parking lots and, in 1960, banning student automobiles. The roads through campus remained busy nonetheless, and some on the faculty still mourned the loss of the trolley, which had ceased operation when the company failed in 1934.

One idea from an earlier era was revived. In 1952, the presidents of Brown, Columbia, Cornell, Dartmouth, Harvard, Pennsylvania, Princeton, and Yale announced that they had agreed to abolish spring football, to begin practice in the fall no earlier than September, and starting in 1953, to play every other team in the group at least once every five years. In the interests of putting athletic contests in proper perspective and promoting the student-athlete, they sought to reduce the number of games scheduled. They also wanted to place athletics under academic authorities and curtail the practice, common at some institutions, of giving athletes financial support. President Malott noted that some of these reforms would make little difference at Cornell, where they were already observed, but it was important to support the "Ivy League" in its effort to keep football in perspective. The Ivy League conference dates from this beginning.

The man leading all this change at Cornell was a person comfortable with stability, with the way things were and had been. In letters written between 1951 and 1953, Malott repeatedly asserted, "I am an extremely conservative person politically and socially . . . all my inclinations are in this direction." Despite his personal conservatism, Malott took a liberal stance in defense of academic and artistic freedom. Good university presidents have always had to safeguard their institutions from efforts by government, business, religious zealots, trustees, or alumni seeking to impose their views. President Farrand had battled Senator McNaboe. President Day had warned off Senate investigators who wanted to censor course offerings. Acting President Wright had called on Congress to show "greater restraint in its investigations." But Malott, who actually viewed the threat of communism as the most dire problem facing the country, defended his more liberal faculty, with whom he was not always in political agreement.

Intrusive governmental probes of the Cornell faculty, originating in the House Un-American Activities Committee (HUAC) and the allegations of Sen. Joseph McCarthy, began with Philip Morrison, professor of physics, and then turned to

Marcus Singer, professor of zoology. Both Morrison and Singer were accused of being communist sympathizers. By the end, the McCarthyites had named and implicated several other faculty members and even some alumni. The *Cornell Daily Sun*, the faculty, and the Cornell Young Republicans supported Morrison. Singer, less well known on campus than Morrison, had fewer defenders; he suffered some hostility and left the university in 1961.

In response to the charges and reports in newspapers, Deane Malott wrote a stirring article that appeared first in the *New York Herald Tribune* and was re-issued by the university in various pamphlet forms. Malott's essay, "'Why Don't You Do Something about Professor X?'" reveals the contradictory nature of his position.

Prof. Douglas F. Dowd, of the Department of Economics, known for his radical positions on a variety of issues, recalled that President Malott would call him into his office to ask, "Did you really say these things?" Malott quizzed Dowd about his public talks on Cuba, the American economy, and the American educational system, among other topics. Had he chosen to do so, Dowd noted, "I could have construed those requests as intimidation"; that he did not probably speaks to the president's genial nature and Dowd's bemused attitude at such direct interrogation.

I am not a social scientist, but from my own conservative point of view I have an uneasy feeling that the American way of life, the freedom which we all hold so dear, cannot and will not return to the simple "free enterprise" of our founding fathers. Our problem rather is to preserve as much freedom, as much initiative, as much self-reliance as we possibly can in view of our present state of society, our material standards of living, our bourgeoning population, and our international responsibilities.

Our only hope, then, is to preserve free speech, the right of independent thought, the right of dissent, without danger of being cast into the gloomy framework of treachery or evil intentions. I am not really concerned about Professor X, singly or in his relatively small group. He may be addled, he may be unwise in his utterances, he may be dangerous in a limited way and in limited scope. He certainly may be wrong in his beliefs.

But who is to say? Heretics have been persecuted throughout history. Truth somehow prevails. We cannot be fearless in the face of truth yet fear the effect of heresy.

From investigation, incrimination and attack, a miserable dissenter may here and there be brought to heel. There may be tracked down a few professors, who, in the early 1940s, espoused some aspects of the Russian cause.

But these investigations may be to such lengths that professors out adventuring on the frontiers of the social sciences, or in any other discipline, will fear to express themselves; they will succumb to the temptation to play it

For his part, Malott believed that it was his responsibility to maintain Cornell University as a free institution. His head and his heart might have been in conflict, but his words and actions showed that he understood that preserving "the university as a safe haven for all sorts of ideas was his proper role." In the end, Deane Malott stated, "Freedom of speech at Cornell or anywhere for that matter, is more important than a dozen Morrisons and we will not be goaded into limiting it by half truths and misrepresentations of the facts either by the sayings of so-called liberals or the inquisitions of so-called conservatives."

Throughout, the faculty backed the president in his support of individuals cited for questionable views. Strong statements of support came from Milton R. Konvitz of Industrial and Labor Relations and Robert Cushman of the Government Department. Cushman observed that in 1918, during the Great War, the Cornell faculty had supported the idea that faculty members had the same rights and duties in writing or speaking out as any other citizen. To the general public, he com-

safe, else in some unforeseen day, in another framework of social and political attitudes, their words may be used to the detriment of their careers.

The teaching profession must not be driven from its traditional stronghold of free speech to a position where it will fear to stand up and be counted. With academic tenure goes the responsibility for a clear and forthright definition of one's views. These professors of ours must have the right to profess; they must not be scourged from the public forum, else eventually only conformists will enter the teaching profession, leadership in the realm of ideas will wane, and the universities will sink to mediocrity.

Thinking citizens must stand behind the principles of freedom of thought and of expression. Implicit is the freedom to make mistakes, to search through error for truth, to express postulates which have not common acceptance.

Academic freedom cannot be preserved by academicians making speeches to each other. It must be maintained by the will of the American people who trust their universities as the citizens of this republic have always trusted, and relied upon, education as a basic tenet of our American culture.

We might remember that there are no non-conformists in the totalitarian segments of the modern world.

—Deane W. Malott, in the NEW YORK HERALD TRIBUNE, June 21, 1953

mented, a professor occupies a "representative position and that in consequence the reputation of the university lies partly in his hands." It was also important, he wrote, that faculty members "in the present crisis . . . safeguard the reputation of the University with especial care." Cushman noted in May 1951 that the faculty affirmed that "academic freedom, like any other human freedom, imposes upon those who enjoy it an inescapable responsibility with respect to its use."

In 1959 the university faced a challenge to artistic freedom. The Russian novelist Vladimir Nabokov taught comparative literature at Cornell for eleven years. In 1959 he published *Lolita*, which incited controversy for its alleged pornographic qualities. Not only did critics attack Nabokov, they attacked Cornell for harboring him and questioned the book's value as literature. Writing to Malott, one man from Ohio labeled the book "notorious" and inferred from Nabokov's continuing appointment at Cornell that the university sanctioned this "sort of trash." Malott responded that the book was a private endeavor by the author, that Nabokov's

The Cornell
Cyclotron, built
in 1935 and de-
commissioned in
1956, ca. 1955.

students praised him as an engaging lecturer, and that the author has "done some credible writing." After the publication of *Lolita,* Nabokov returned to Ithaca to gather notes he had left in storage, but by his choice he never returned to the faculty, his finances suddenly so secure that he was able to retire from teaching to write. President Malott, despite his personal conservatism, earned for himself and Cornell the reputation as leaders in the defense of liberalism, freedom of conscience and artistic expression—all very much in the Cornell tradition.

During the 1950s students expanded their role at the university and, as Carl Becker would have put it, began "thinking otherwise." Acting President Wright had observed that Cornell "has a very aggressive student body which takes an interest in every area of life." The political currents that swept across the country in the 1960s originated in the earlier decade. To speak of students as a monolith, of course, is to blur the distinctions between them, for while some students adopted liberal causes, many others did not.

In 1951, Howard Fast, novelist and political radical, arrived in Ithaca to lecture at Willard Straight. President Malott, obviously not in harmony with Fast's politics, reported that Fast "had a good sized audience, eighty or ninety percent of whom were entirely out of sympathy with him and heckled the poor man until he finally had to plead a sore throat and leave the platform. To my mind," noted Malott, "this is better education than saying to these youngsters, 'No don't listen to that man.'" Malott trusted that most students would react just as these had. The faculty on the whole, judged Malott, was full of "conservative, able people, just as much interested in preserving their freedom as you and I are." He wrote more approvingly, "You will be interested to know that a faculty committee on lectures has invited Senator Taft to speak here" to provide a contrary view.

There were always visitors to the university who gave Malott and some others pause. In 1957, John Collyer, chairman of the Board of Trustees, heard that Pete Seeger was scheduled to perform at Willard Straight. Seeger, he was told, was "one of the most widely-known and publicized Communists in this country, who has been cited endless times." Collyer alerted Malott, who was assured that no information about the concert had gone out from the Office of Public Information, the only publicity being a small notice in the *Sun*. The problem was that Seeger performed "songs with social significance along with traditional selections." Four hundred people attended the concert, which was "not [a] lecture but merely entertainment." Malott noted that a parade of questionable visitors came to the university and that they always presented difficulties: "We could, of course, ban people of this sort," but the resulting ruckus would be "more harmful than the cure."

Students live in a very different world from their professors and university administrators, and the campus at night is a place unfamiliar to the adults who work there by day. Those who would discover something about students have long resorted to surveys. Studies in 1951 reported that forty-seven percent of Cornell students had cheated at one time or another, on examinations or paper assignments. A study in 1952 found that thirty-eight percent of undergraduate men cheated at least once and that fraternity men were more likely to have cheated than independent male students. The results enraged Malott; he denied that cheating was common and defended the university's reputation, believing such information harmful to Cornell.

Students created much worse publicity for the university later in the decade, when the administration attempted to regulate student life. In 1956 the university enacted a ban on drinking beer and alcohol in Schoellkopf Stadium. This brought chortles from the students, and absolute noncompliance. In December 1957 the university attempted to enact a code for fraternities that the *Cornell Daily Sun* deemed "dangerous and foolhardy." Then in 1958, student uprisings greeted the university's attempt to end coed parties in off-campus apartments. Students did not take kindly to such attempts to curtail their behavior and dubbed it the "girl ban,"

The Big Red
Barn, originally
the A.D. White
carriage house,
ca. 1956.

shouting, "We have parents already." On campus Malott was compared to Carrie
Nation, and students with placards urged him to return to Kansas. Among President Malott's perceived faults were his frequent absences from campus. Students
also noted, surely in an attempt to convert the faculty to their way of thinking, that
Malott had even denied the faculty the right to vote for its own representatives on
the Board of Trustees.

Protests continued throughout the spring. In June three thousand students
responded in fury to a tuition increase and a ban on unchaperoned parties in "bachelor apartments" by throwing eggs, stones, and a smoke bomb at the president's
house. National newspapers picked up the story and alarmed alumni; local residents, who regarded the demonstrations as rude misbehavior, complained. Most of
the president's mail supported firm action, and some writers excoriated the student
leader, Kirk Sale, son of a Cornell English professor, for not knowing better. To one
correspondent, Malott wrote, "We'll live through it but it's rough going!"

The reports of student demonstrations published in the national press were "grossly exaggerated," insisted one administrator, but there were other indications of a widening gulf between the president, under whom rules proliferated and administrators flourished, and the students and faculty. An alumna wrote in 1958 that she worried about the tendency of Cornell's administration to promote "stultification of the right of students to govern themselves and thereby emerge as responsible citizens." She had heard from a trustee, she told Malott, "that two-way communication between you and the faculty had diminished," and she had noticed that in the administration's view, students were persons to be ordered about rather than asked for their ideas. From another writer came the observation that "one of the values in attending Cornell comes from the freedom that students have had in handling their affairs through a cooperative student government–administration relationship." In defense of students, this writer commented that the "decisions made by the student government are usually carefully arrived at and are usually sensible solutions to problems which they and the administration face." Shouldn't the president pay attention?

One alumnus diagnosed the problem at the university as the result of matriculating women—the perennial target for some few students and alumni. E. B. White '21 observed that in his time a "little band of supermen" thought it was the women's fault that the football team tended to drop the ball. In this 1950s outbreak of sexism, one old Cornellian sputtered that "the manly characteristics of the student body" declined as the influence of women students increased. The boys, he lamented, were too much occupied by drinking and dating, "which in my estimation have no proper part in a man's college." The women too, according to this alumnus, showed "excruciatingly poor taste" in their "sloppy and dirty attire and juvenile antics, especially when they are together [with male students]." The writer had seen Cornellians at a Princeton football game and thought them wanting, especially when they paraded about with gin glasses following a cow, "women students tak[ing] a *pari passu* part in the performance." His parting shot was that "it was enough to disgust people" in the stands, and such displays, combined with the media attention given riots on campus, "can not fail to bring discredit to the University."

The women students had complaints of their own, and some of their issues anticipated causes and crises to come. In 1962, the Women's Self Government Association petitioned for the end of curfew for all seniors in good academic standing. Over the next four years, this and other issues would grind on as women argued that rules be dropped on the basis of fairness and of equality with the men.

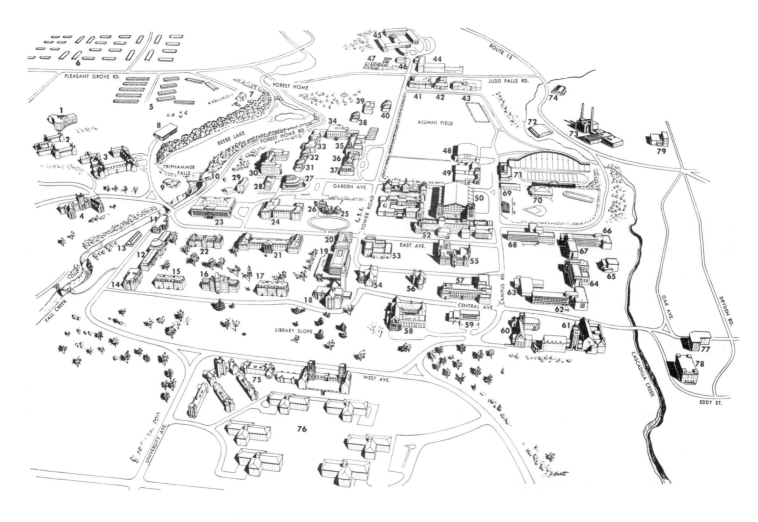

Cornell University campus map, 1962.

CHAPTER SEVEN

Many of the letters Malott received from townspeople and alumni supported his actions, but not all. Instead of praising the president's firm handling of protesters, some perceived instead an impasse between the administration and the students, which one alumnus attributed to an "autocratic, doctrinaire theory of administration" at a university accustomed to "the theory that the faculty should run a school and a President should be the brilliant spokesman for the faculty and students." The president, this writer observed, failed to realize that a university is "not a business but a gathering of brilliant scholars to teach willing minds the great truths of life." The only constructive path now open, observed this writer, was that Deane Malott resign.

By 1961 Malott was ready to do just that, announcing that he would leave his office in 1963. His last statement to the trustees concerned the administration of the university. Jacob Gould Schurman's system of managing university affairs by faculty committees, he pointed out, had become cumbersome because the university had grown in size and complexity, as had the nature of academic life. It was often difficult to call meetings because faculty members were sometimes off campus or otherwise engaged—conducting research, attending professional meetings, and delivering lectures elsewhere. Logistics aside, Malott found faculty committees ill prepared to conduct the essential task of attracting outside money to campus.

Despite the need for additional funding, Malott identified a potential danger: external money brought with it the "slow erosion of the University's ability to determine its own direction of development." Malott's suggestions were to strengthen the authority of the central administration to manage the university and to increase the prestige and power of the office of dean of faculty. This in turn would allow the faculty more time to devote to teaching and research, and to publication, which had become increasingly important for earning tenure—another indication of the ways in which the academic world had changed.

Concerning the deteriorating relationship between the administration and the students, however, Malott had no advice to leave for his successor.

Chapter Eight

Fault and error clear revealing

Cornell, like other universities across the nation, seethed during the mid- and late 1960s with campus concerns, with issues of national and international dimension —with causes good and just, harmful and even wrongheaded. The wounds inflicted by such divisiveness would eventually heal, but they left indelible scars.

In retrospect, we see that although protests appear to have dominated the era, many students were indifferent to the turmoil, and life at the university went forward: classes met, fraternities initiated new members, athletes appeared on the field, students read assignments in the library. The university also proceeded with its scheduled program. In 1965, for example, throughout the fall and spring semesters, Cornell celebrated Latin American Year with lectures, conferences, exhibits, publication of a book, and campus events. Cornell's deepening interest in the region and the growth of area studies programs as a recognized university strength led to the establishment of a Latin American program. Writing to the deans, James A. Perkins, the university's seventh president, heralded the university's new approach to international relations, especially its focusing of the entire academic community "on contemporary affairs of a major world area."

Concentration of effort can also be seen in the biological sciences, a concern of both Perkins and his provost, Dale Corson. A committee charged with studying the duplication of courses and research in various university departments recommended a radical reorganization and creation of the Division of Biological Sciences. Once this approach won approval in Albany, some professors in the College of Agriculture moved into the new division, taking their state-funded lines with them. The result was more collaborative research and a unified program for students. Corson commented somewhat ruefully that during the 1960s, "we could do anything we had good ideas for"; later, money for new approaches and endeavors became scarce.

Other centers with similar structures followed this first intracollege division. In 1965, the trustees approved the Materials Science Center and the Center for International

James A. Perkins (president, 1963–1969) in the Temple of Zeus, Goldwin Smith Hall, ca. 1965.

Studies, and at the medical school, the Clinical Research Center was the first of numerous other combinations that brought researchers together. These centers' faculties were drawn, for the most part, from existing departments and schools.

The increasing importance of science during these years can be seen in the construction of new buildings and new wings on older structures. Because planning, fund raising, and construction spanned years, new programs often assumed no physical form until well after their creation. During the early 1960s NASA offered money for a radio physics and space research building. The Arecibo Ionospheric Observatory in Puerto Rico became a reality, as did buildings on campus for molecular biology, a new laboratory for nuclear studies (the first one had been erected in 1946), and the cyclotron. A capital campaign at the medical school raised funds for new programs to match the expansion of medical science and for the Harkness Research Building. In 1966 the trustees authorized the creation of an office of computer services, and the computer, regarded initially as exclusively a scientific tool, made its appearance.

Discussions about the ideal educational experience at Cornell in the 1960s ranged from the concrete to the philosophical. Should the student population grow, and if so, by what number? Was the education offered at Cornell what it should be? A committee on undergraduate education posed a familiar question: was the "primary purpose of a university education to train man to better himself and his environment or to train man to better earn a livelihood"? This question recalls Schurman's and Farrand's struggle with "careerism" and even the earlier division between Ezra Cornell's practicality and White's liberal academic vision. Both views, of course, found a home at Cornell.

In 1965, a speech by President Perkins during which he announced the university's priorities—placing social improvement as a primary goal and mentioning education last—provoked a reaction from students: "We were appalled and dismayed to read your statement that instruction was the last of the four major purposes of this university." A student committee sought to reestablish the primacy of education and listed several other reasons for their discontent. They pointed to a general disrespect by the administration for student government and for students' opinions in general. They commented bitterly on the inaccessibility of university administrators to students, arguing that if students had no access to those in charge of running the university, they had no recourse other than protest. They charged administrators with a lack of communication concerning other campus issues, including the university's policy on marijuana, the operation of the campus store, the high cost of doing laundry on campus, and problems with campus housing. They asked that

Construction of Clark Hall, physical sciences
building, with Baker Lab (front right) and
Newman Lab, Savage Hall, and Bailey Hall
(left, front to back).

The earth art exhibition at the A. D. White House, January 1969.

the position of vice-president for student affairs, vacant for some time, be filled. They complained that the university was interested in "other matters than its undergraduates. In a nutshell, the undergraduates feel they are second class citizens—forgotten men in the huge complex of a multiversity." In response, the administration added new faculty positions to broaden the curriculum and reduce class size. Faculty salaries rose and the university created twenty-three newly endowed chairs. The administration initiated a program of enrichment by naming outstanding individuals Andrew D. White Professors-at-Large, invited to come to campus for extended visits, reviving White's plan for external faculty.

A special committee addressed the problem of campus planning as problems accelerated, some of them cosmic, some more mundane. In 1964–65 the university created two peripheral parking lots and purchased six campus vehicles—the beginning of the Cornell bus fleet and traffic division. New buildings opened, including Clark Hall in 1965, Space Sciences in 1966, and Bradfield and Emerson halls in 1968. Based on plans made earlier, in fall 1966 Perkins presided over the creation of the Society for the Humanities, housed initially on Wait Avenue. The Society opened in fall 1967 with a symposium on the morality of scholarship. The College of Home Economics underwent a transformation in 1969 and became the College of Human Ecology, a name better representing its varied program and staff and drawing men as well as women applicants.

During the 1960s we can also observe the growth of the central administration. When James Perkins became president, there were two vice-presidents; in 1966, there were five; by 1969, six—a sign of the complexity of the university's operation and of shifts in university governance. At the beginning of the twentieth century, finances had not dominated the meetings of the Board of Trustees—not even during the lean years of the Depression—and had been handled by a committee of the trustees. By the end of the decade, however, issues of finance and fund raising had become crucial; improvements and innovations now depended upon outside funding.

On April 5, 1967, a fire at the Residential Club, home of students enrolled in an experimental six-year Ph.D. program, took the lives of eight students and one faculty member. The program, about which many faculty had been skeptical, ended as its first and only class graduated. A safety survey of all campus buildings followed. Perkins pursued other initiatives concerning students, including raising entrance standards and reappraising transfers between university colleges, the honors programs, and independent study. Because he was concerned about the number of students who were dropping out, he prompted a new look at freshman orientation at Cornell and at advising.

Faculty and trustees also drafted several reports concerning campus life. One, "Report of the University Commission on Residential Environment," dealt primarily with discrimination found in the fraternity system. Another, "Principles and Policies Governing Student Conduct," distinguished university regulations from local, state, and federal laws. For all but severe breaches of the law, the student code would prevail, but students whose misconduct grossly violated standards of behavior would be discontinued in the education community. Issues of campus discipline would soon become critical.

In thoughtful discussions some faculty and trustees considered the changing relationship between university and student, just as Students for a Democratic Society and others challenged the contents of the university investment portfolio and questioned the morality of President Perkins's seat on the board of Chase Manhattan Bank, which had significant investments in South Africa. "Today's students," asserted Ralph Bolgiano, chairman of the faculty committee on student affairs, "are seriously and sincerely challenging the present order of things as they exist both within the University and on the outside. One question growing out of current episodes is whether it is the role of the University to provide and enforce standards of conduct or to provide a sanctuary within which the student may develop on his own with a great sense of freedom with full responsibility for his own acts."

Despite all the achievements of the 1960s, the tenure of James A. Perkins is remembered almost exclusively because of the events of 1969. So explosive was the situation that the date has become an emblem for the era and the topic of several books, most recently a scholarly work entitled *Cornell '69: Liberalism and the Crisis of the American University*, by Donald A. Downs '71. Downs demonstrates that 1969 is only shorthand for a longer period and for more than one issue and one event. What occurred at Cornell can be seen as part of a generation's discontent triggered by war, social change, political failure, civil rights, generational conflict, and liberated sexual attitudes. The children proved that they had minds of their

own, and most particularly that they were not children. As Jack Lewis, director of the Cornell United Religious Work, observed, "*In loco parentis* is dead."

James Perkins had come to Cornell in 1963 from the Carnegie Foundation, where he had been a vice-president. His Quaker background and his humanitarianism led him to attempt to work out at Cornell solutions to some of the acute social and racial problems facing the nation. In doing this, Perkins was echoing Andrew D. White's belief that a student, given the opportunity and with kindly guidance, would take advantage of all that was available to gain an education. It would not be that simple, however. During this tumultuous decade, there was more to gaining an education than attending classes and participating in the life of the mind. The good that Perkins hoped to do at Cornell and that which he actually accomplished are often hard to see in the smoke from the conflagration of April 1969. He was, most assuredly, ahead of his time, and Cornell was probably the right

Candidates for the Peace Corps running through the White Gateway ("Andy White's chocolate layer cake"), designed by William Henry Miller in 1896, at the north end of Eddy Street.

institution for such experimentation. That it would go so wrong, no one could have foretold, for the omens indicated that Perkins understood the complexities and there was much goodwill on campus for the effort. But when strong leadership was needed—at Cornell as well as at Harvard, Columbia, Berkeley, and other universities facing similar problems—it would not be there.

With money from the Rockefeller Foundation, Perkins instituted a program that came to be called the Committee on Special Educational Projects (COSEP), to enable minority students to attend Cornell and to support them while on campus. From the 1880s to 1964 fewer than three hundred African American students had attended Cornell. In 1965, as a result of initiatives by the university to provide educational opportunities to young people of color, two hundred and fifty African American students arrived on campus. Money to fund their tuition came from the

Ford Foundation, and the COSEP program proved so attractive that even Puerto Rican students at Cornell sought representation within it. The university was pleased with this initial minority program. In a 1968 report Perkins noted that Cornell was now in the position to "make a larger contribution to the education of qualified students who have been disadvantaged by their cultural, economic, and educational environments." Cornell instituted COSEP in good faith and was a leader in a national movement to offer higher education to those who had previously been denied it because of color or poverty.

Student activism at Cornell—and elsewhere in the nation during the 1960s—addressed just such social issues. The protests of the 1950s had primarily targeted President Malott, his administration, and what students considered autocratic rules that intruded into their personal lives, although even in that more innocent decade a growing awareness of social issues was evident. By the 1960s campus protests focused more particularly on national events and issues while not ignoring conditions at the university. In voicing opinions about world and national affairs, civil rights and equality, war and national duty, students attempted to effect change in a society they saw as flawed and run by people for whom they had little respect. "Any student who can sit through four years of college without once getting excited enough about the war in Vietnam or Communism in Cuba, voting discrimination in the South or the plight of the Jews in Russia . . . to make some public protest . . . has undoubtedly been wasting his time," wrote Mary D. Nichols '66.

Students protested, boycotted, and marched. Joining with like-minded faculty, they became activists—for peace, for an end to the draft and the war in Vietnam, for equality for women, for civil rights for African Americans. "Freedom buses" left from many northern locations, including Cornell, to take activists south. In 1964, Klan activists in Mississippi killed Cornell student Michael Schwerner and his companions James Chaney and Andrew Goodman during a voter registration drive. Students were next stung by events at the 1968 Democratic National Convention in Chicago, and as anger in American cities erupted in ugly and

Students in Upward Bound, a federally funded summer program to prepare minority students for college, 1965.

Cornell Vietnam Mobilization Committee, 1969.

unsettling ways, the gulf between generations widened. One of the victims of the times was civility.

When students at Cornell and elsewhere burned their draft cards and worried about their vulnerability to military service, Perkins had little sympathy. Although Perkins was a Quaker, he did not condone students' refusal to serve, seeing that as "an incorrect stand." He complained that the national leaders admired by the students encouraged their disobedience. The students were not just mirroring the national protest movement, however; they were also creating and leading it, and Perkins, along with many others, failed to understand that their approach to problems would take active and uncomfortable forms.

By the mid-1960s, national student unrest had led to acts of violence. These were startling occurrences, unprecedented on college campuses. When troubles erupted at Berkeley in 1964, the Cornell faculty passed a resolution of concern and sent to California a letter worrying about a "breakdown of communication between faculty, administration and important segments of the student body." Less than a year later Cornell faced its own problems: during a review of Cornell's ROTC in Barton Hall, protestors sat quietly throughout the military exercise. To those in the administration and the military, the seated, silent students were attempting "to interfere" with a legitimate function. The students of the Committee to Block the Presidential Review saw it as their "duty and legal right to stage this demonstration." They hoped to drive military activities from campus.

Following the ROTC protest at Barton Hall, the university charged sixty-three students with disorderly conduct. Alumni flooded the president's mailbox with letters of support for his decisive action against the "unruly" students. The letters reveal a good deal about the times: "Is this [student]," asked one alum, "a Jew?" Perhaps, a writer suggested, the university should "kick out this bunch" and "take in more students from the Middle West." The capital letters of a writer who did not sign his name indicate his emphatic belief: "THERE IS NO DOUBT THAT

THERE IS AN ALL OUT COMMUNIST MOVEMENT IN ALL AMERICAN COLLEGES." Gov. Nelson Rockefeller received complaints about Cornell that he forwarded to Perkins. One taxpayer sputtered that the "display by students at Cornell is a damn outrage. I do not choose to pay taxes to send such ill-mannered, uncouth slobs to a tax supported school." Other writers urged stern action; some threatened to withdraw donations they had given or planned to give. Surely Perkins was encouraged by the general response to his handling of the protest as the generations lined up facing each other.

Not all students, of course, were involved, or even sympathetic to the protest. And not everyone was appalled at the protestors' strong sentiments, or even by their actions. Some letters to Perkins urged caution and understanding. A particularly thoughtful appeal to the administration from members of the Department of Philosophy recorded their distress at the violence that had occurred but contended that "most of the students who sat in at Barton Hall were motivated by a grave moral concern." There had been no desire, these professors pointed out, to hurt the university. These faculty members pleaded for understanding and dialogue. But the majority of the letters Perkins read, and the advice from those on campus with whom he was close—a small group of mostly older faculty—reinforced his sense that he understood the situation at Cornell and that, as president, he was responding appropriately. This certitude on the part of the administration would come back to haunt it.

When the university placed those charged at the Barton Hall protest on disciplinary probation and warned that a repetition meant suspension, students complained: the university—meaning the president—"inhibits free discussion." Perkins wrote in late June that "it has been a complicated matter to handle so that the interests of freedom of speech were protected at the same time that the interests of the community were not infringed." The interest of everyone, he insisted, was "to protect individual freedom but not at the expense of either freedom of others or the proper functioning of the institution. This rule is now pretty well imbedded in University thought." Perkins believed that valuable lessons had been learned during the Barton Hall protest; he lamented the unfavorable publicity, but he insisted that Cornell had "come through the matter with dignity."

Protests continued the next year. On April 27, 1965, students interrupted events of the Charter Day celebration by shouting down the speakers. The level of protest increased, and in early May, during a question-and-answer period following a lecture, students hurled abuse at W. Averell Harriman, the U.S. ambassador to South Vietnam. These acts impinged upon the long-held academic tradition of freedom of expression. Even those faculty who agreed with the students' position on the war found their curtailment of free speech objectionable.

A diagram of these years would show growing anger about the war over a layer of agitation concerning racial issues resting upon a base of other social problems. Some individuals were concerned with all issues and would span all layers, some would be placed in just one level, some, both students and faculty, would stand outside looking in. These layers of issues and the figures associated with them were constantly in flux. To complicate matters, there were several student organizations, such as the Afro-American Society (AAS), founded in 1966, and Students for a Democratic Society, founded at Cornell in 1964, whose leaders sometimes worked on strategies in cooperation with each other but at other times were at odds.

Amid this turmoil, in fall 1966, the chief of the Cornell Safety Division declared *The Trojan Horse,* a student literary magazine, obscene, delivering all copies he could find to the Ithaca City Police. Students protested, and the faculty defended the students' right to artistic freedom of expression and voted "not to prohibit its sale." *The Trojan Horse* generated a fierce administrative battle concerning the jurisdiction of the Office of Proctor and the Safety Division, leading to resignations, a reassignment of duties, and finally the consolidation of these two offices. In court, Judge Harold Simpson declared *The Trojan Horse* "not obscene." He wrote, "It lacks the quality of prurience—that is, it did not create sexual cravings or desire." It was, however, distasteful to many, boring to others. Deeply concerned about the events on campus, the growing lack of trust between administration and students, and the deteriorating situation, Prof. Edward Morris wrote to Perkins asking sadly, "who runs Cornell?"

Allan Sindler, a professor of government, chaired a commission of fifteen charged with investigating recent campus events. In September 1967 his committee issued its report, which addressed *The Trojan Horse* issue, marijuana use, civil disobedience, and forms of political dissent. The commission sought to prevent dissent from impinging on the rights of others and recommended a new judicial system, which was approved by the faculty in spring 1968.

The campus cauldron boiled with issues, and Perkins called the situation "sensitive and explosive." As debate about a new black studies program was in progress, on April 4, 1968, black students took over the Economics Department, protesting racism they perceived in lectures given by a visiting professor. As administrators discussed solutions with irate students, they bypassed established procedures for complaints against professors, generating charges of impropriety by the local chapter of the American Association of University Professors. That same day the Reverend Martin Luther King, Jr., was assassinated in Memphis. Downs calls the memorial service for King, held April 5, the "death knell for the politics and pedagogy of integration at Cornell" and the inauguration of direct racial confrontation.

Negotiations between AAS and the university over the shape of the black studies program heightened tensions and fostered suspicion. There was also an internal struggle among the black students for leadership of AAS. Tactics grew more confrontational, with AAS members demanding a separate black college and naming James Turner, a Northwestern University graduate student they had met at a national meeting, as the person they wanted as director. In December 1968 black students carrying toy guns engaged in demonstrations on campus during which several vending machines were overturned and damaged. There was a sit-in at the president's office, books were removed from library shelves and dumped at the circulation desk, students danced on the dining room tables at the Straight. Before Christmas, Perkins met with the black students and said there would be no separate black college. He appointed Vice-Provost Keith Kennedy to head a new committee on black studies, and AAS leaders agreed to meet with him.

The new year began with a change of AAS leadership. At the end of January the Conduct Board directed that five students appear at a hearing regarding the December vandalism, which they failed to do. Late in February black students confronted and physically shook Perkins as he was opening a symposium on South Africa, once again violating free speech on campus. In March, the five students were again summoned to a judicial hearing under the threat of suspension if they failed to appear. When white students disrupted recruiters for Chase Manhattan Bank and were not charged by the administration, black students alleged racial inequality. At an emergency meeting the faculty voted to support the judicial system, which the Faculty Committee on Student Affairs (FCSA) affirmed. The five students were instructed to meet with the Conduct Board on April 17, and when they failed to appear, FCSA tried them in absentia and issued reprimands to three.

False alarms were set off on campus, and a cross burned in front of Wari House, the residence for black women students. Then came the confrontation at Willard Straight Hall on Parents' Weekend.

The incident began at six A.M. on Saturday, April 19, when AAS took over the Straight, evicted the parents sleeping in the guest rooms, and repulsed an attack by men from Delta Upsilon, who invaded the upper level to "liberate" the building. At that point, the administration learned that the black students in the Straight had guns. On Sunday, Vice-Provost Kennedy agreed to nullify the FCSA reprimands

Eric D. Evans '69, Afro-American Society leader, addressing the press in front of Willard Straight Hall, April 20, 1969.

against the students and AAS agreed to end its take-over. Those in the Straight received amnesty, and at four P.M. AAS members left the building, their guns in full view, with the press in attendance. The image haunts the university to this day. Dale Corson said bluntly, "it was a public relations fiasco." It was that, of course, and much more.

At a convocation in Barton Hall on Monday, Perkins failed to address the issues. Almost nine thousand people looking for clarity and leadership heard Perkins speak only about humane studies—a speech he had intended to deliver during Parents' Weekend. Perhaps he feared being forced from the stage, as he had been earlier that year, or having the microphone wrested away and given to AAS, as an unidentified caller had threatened. Whatever his reason, Perkins stunned the crowd with an irrelevant speech that demonstrated his inability to distinguish routine from extraordinary events. His opportunity to calm the situation was squandered.

Some twelve hundred faculty members met in Bailey Hall at four on Monday afternoon. Perkins reviewed the history of the judicial system at the university and justified the administration's actions. At issue was the agreement that had been brokered with AAS nullifying the reprimands, reached "by negotiating with armed students." Had the administration's representatives given too much away? Were there to be no consequences for students' totally inappropriate actions on campus? Speeches, resolutions, and motions followed, and in the end a compromise motion of eight points passed by a voice vote. The resolution affirmed that the faculty sympathized with the black students at Cornell but condemned the takeover of the Straight, the cross burning, and the presence of weapons on campus. The guns, the resolution read, "make it impossible for the Faculty to agree at this meeting to dismiss the penalties imposed on the three students" by FCSA. The faculty affirmed its desire to review the AAS complaints, to meet with its representatives, and to support law and order on campus. This resolution did not please everyone, nor was its vague language understood the same way by all. There were already some resignations from the faculty, Allan Sindler's being the first. Far from promoting healing, the faculty resolution caused further confusion and dissention.

On Tuesday, as factions met to consider their positions and strategy, AAS leader Thomas Jones announced on a local radio broadcast that Cornell was on the edge of destruction if the faculty did not reconsider its Monday vote. In Barton Hall students and some faculty demanded that the resolution be nullified and then threatened to take over Day Hall if it was not.

On Wednesday, April 23, the faculty voted to nullify the reprimands. Milton Konvitz, a professor in Industrial and Labor Relations, said that in the meeting he was both intent and numb, believing the campus had reverted to a state of nature. It was as if, he wrote, "we were being asked to declare on Wednesday that 1 + 1 = 3, though on Monday we had said firmly and decisively, that 1 + 1 = 2." Knowing that the students were "ready to throw the campus into utter turmoil," many in the faculty made that different calculation. Although some pledged to hold fast, believing that the rule of law counted and all should be judged by the same standards, others wanted to avert the greater tragedy of destruction and possibly death. In the end, the faculty voted to step back from the brink of chaos. Konvitz mused that "life today offers little stability in any respect. The quest for certainty ended some years ago. We live permanently in an encircling gloom, and the kindly light that we have is only a feeble candle of short-range vision."

What had happened? The easy answer is that the faculty voted for resolutions that contained too many points, that individuals responded to one or several but not necessarily all of the reasons to stand firm or to retreat from danger. A more complicated answer is that the faculty voted overwhelmingly to step back from the prospect of violence, of destruction of the institution they loved. Others held firm to principles that most of them shared, fearing that any breach of academic freedom was the death knell of the university. Still others refused to accept the assaults on freedom of speech or to bend to physical threat. Did any of them think about the words of George Lincoln Burr in 1921 after the student mob had attacked young Morelli for not wearing his freshman cap? What lies before us, Burr had written,

PLEDGE

We declare that the University cannot function when decisions are reached by negotiating with armed students.

Notwithstanding the President's statement this morning (April 21), belatedly forbidding the carrying of guns outside student rooms or the seizing of buildings, if Dean Miller's motion to declare the Conduct Board's judgment null and void is endorsed by the faculty, we pledge ourselves to cease classroom instruction and to undertake a review of our relationship to the University in the light of this intolerable and, one would have thought, unthinkable situation.

We are, of course, mindful of our obligations to our students and will do our best to carry out this policy without damage to their academic interests.

—Statement by thirty-one faculty members, April 21, 1969

For me academic freedom has never previously seemed threatened at this university. But today, I think it is. And it is primarily because of this, rather than any threats made over the radio, that my colleagues are leaving Cornell. You have asked us to understand why it was that the black students acted, to understand the fear they felt. It is fair that you ask this, and I'm sure a good many faculty and students did not sufficiently appreciate this before. But empathy must be two-sided if mutual understanding is to be achieved, and you too have an obligation to appreciate our views on the issue which we regard as every bit as crucial. What so many members of the Cornell faculty saw at stake in their meeting last Monday was, I can assure you, not the Cornell judicial system, nor was it the matter of justice for the blacks, something that most of those who voted as I did wanted as much as you. The issue that we saw as paramount was rather different. . . . At Monday's meeting what so many members of the faculty saw before them was not a simple picture of a university official who felt obligated to sign an agreement against the background of firearms; the backdrop was hardly that simple. Because in the minds of most of us, behind men armed with guns (and for us it did not matter whether they were whites or blacks who held the guns)—behind them was the background of a very recent incident that cannot be washed away—the sordid spectacle of a colleague physically pulled from a platform because he expressed views which some of his listeners didn't happen to like. That action was a direct assault on academic freedom. If

is a regime of lynch law, and the liberties of us all will not long be sacred. In 1969, each vote cast at that Wednesday meeting required courage. The choice was not easy, and after the faculty made their collective decision to retreat, all were plagued by lingering doubts.

The following Sunday Tom Wicker titled his *New York Times* column "Humanity vs. Principle at Cornell." Wicker paraphrased an administrator, writing that "Cornell ultimately will find itself the better for its week of upheaval—its students and faculty more nearly the free and open community that is the university ideal, and its blacks more fully a part of that community." His remarks seemed a benediction after the trauma of the previous week, but the week of upheaval was to stretch into a long time, and Wicker's interpretation was definitely not shared by all.

Still, nothing was settled: members of the faculty who called themselves the Group of Forty-One voiced concern about academic freedom; several professors

it is to be condoned and excused as a political act, then academic freedom is in even greater jeopardy. It is that spectacle of force and intimidation and what it symbolizes that is uppermost in our minds, and which inevitably affected our perception of the relationship of guns to the agreements we were asked to endorse. We voted for the maintenance of academic freedom, believing that without that essential quality there can be no relationship of any kind between blacks and the university, because without that quality you don't have a university. . . .

On Wednesday your faculty voted under what most of them perceived as continuing pressures of a threat of violence. . . . I resented deeply having to act under the threat of violence, and that action cost me too some of my self respect. Not simply because I was capitulating under force, but because I felt in doing so I was further undermining the foundation of academic freedom at Cornell. I voted differently on Wednesday because I discovered in talking to students on Tuesday and Wednesday morning that they had no realization that our Monday's stand was for academic freedom and against threats to compromise it, and that most of these students were completely confused . . . and assumed that Monday's vote had to do with the ends of the black students, rather than the means to be used in attaining them.

—George McT. Kahin, address in Barton Hall, April 25, 1969

met privately with members of the Board of Trustees to discuss the situation on campus; faculty at the law school wrote to Perkins voicing their lack of faith in his ability to lead the university. The trustees identified a lack of planning during the crisis and especially a "lack of visibility of the leadership of the University." The board sanctioned the creation of a constituent assembly comprising all segments of the university—faculty, students, and staff. Some faculty members refused to teach classes and held teach-ins instead, following the example of George McT. Kahin, professor of government and a Southeast Asia specialist, who began campus teach-ins as a way to discuss U.S. involvement in Vietnam.

In May 1969 the trustees voted to affirm a declaration of governing principles for the university. There were ten: that all students and faculty were guaranteed the right of free speech; that the freedom to teach in accordance with the dictates of intellect and conscience was fundamental to the university, and that no one had any right to inhibit the rights of others to teach or to interfere with the freedom to

HUMANITY VS. PRINCIPLE
AT CORNELL

. . . .

Cornell ultimately will find itself the better for its week of upheaval—its students and faculty more nearly the free and open community that is the university idea, and its blacks more fully a part of that community. And although he [Steven Muller, university provost] is saddened that a number of Cornell faculty members, including some with high standing, plan to resign in protest, Muller believes that they have the opportunity to stand on principle this week only because university officials were willing, last Sunday in Straight Hall, to put a real concern for humanity above abstract principle.

—Tom Wicker, THE NEW YORK TIMES,
April 27, 1969

April 28, 1969

To the editor of THE NEW YORK TIMES:

The events of this past week are but one part of a pattern over the past eighteen months of the incapacity of the Perkins administration to contain and resist coercion-based demands. Militant student groups have rightly concluded that this is the sure way to extract concessions. Given the ideology of these groups, and their insistence on "cleansing" the campus of all vestiges of what they call "institutional racism" and the "military-industrial complex," no academic freedom is maintainable. These are the issues, Mr. Wicker, and not "humanity above principle."

—Allan P. Sindler, Professor of
Government, Cornell University

learn; that bigotry and racial discrimination had no place on the Cornell campus; that every member of the Cornell community was to be judged individually as to his conduct and performance; that the university was not a sanctuary from the law; that duress, intimidation, violence, and the threat of violence were inimical to the life of the university and unacceptable as expressions of dissent; that disruption and the tactics of terror would be met by firm and appropriate response; that orderly change was essential to the life and the growth of the university; that Cornell encouraged faculty and student ideas for adapting the structure, curricula, and programs of the university to the changing needs of the times; and that all university policies had to be consonant with the basic Cornell principle of freedom with responsibility.

On May 28, Perkins spoke of his expectations for the fall term. This signal that he intended to remain at Cornell prompted open calls for his resignation. Concurrently, the *Alumni News* carried a full and searing report of the events of the spring. Perkins and the administration were stung, and alumni enraged. Sensing the crumbling situation, on May 31 James Perkins offered the Board of Trustees a letter of resignation, which the board accepted.

Writing about those days thirty years later, a student of the class of 1969 commented, "I have few clear recollections of the events associated with the takeover of the Straight." His memory of the events that spring is representative: "all of those events are somehow wrapped up in a foggy memory of racial separation, Vietnam protests, and the 'hippie' generation."

Donald Downs ends his *Cornell '69* with two lessons that he believes emerged from those difficult days. One was that "the principles of liberal education need strong, publicly proclaimed support from campus leaders who actually hold such principles dear," and that "professors, administrators, and students must have the courage to speak out against the forces that would compromise these principles in the name of whatever moral vision holds sway." This testifying must be done, asserts Downs, in good faith so that it is utterly defensible. "Liberalism must maintain its racial conscience," he insisted, but at the same time—and this is Downs's second point—liberalism needs to retain confidence in its "commitment to individual freedom if the drive for social justice is to recapture the moral authority of the constitutional order." Remaining silent, Downs maintains, is morally untenable. "The university can lead us out of our respective caves only by being true to itself."

"I have thought of you many times," Thomas Jones, a leader of the African American students in 1969, wrote to James Perkins in 1980. "I have been pained and shamed that a friend of Afro-Americans paid the highest price for that confrontation. I give you an apology for not having stood with you against the tide of emotionalism and racial fear." In 1995, Jones donated one hundred thousand dollars to the university to sponsor the James A. Perkins Prize for Interracial Understanding and Harmony. Some found this soothing; others found the irony of the gesture bizarre and altogether disturbing.

Pledge we faith and homage ever

Cornell was in a fragile condition following the events of the spring, but sometimes an institution is fortunate to get the leadership it needs. Dale Corson, one of the nuclear physicists about whom President Day had so happily complained, became Cornell's eighth president in 1969. He was the second president, after Schurman, to come from the faculty. Corson's mandate was to pick up and reassemble the pieces into which Cornell community had fragmented. From the start, it was impossible to please everyone—not even most of the time—but a mirror held up in Ithaca would have reflected troubles of similar intensity elsewhere in the country. The era might be thought of as America's second war against itself.

That fall, as always, students returned to Ithaca to take up their studies, to join fraternities, to engage in the rites of the young. Although many returning students had taken part in the events of spring 1969, not all had been involved, and some—most probably even the majority—had gone on with their schoolwork and jobs, with fraternity life and with romance. Not even the partici-pants could agree on the nature of the turmoil through which they had just passed. The Ithaca community had been stunned by what had happened so close to home, and the faculty remained divided along the lines taken the previous April. Many voiced a lack of faith in the university's administrators and in one other.

Dale Corson, quietly confident and steady, had served the university as professor of physics, dean of engineering, and provost. He had formulated the innovative Division of Biological Sciences. His thorough knowledge of the insti-tution, its policies, and the situation on campus gave him perspective; most on campus trusted him. These attributes helped Corson address Cornell's problems in the 1970s despite the compounding effects of widespread distrust of the nation's political leaders, the struggle for civil rights, and the war in Vietnam.

Cornell faced needed repair of campus buildings, insuffi-cient space for new research interests, shrinking funds caused by high inflation and a national recession, extensive drug use

Dale R. Corson (president, 1969–1977) with Jose Azel '76, at the Herbert F. Johnson Museum of Art exhibition of his photographs, 1974.

I came to Cornell in the fall of 1946 as an Assistant Professor of Physics, eight years after completing my graduate study and after five and a half years of war-related activity. The invitation to Cornell was a great honor and being at Cornell has continued to be an honor throughout the intervening 57 years.

Before WWII I had been an instructor at the University of California at Berkeley, teaching highly able students. When I came to Cornell the students were of even higher quality. In 1946 we had an influx of war veterans who knew exactly why they were here and they were top students. A few years later they were of still higher quality. For thirteen years I taught freshmen and/or sophomores and not a semester passed without some student com-

ing to ask "have you thought about looking at this subject or this problem this way?" Year after year the students led me to new insights into subject matter I thought I understood in depth. I had two students in the same class who later shared the Nobel Prize. Sometimes the students taught me more than I taught them.

I might have been a logical choice when I became Chairman of the Physics Department but when President Malott selected me to be Dean of the Engineering College it seemed an irrational move. I had done a great deal of engineering in building particle accelerators, cyclotrons and synchrotrons, both before the war and after. My wartime work was largely engineering so I had experience in the field. Applying that experience to the problems of

and sexual freedom among students, and continuing political activism. Another challenge was Cornell's public image. The picture of an idyllic campus sprawling across East Hill had been replaced by the image of armed students emerging from the Straight, with implications for applications and alumni support.

One priority was to strengthen and expand the Committee on Special Educational Projects (COSEP) and understand the needs of those students. In addition, Cornell was now competing with other schools in the recruitment of black students. The university made a commitment to create a Center for Afro-American Studies, which shortly became the Africana Studies and Research Center, to be administered not by a college but to report directly to the university provost. It needed facilities and staff.

Another concern was finding the proper role for the university in addressing the environmental concerns facing the nation and the world. This new initiative involved faculty and students from many parts of the university and required significant resources. Corson also saw the need to strengthen the humanities at the

an Engineering College was a big leap but I decided to give it a try.

After only four years in the job President Perkins asked me to be Provost and that turned out to be the best academic job I ever had. It gave me a chance to study the entire university and to learn about fields that had been no more than names before. I believe the Provost's position is the best one in the whole university.

I would never have become President if we had known how to deal with the campus disruptions of the late 1960s. I became president at a time when there were probably no other candidates for the position. In the first campus protests, when I was Provost, I made a decision that proved vital. I decided I wanted to know, to talk to and, where possible, to work with the protestors. When the crises came I knew the protest leaders and they knew me. I continue to see and to correspond with some of them. Many of them are now "establishment" types, in positions of leadership. I like to think that their Cornell experience, even in protests, contributed significantly to the roles they play today.

Finally, a comment about my associates: the faculty, the university administrators, the university work force, the Board of Trustees and the alumni. These are the ones who have made it such a privilege to be at Cornell. Thank you.

—Dale R. Corson, 2003

university; he had participated in the growth of the sciences and believed in parity. He set out to review and revamp the structure of the university and appointed Ian McNeil, professor of law, to chair a task force on the curriculum, student life, extradepartmental centers, residential needs—now taken for granted as a university responsibility—and faculty, student, and staff governance. The working groups coordinated by McNeil pulled many on the faculty into a common effort, generating the excitement that comes from responding to new times. Professional staff support for student life increased, but faculty withdrawal from the day-by-day running of the university was accelerated, ending the organization created sixty years earlier by Jacob Schurman.

During Corson's first year as president, the campus was calm until April 1, 1970. When the Africana Studies and Research Center building on Wait Avenue burned, black students protested in the president's office, rampaged through the newly opened Campus Store, and rallied at Willard Straight. Some protesters attended the university faculty meeting to present their concerns. A week later

Africana Studies and Research Center brochure.

students returned to the Campus Store, where they built a bonfire of items taken earlier. President Corson declared a curfew and sought an injunction—the first ever for activities on campus—from the New York State Supreme Court against all persons perpetrating violence on campus. To show its support of COSEP and the Africana Center, the university trustees voted to locate a new headquarters for the center and fund its programs.

The final segment of the 1969–70 year brought news of the expansion of war in Indochina, an American invasion of Cambodia, and the deaths of four students at Kent State in Ohio and two at Jackson State in Mississippi. So much violence was like a spark on dry kindling. Faculty and students on campus were ignited once again. Classes at Cornell continued, but with consideration given to students whose reaction to national events made study difficult or even impossible. The trustees, recognizing the changed nature of student involvement in national affairs, voted to permit students and faculty to engage in political activity by declaring a break during the coming semester; this "Citizenship Break," as it was known, eventually became Fall Break.

War and student protest were only two of the issues on campus. Corson also supported the aspirations of women for better representation in the curricula, and one outcome was a new course, The Evolution of Female Personality: Its History

and Prospects, offered in spring 1970. Fully approved and accredited, it had an
enrollment of two hundred students. It was "unique not only in its content but in
its origins," for it "had been forged by a *collective,* a self-appointed group of thirty
staff women, graduate students, and adjunct faculty, most of whom were, like the
women whose nature and history and status the course was designed to explore,
on the margin of academe." Female Personality had a firm place in the curriculum because Professor Harold Feldman of the College of Human Ecology offered
it an academic base. "We'll call it my course," he had said, "and you'll teach it."
Cornell's approach was more straightforward and direct than that of other institutions, where women's issues were incorporated into existing seminars or taught as
a segment of an established course. Within two years, Cornell had a full-fledged
women's studies program.

In 1971 Provost Robert A. Plane remarked, "perhaps our most pressing need
is for increasing numbers of women faculty members in areas where we have large
numbers of women students." Trustee Constance Cook '41, J.D. '43, headed an
ad hoc Committee on the Status of Women, whose 1972 report found only 107
women—52 of them in the College of Human Ecology—among the 1,453 faculty
members, and no highly placed women in the administration. The committee challenged the university to accommodate the trajectory of women's lives with options

Women's art festival, 1972.

for part-time appointments and a maternity leave policy, and to provide better job and career training for women. It also called for the hiring of more women professors, administrators, and staff, especially in the area of mental health. In addition, the Cook committee recommended that the university seek grants to fund positions for women on campus. Along with hiring more women came the problem of dual-career marriages and partnerships. Soon the issue of nepotism became moot.

The Cook report found a general belief among administrators that women faculty were appropriate for curricula that attracted women students—much the same sentiment expressed by Jacob Gould Schurman fifty years earlier. It would take time for this restrictive attitude to fade away, yet women, who had always taught in the College of Home Economics and in its successor, the College of Human Ecology, were beginning to be seen elsewhere on campus and in gradually increasing numbers. Constance Cook eventually served from 1976 to 1980 as university vice president for land grant affairs.

Other changes in the 1970s were intended to make the university more responsive to student, faculty, and staff needs. The administration began publication of the *Cornell Chronicle* in fall 1969 as part of Cornell's commitment to improve campuswide communication. In 1970 the trustees created the position of university ombudsman—a relatively new concept adopted from Swedish practice—and approved the Division of Campus Life. This new entity was to oversee housing, dining, student unions, registered campus organizations and activities, religious groups and organizations, athletics and physical education, university health services, the Campus Store, public lectures and performances, traffic and parking, student orientation and counseling services, and the nonteaching functions of the museums. In 1971 the university appointed an affirmative action officer to ensure that Cornell met its professional and legal obligations regarding diversity. Liaisons with the city and county were concentrated in an office of community relations. Several innovations seemed, at first, little more than interesting experiments.

Computers, initially mysterious to those in fields other than science, became more evident, and televised courses were recorded for off-campus instruction. The trustees created the Office of University Bursar in 1971 and introduced the student charge card.

Changes in the nature of student life elicited anxious comments and even complaints from parents and the press. One legacy of Andrew Dickson White's belief that men should house and board themselves—"govern themselves" had been the term used in the charter—was that dormitory space for men at Cornell always lagged far behind enrollments. The options for upperclassmen included fraternity housing and off-campus apartments. The startling shift in 1972 was from single-sex dormitory units to coeducational housing. Student lifestyles, commented Dale Corson, "sometimes shocked us," but he credits the efforts of Ruth Darling, the associate dean of students, for making this shift palatable to doubting parents. Corson recalls "very few confrontations" over coed dorms, but Cornell retained some single-sex dormitory space for students who wanted it. A 1974 study reported that many students preferred off-campus apartments to university housing, and thirty-one percent of the four hundred Cornell students who took part in the survey (of an undergraduate population of eleven thousand five hundred) admitted to having participated in "cohabitation." This was not, insisted the researcher, trial marriage, and it was far more than sexual convenience. Rather, the students believed that they were avoiding the superficiality of dating by cultivating emotionally satisfying relationships at a university they regarded as large and impersonal, in a nation many saw as repressive and hypocritical. These students reported a desire for deeper personal relationships while expressing doubts about the institution of marriage.

Dale Corson recorded what he observed among current students. Despite all their present-mindedness, verve and idealism, impetuousness and irresponsibility, Corson thought Cornell students lacked the lightheartedness of previous generations. Their optimism, he wrote, "is at a low point." They were "biologically and socially more advanced" than their predecessors, yet they were still, at heart, adolescents. He found them basically conformist despite their greater degree of independence. On the other hand, he insisted, they had "more potential for leadership than any previous college generation." In January 1972 Corson reported to the Board of Trustees that the campus was quiet; that there was "no indication of [a] return to extremes of political activism or confrontation." The students, he thought, were engaged in study.

That spring, however, tensions arose between African American basketball players and their white coach, necessitating intervention by the university ombudsman.

The campus grew edgy. Then on April 26, at one P.M., between fifty and seventy-five students and some non-students occupied the library in Carpenter Hall. They complained about U.S. military and Central Intelligence Agency recruiting on campus, secret government research conducted at the Cornell Aeronautical Laboratory (CAL) in Buffalo, and always, the war in Vietnam. Corson answered the takeover with firm guidelines. He declared that no outside force was to be used to evacuate a building, with all actions to be taken by Cornell Safety personnel only. He declared that there would be no amnesty and no negotiation with those inside the building, but he proclaimed a willingness to discuss the issues once the building was vacated. The students knew exactly the consequences of their actions and understood how to proceed.

On May 1 the students left. No one had been hurt, no outside police had been called in, there had been no negotiation of impossible demands, no amnesty had been granted. Instead, both sides had agreed to discuss the issues, and only campus judicial procedures were involved. There was a collective sigh of relief, and the episode demonstrated that Corson's way of handling such situations would work to the advantage of everyone.

President Corson following Lowell George out of Carpenter Hall, April 1972.

While many at Cornell focused on campus life, Corson believed that the larger challenge for the university was financial. Inflation was high, some alumni had discontinued their support because of student unrest, and taxpayers and politicians were loath to allocate more money to state schools. At the same time, new circumstances required more student services at higher costs. Across the nation, more and more students sought admission to universities, and competition for the best of them intensified among the nation's top schools. In 1955 there had been three million students in U.S. institutions of higher education; in 1970 there were seven million five hundred thousand. Besides absorbing the higher enrollments and providing aid for disadvantaged students, universities had assumed costly research commitments. Cornell's deficit was approximately one million two hundred thousand dollars in the endowed budget, and the statutory colleges had suffered "indiscriminate budget cuts" from the state.

Finances were but one area of concern in 1973. In what he considered a year of decision, Corson presided over a quiet revolution in the university's governance and curriculum. Student representatives took seats on an expanded Board of Trustees. There were discussions about the curriculum and course offerings, and the organization of some departments changed. Geological Sciences became Earth and Atmospheric Sciences. Computer Science emerged as an important program. The College of Agriculture became the College of Agriculture and Life Sciences to signify its expanded scope. Limnology merged with Entomology. The School of Civil and Environmental Engineering appeared. The trustees discussed the merits of interdisciplinary programs, which were generally acknowledged to be the future direction of education at Cornell, but their creation was not always smooth: some mergers threatened people in entrenched positions.

The alterations made in the curriculum reflected the new president's vision for the university. Corson's view of what a university might do was the opposite of his predecessor's: it "should not be the agent of change, it should study the problems of society and means of change." A 1976 review of undergraduate education at Cornell questioned class size, limits on library facilities, and specialization, and expressed concern about some students' inability to write clear prose. Administrators worried about a decline in SAT scores. At the same time, academic critics questioned the value of prescribed graduation requirements. National attention focused on changes in grading standards—a subject that would continue to engender debate for years to come.

As part of his plan to provide a more stimulating intellectual atmosphere at the university, Corson established the Committee on Undergraduate Teaching. From 1971 on, the Institute for Environmental Studies offered courses and lectures that drew faculty

STATE OF THE UNIVERSITY

· ·

Cornell will also feel the impact of the change in interest from traditional to nontraditional education, from education exclusively for the 18 to 22-year-olds to education for the adults. In the next 15 years I anticipate an increased emphasis on the nontraditional, an emphasis away from the liberal arts and toward career-oriented education, a trend I don't like. . . .

We live in a world that's changing. This is a period of retrenchment in higher education. We will not be able to do things the way we did them before. The era of growth is over. It will be difficult to make the adjustment but we must be aware of the need to adjust and be sensitive to the severity of the problems which face our students, our faculty and our whole University. It will be difficult to accept the facts and even more difficult to make the necessary adjustments. We must work together to establish University priorities and to implement them. We must determine what's vital to the University's future and decide what we need most to do and in what order and then do it. When we do what has to be done, we can do so knowing that Cornell will stand, as in the words of the Shakespeare sonnet, "still constant in wondrous excellence."

—Dale Corson, Trustee-Council Weekend address, October 11, 1974

Construction of the Herbert F. Johnson
Museum of Art, designed by I. M. Pei, 1972.

CHAPTER NINE

and students from across the campus. The Society for the Humanities took up its home in the Andrew Dickson White House in 1973, when the university art collection moved to the Herbert F. Johnson Museum. There was considerable talk about I. M. Pei's startling design for the building, which invited viewers to peer into its open spaces as well as to look out from them. People looking up from the city below dubbed it the Sewing Machine.

An exciting expansion of both the curriculum and the physical plant in 1966 offered undergraduates in landlocked Ithaca field opportunities in marine science. Cornell and the University of New Hampshire joined to build the Shoals Marine Laboratory on Appledore Island, six miles off the coast of New Hampshire. That facility opened in 1973 and immediately drew not only students but also those seeking adult education. Where the School of Agriculture had pioneered in reaching out to nontraditional students, other segments of the university now followed.

Corson later mused, "A Cornell student is a fortunate student. A Cornell student can study poetry with Archie Ammons. Or hear a lecture by Efraim Racker on mitochondria. Or William Brown on the evolutionary niches, which have permitted the survival of certain species of insects for millions of years. Or Irving Younger on the technique of cross-examination." The list of eminent professors was long, and the opportunities in library, lab, and classroom were vast. "Cornell students have a rich plate before them. They can nibble or they can eat voraciously." He concluded that it was the duty of the institution to see that the array of courses remained broad, challenging, and interesting.

The quality of people on the faculty might well be glimpsed in a conversation between Robert Wilson, professor of physics and director of the Cornell Laboratory of Nuclear Studies, and Sen. John Pastore in Congress, after Wilson had testified in favor of greater government funding:

Senator Pastore: Is there anything connected with the hopes of this accelerator that in any way involves the security of this country?

Professor Wilson: No sir, I do not believe so.

Senator Pastore: Nothing at all?

Professor Wilson: Nothing at all.

Senator Pastore: It has no value in that respect?

Professor Wilson: It has only to do with the respect with which we regard one another, the dignity of men, our love of culture. It has to do with those things. It has to do with are we good painters, good sculptors, great poets.

I mean all the things we really venerate and honor in our country and are patriotic about. It has nothing to do directly with defending our country except to make it worth defending.

There is no report of Senator Pastore's reaction.

There were constraints on what the university could do to change and expand its mission, however. The answer to Cornell's financial situation and the vicissitudes of state and federal funding was to raise more money from philanthropic organizations and alumni. The Cornell Fund and the Cornell Campaign were both successful, jump-started by Nicholas Noyes, who had pledged a million dollars to the university with the challenge that his donation be matched by alumni who had not donated before or who donated more than their previous levels. Coming as it did on the heels of the turmoil of 1969, this gift inspired extraordinary support from the alumni. For his part, Noyes requested only a place on the fifty-yard line for the Cornell-Yale game—dubbed the most expensive seat in collegiate football history.

Hans Bethe and Boyce McDaniel bicycling in the Wilson Synchrotron, 1968.

Some faculty found the University Senate, created in 1971, an effective body and devoted considerable time to it. Senate President Arthur Spitzer listed its achievements during its initial months, which included resolutions on sex discrimination and the sophomore residence requirement, a bill to encourage open meetings throughout the university; a proposal regarding parking and traffic on campus, recommendations for fellowships for South African students (promised by President Perkins in 1968), and a firm statement regarding the university's financial investments in South Africa—an issue that was to absorb the energies of many students, faculty, and staff for some time to come. The Senate also heard a complaint about the placement of poisonous ornamental plants near graduate student housing, where there were likely to be young children. By the mid-1970s, the Senate appeared to have lost its focus; faculty interest dwindled, and attendance fell. The Senate was also found to be costly. The McNeil Task Force suggested in a report to the trustees in March 1975 that it be abolished.

At the same time the faculty's presence in the operations of the university diminished. Disillusioned after the events of the past decade, the faculty showed more loyalty to disciplines than enthusiasm for the political activism and campus activity that had engaged so many. Whereas a student in 1911 could comment that "when the faculty sets down its professional foot on a question, that question is about decided," new conditions prevailed. The faculty of the 1970s was more numerous and scattered across a broad campus. Interaction between components of the university became less frequent, and questions of academic professionalism claimed faculty attention. This shift from community to separation was cause for dismay as the links between individuals in different departments weakened.

The state's declining financial situation in the 1970s prompted a reassessment of the university's land grant function. In 1974 Provost David Knapp recommended expanding the focus of Cooperative Extension from rural issues to urban problems. He also thought it the right time to reexamine extension's research function and improve the working relationship between campus students and those in Cooperative Extension courses, and to improve coordination between the university and the state's community colleges. In addition, Knapp recommended that the university institute adult education for professionals already in careers.

Throughout the decade, Cornell continually attempted to resolve questions raised by race. COSEP, created to aid minority students, declined in effectiveness, and the provost reassigned academic advising and counsel of minority students to individuals in the colleges. A black undergraduate suggested to Corson the idea of Ujamaa, a residence hall that would provide housing and activities for students interested in African American culture. Although not limited to black students, Ujamaa housed few nonblacks and was challenged by the American Civil Liberties Union for fostering segregation. Concerned, the Board of Regents investigated but declined to recommend any changes. The trustees reaffirmed a commitment to minority education and sought ways to further diversify both students and faculty.

Affirmative action initiatives did increase the number of women faculty and staff. Personnel services for women employees were enhanced and special programs initiated for women students. Additional medical facilities for women students became available. Cornell also complied with federal Title IX, which required equal athletic opportunities for women. As the women's sports program grew,

The 1969–70 Cornell hockey team (the only undefeated, untied team in modern collegiate hockey history), with Coach Ned Harkness, at the NCAA championship game in Lake Placid, 1970.

some traditional men's teams were necessarily designated "club" rather than varsity sports and lost their university funding. Bob Kane, director of Athletics, noted that by 1972 there were fourteen intercollegiate teams for women, some doing very well. Ivy League competition for women started in 1975, and by the late 1970s there was a trainer for women, a training room at Helen Newman Hall, locker space for women at Lynah Rink and Teagle Hall, and a boathouse for women rowers on the inlet. By 1980 Kane believed that the university was in compliance with the law even though achieving fairness—a university goal and a federal regulation—did not suit everyone.

Despite the success of the Cornell Fund and the Cornell Campaign, budget cuts were made across campus. Losing funding from the New York Hospital, with which it was affiliated, the Cornell School of Nursing was particularly hard hit. It celebrated its centennial in 1977 but ceased to award baccalaureate degrees after June 1979. On the Ithaca campus, the Sloan Institute of Hospital Administration was folded into the Graduate School of Business and Public Administration.

Having put back together the pieces of the university—or at least rearranged them in a workable fashion—Dale Corson resigned as president in 1977. The trustees accepted Corson's offer to oversee the medical school until 1978 and named him university chancellor, making him the second man after Edmund Ezra Day to hold that position. Not everything promised had been undertaken or completed; the university was still in the process of healing, and rifts within the faculty remained. But Corson had managed to restore Cornell's stability. He foresaw the financial exigencies of the future and knew that many of the problems faced during his years in Day Hall would continue to challenge the university.

Chapter Ten

Name and fame be honored

With the university on an even keel, the presidential search committee in 1977 sought an individual with dynamic leadership, strong academic credentials, a proven record as an administrator, and a stand on affirmative action in harmony with Cornell's commitment to diversity. The new president would have to move the university forward through difficult economic times, and thus Cornell needed a president who could raise funds. Being a Cornell graduate was not necessary, stated the trustees, but of course, it would generate considerable enthusiasm.

Within a short time, the committee identified Frank H. T. Rhodes as a "formidable candidate," despite his lack of any prior Cornell affiliation. With the announcement of his election, a *Cornell Daily Sun* columnist noted that while "you can't please everyone all the time," in this case that truism "seems to have been violated by the overwhelmingly favorable response."

Rhodes came to Cornell from the University of Michigan, where he had been vice president for academic affairs and a professor of geology and mineralogy. Installed in 1977 as the ninth president of Cornell University, he served eighteen years, until 1995. Many of the criteria identified as important to the search committee proved to be exactly the qualities needed for these years, which featured financial constraints, nascent labor unions, special interest groups, student protests, and diversification. The trustees wanted someone who would lead the "inner" university and represent Cornell to its outside constituencies. That Rhodes would meet the trustees' expectations in so many ways, especially in connecting the alumni more closely to the university, no one could have foreseen.

One of the most striking features of this period was the expansion of the academic vocabulary. Through new words and old words used in new ways we can chart intellectual changes in many academic fields, from technology to the humanities. *Global warming* and *biodiversity* were associated with courses, new centers, and even buildings. *Database, PC, Mac,* and *teleconferencing* signaled technological change and opportunity. *Deconstruction, discourse,* and *intertextuality* stretched the humanities curriculum with broadened and sometimes surprising scholarly concerns. *Rational choice, critical thinking*, and a new absorption with theory caused disciplines to reexamine traditional concepts and reach beyond academic borders to explore the multidisciplinarity of knowledge. Teaching methods also changed because of an expanded reliance upon technology. Familiar words took on special

significance: *minority, diversity, regulatory, multicultural, interdisciplinary, nontraditional, feminism, political correctness* and its opposite. Each reflected challenges to assumptions about the nature of academic life and society, and about how the university addressed problems and issues as the century neared its end. Cornell, along with other institutions, diversified its student population and faculty while expanding the curriculum and academic opportunities in ways previously unforeseen. Most of this happened not because of any single person but because of the times. The new words and concepts became the language of an evolving academic universe.

The best word to describe the student body during the last quarter of the twentieth century

Frank H. T. Rhodes (president, 1977– 1995) with James Stirling, architect, and Alain Seznec, dean of the College of Arts and Sciences, reviewing plans for the Sheila W. and Richard J. Schwartz Center for the Performing Arts.

is *diverse.* Some administrators voiced a concern that if the pool of qualified students was shrinking, as some believed, just as university costs were on the rise, the consequences would be less tuition money to support the academic program. At the same time, others feared the Cornell experience could not be maintained if the student body grew too large or too diverse—the very same concern expressed following the university's expansion after World War II. Total enrollment—undergraduates, graduate students, students in professional schools and at the medical school in New York City—in fall 1977 was 16,343, which many thought optimal; in 1986, it reached 17,902, and by 1995 the figure was 18,914. In 1986 there were 54 American Indians or Alaskan Natives, 672 African Americans, 570 Hispanics, 1,345 Asians or Pacific Islanders, and 13,136 Caucasians. There were, in addition 1,782 students from foreign countries. That year, too, 48.6 percent of all students were from New York State, 14.5 percent from the Middle Atlantic states, and 10.5 percent from New England. Far fewer students came from the other regions of the United States. By 1995, the number of minorities had greatly expanded, to 86 Native Americans, 733 African Americans, 968 Hispanics, 2,603 Asian or Pacific Islanders, and 10,583 Caucasians; 2,511 were from foreign countries. The number of students from New York State fell to 37 percent of the student body; those from the Middle Atlantic states totaled 15.3 percent, and from New England, 9.1 percent. Increasing numbers of students came from the Midwest, the West, the South, and the Southwest.

Engineering students watching the annual truck race.

Another shift was the entry of more women students into what had been traditionally male majors. In 1981, for example, the Cornell College of Veterinary Medicine graduated its first class in which more than 50 percent of the degree candidates were women.

As the number of students rose, administrators found that a greater percentage of entering freshmen could no longer afford tuition and housing. Trustees instructed admissions officers to disregard need when considering applications, leading to the term "needs-blind" admissions—a policy now followed by many universities. Cornell offered scholarship aid, work opportunities on campus, and summer jobs—the modern equivalent of Ezra Cornell's idea of student labor. In 1987 trustees broadly defined those eligible for financial aid as students of "outstanding merit, unique talent, commitment to work and community service" as a way to demonstrate the university's commitment to diversity in the incoming class, of whom seventy percent that year sought financial aid. This was an admirable but costly shift, especially for an institution whose endowment could not match that of some other schools.

Federal regulations, beginning with the Civil Rights Act of 1965 and extended thereafter, encouraged the university to diversify faculty, staff, administration, and the student body, as it had begun to do early in the 1960s. The university of 1990 or 1995 was nothing like Cornell a generation earlier: there was greater gender parity, and the students represented many ethnic backgrounds. But with diversity came costly problems, as each group sought to promote itself through clubs, news-letters, living centers, or academic programs, which necessitated the search for qualified faculty. Fragmentation of the student body became a concern, especially when offensive graffiti against ethnic groups and women appeared around campus. Minority students, feeling uneasy, sought assurance from the university that there would be adequate financial support for the Africana Center and recommended its relocation close to campus. In response, the trustees adopted an Equal Education and Employment Policy, which stated that no person would be denied admission to any educational program or activity on the basis of race, color, creed, religion, national or ethnic origin, sex, age, or handicap, nor would employment be restricted in any way. With this announcement, the Cornell Gay Liberation asked for a similar statement "prohibiting discrimination on the basis of sexual or affectional preference." In March of that year, the trustees passed a revised policy of Non-Discrimination for Student Organizations and Fraternities and Sororities, thereby updating an earlier regulation approved in 1967. In 1982 the university appointed an associate provost for equal opportunity and minority affairs officers in each college. In 1983 nondiscrimination regulations appeared regarding membership in student organizations, especially Greek letter societies.

The academic response to the times and to the diversification on campus was also varied. The Africana program had begun in fall 1969; a Native American program began in 1982, growing out of student and Iroquois community interest; Latino Studies began as Hispanic American Studies in 1987, then changed its name in the early 1990s; the Asian American Studies program began in 1987. The Latino Living Center on West Campus opened in 1994; Akwe:kon, the Native American house, opened in January 1987. In 1994 these living units attracted the attention of the American Civil Liberties Union, which investigated what it thought might be segregated housing on Cornell's campus. After an investigation, the New York Civil Rights Coalition ruled that Cornell's living units did not violate any federal or state statute. In 1993, in response to a student petition requesting a gay, lesbian, and bisexual living center, Rhodes argued that the campus had become "factionalized with students defining themselves as racial or religious or ethnic groups rather than seeing their common humanity." The trustees denied the request. Special housing for groups had long been defended at Cornell, however, and fitting everyone into one pattern had never been the Cornell way. When denying the housing request, Rhodes invited representatives from the coalition of gay, lesbian, and bisexual to meet and prepare guidelines for fair and equal treatment at Cornell.

History matters. So let me offer a historical fragment. My first contact with Cornell was not in Ithaca, but in England, more than sixty years ago, where as a schoolboy I was a regular listener to a BBC program called "Birds in Britain." What struck me then, and still impresses me now, is that virtually all the recordings of bird songs played on that program were provided by the Cornell Laboratory of Ornithology. I marveled that a university in a town too small, apparently, to be included in my atlas could contain such treasures and share them freely with the rest of the world. What an extraordinary tribute to the capacity and breadth of a great university. I mention that personal history because it seems to me that capacity and breadth, worldwide reach, and intellectual range remain defining characteristics of Cornell. And the more I come to know Cornell, the more I marvel at the remarkable way Ezra Cornell and Andrew Dickson White achieved that notable balance.

Any university would be proud to have programs of international stature, but for one university to have programs of that quality in fields ranging from art to agriculture, from history to hotel administration, from linguistics to labor economics and from medicine to materials science and engineering, is truly extraordinary. Few other institutions display that spread. None comes close to the quality that is Cornell.

Nor is that all. By and large, the people in these disparate programs teach together, work together, study together, and tackle tough issues together. And that is just what our founders wanted.

Ezra Cornell would have opted for the useful: metal fabrication, animal husbandry, engineering, surveying and mining. White, on the other hand, leaned in the other direction: the scholarly, the reflective, the academic. The compromise they truck was greater—far greater—than the sum of its parts. "Don't forget the horse doctor," Cornell is said to have called as White left on a journey to Europe to purchase books and scholarly materials. White did not forget. He found James Law in the veterinary college at Edinburgh, but he also brought back Goldwin Smith, Regius Professor of History at Oxford. And he brought back treasures: not only "pictures and statues of the nobler sort," as Morris Bishop describes, new architectural materials and a mountain of books, but also anatomical and engineering models, laboratory apparatus, chemicals and miniature ploughs.

This remarkable balance of the pure and the applied, the aesthetic and the useful, is part of the inherent genius of Cornell as we know it today. "I believe," declared Ezra Cornell at the university's opening, "that we have laid the foundation of an institution which shall combine practical with liberal education, which shall fit the youth of our country for the professions, the farms, the mines, the manufactories, for the investigations of science, and for mastering all the practical questions of life with success and honor. I believe that we have made the beginning of an institution which will prove highly beneficial to the poor young men and poor young women of our country."

And they had: without knowing it, they had created what Frederick Rudolph was later to call "the first American university."

But it was not just the programs that set a new pattern; it was the people. Cornell University was to be inclusive; its membership was to be as cosmopolitan as its programs: an international faculty, students of both sexes and all races, the poor as well as the wealthy. This was not only a novel education scheme; it was a revolutionary manifesto. And if today it seems commonplace, the familiar pattern of every great university, it is because of the vision and boldness of Andrew D. White and Ezra Cornell.

Generations of men and women from across the face of the earth have been the beneficiaries of their courage. The institution they created has become a mighty engine of personal growth and pubic good. We still stand in their shadow. That's why history matters. How important, then, that each new generation should understand the history of this remarkable university and so cherish and promote the goodly inheritance that we have received.

—Frank H. T. Rhodes, 2003

Factions of concerned students staged continual protests sparked by racist acts and tuition hikes. They sought greater minority enrollment and more minority faculty, and support for the COSEP program and minority students' needs—especially acute because of the high attrition of minorities. Other protests focused on national and international issues, the most prominent being the university's investments in South Africa. Student actions were always colorful, imaginative, and noisy, featuring petitions, signs and posters, speeches, and gatherings in front of Willard Straight Hall. In April 1985, students occupied Day Hall for three days and built a shanty-town to dramatize the conditions endured by the poor. The faculty recommended a policy of divestment to the trustees, but the board took no action. Again in 1986 students demonstrated in support of divestment, which a trustee committee finally took under consideration. In spring 1990 a small group of students and faculty, protesting inaction, occupied the Johnson Museum during Trustee Weekend.

The maintenance needs of the older buildings on the Arts Quad strained the university's finances. New scientific disciplines also had to be accommodated, and the open spaces on campus began to shrink. Even the library, thought to be commodious when it opened, faced space constraints. One solution was an off-campus storage facility placed in the apple orchard. An extension jutting over Library Slope expanded reading space in Uris Library, creating what students called the cocktail lounge. A stunning underground extension of Olin Library, named for its donor, Carl A. Kroch, gathered into one building the university's rich Asian and East Asian collections, the university archives, manuscripts, and rare books; it opened in 1992. Computer digitization, necessary to open the library's vast collections both to those on campus and to scholars elsewhere, proved costly. The shift also required extensive upgrading of the skills of both staff and patrons.

The federal government became ever more visible at Cornell, its money evident in programs, its jargon familiar. The government funded new scientific initiatives and supported some of Cornell's laboratory programs. Reflecting civil rights legislation, Washington also issued guidelines and mandates to prevent discrimination and promote equality. Similar legislation was approved in Albany and by even the City of Ithaca's Common Council, all of which required compliance. Federal inspectors visited campus in January 1979 to review the university's adherence to regulations, asking questions especially concerning "upper-level exempt administrators," who were still primarily white males. The investigators also noticed the "underutilization of minority faculty, especially Hispanics and Native Americans, and low participation of minorities and women in apprenticeship programs in the unions."

The Carl A. Kroch Library, built underground in 1992 to house Cornell's renowned Asia Collections and Rare and Manuscript Collections.

Changes in federal statutes invalidated the mandatory retirement age. One professor, taking advantage of this legislation, filed suit to enjoin the university from requiring his retirement at age sixty-five. In considering the issue, the university argued that the new regulation posed a burden of added expense, and that allowing faculty to remain longer would compromise the university's ability to strengthen and alter academic programs. A year later, however, Cornell revised its policy to adhere to the law and raised the age of retirement from sixty-five to seventy. In 1982 came a ruling that senior administrators and those with indefinite tenure were exempted from mandatory retirement even at age seventy.

The federal government issued other mandates, such as regulations requiring gender equality in employment and pay, necessitating a trustee policy in 1978 affirming both changes. A 1982 federal team investigating the university's compliance with the Civil Rights Act found nothing illegal but declared the student humor magazine, *The Lunatic,* offensive to minorities and women. Then, in 1985, the state raised the minimum age for the consumption of alcohol from eighteen to twenty-one, placing Cornell in the position of regulating campus drinking and thereby tempting students to find creative ways around the legislation.

The Federal Deficit Reduction Act of 1986, more familiarly known as the Gramm-Rudman Act, imposed restrictions on federal funding to universities. Together with President Ronald Reagan's tax policies, these financial cutbacks caused distress at universities all over the country. New federal guidelines in 1987

The Uris Library "cocktail lounge," 1989.

and 1991 limited the amount of overhead that could be charged on research grants—a regulation that cost Cornell more than three million dollars. Compliance with the Americans with Disabilities Act of 1991 meant costly physical alterations to make a perilous campus somewhat less so. In 1994, the City of Ithaca banned exclusion from housing based upon sexual orientation. Regulations came from every level of government; money for compliance did not follow.

Federal legislation targeted women and minorities for affirmative action. Since 1900, there had been women on the faculty, with professorial rank from 1911 on. Women had worked at Cornell in various administrative positions, in laboratories, and in the library and in the infirmary, but for the better part of the twentieth century, few were members of the regular faculty, aside from those teaching home economics. It took the civil rights legislation of 1965 and subsequent laws to bring about greater representation of women in all aspects of university life. By the 1970s there were women administrators and more women faculty members. What had begun in the 1970s as an annual report on the status of women and minorities by the 1990s was indexed in the *Proceedings of the Board of Trustees* under affirmative action. From 1992 on, it was called the diversity report.

The new federal and state legislation, especially laws prohibiting discrimination, generated lawsuits. From 1969 to 1980 sixty-one people filed seventy-seven claims against the university, some involving themselves in more than one suit. Forty-five of those cases were dismissed or withdrawn, and thirteen cases were settled. One case, known as the action of the Cornell Eleven, began in 1979, when women in several departments were denied tenure. The Cornell Eleven sued the university, complaining that these decisions proved that women as a group were being unfairly treated. In 1984 the courts found that there had been no discrimination in these cases against women as a class or group, and the university negotiated settlements with most of the participants. Seeking to head off similar confrontations and ensure uniformity for tenure decisions across campus, the administration required that academic departments follow a more careful review procedure.

Union activity on campus was one of the ramifications of the discussions and investigations concerning fairness within the university community. Representatives of labor unions came to campus seeking membership and affiliation. During Dale Corson's term as president, a union began representing the university's craft workers—carpenters, plumbers, and others—and negotiations between the administration and union leaders had been informal and friendly. Corson remembers discussions over coffee breaks, but this casual relationship soon ended. An attempt by the Civil Service Employees Association to unionize technicians and cleaning personnel did not succeed. Early in 1979, however, employees of the heating plant joined the International Union of Operating Engineers, which was certified in September 1979. Their strike in March 1980 threatened to precipitate campuswide organizing of the four thousand nonexempt employees. Cornell entered into collective bargaining with nonunion workers, who now sought their own representation. By 1983 the university was negotiating with the Security Employees Union and the United Auto Workers, which represented service and maintenance workers. The former group filed suit when Cornell, facing a more than two-million-dollar shortfall in state funding, eliminated the positions of thirty-nine employees. Inflation accounts for much of the difficulty: it diminished the value of wages, raised costs for the university, and made housing throughout Tompkins County more expensive, forcing some workers to commute from greater distances. Accompanied by some protests, discord, and litigation both against and by the university, the unions came into being at Cornell, as they did at other universities.

In the midst of all this activity, Rhodes listed his priorities for the university. Maintenance of existing buildings was one, for which he sought increased state aid, especially for the College of Veterinary Medicine. In the statutory colleges he identified a problem in the salary levels of senior faculty members, whose pay had not kept up with that in the other New York State universities because of the ways in which their jobs were defined, those at Cornell having an important research component. He recognized that the library was challenged by new and costly technologies. He wanted the research strength of the university to grow and hoped to provide more opportunities for graduate education.

Other areas of campus needed attention. The state voted funds to the College of Agriculture to replace older buildings that could no longer support modern science. Yet as Cornell made plans to erect new buildings, community protests erupted over the proposed razing of old structures. In 1984 Historic Ithaca, Inc., the local preservation organization, won Historic Site status for the College of Agriculture campus. Encouraged, the preservation society brought suit to prevent the destruction of Stone, Roberts, and East Roberts halls. Cornell won the court case in 1986 and demolition began immediately. There were lawsuits regarding university-owned property, but the state Supreme Court upheld Cornell's contention that university-owned fraternity houses were exempt from taxes, and in a separate case the courts upheld the university's right to use properties for educational purposes even when those buildings were located residential zones of the City of Ithaca.

Discussions in 1989 concerned the creation of housing for retired faculty on Savage Farm, located along Triphammer Road in the Village of Cayuga Heights. When this proved impossible, in 1992 Cornell sold the Savage Farm property to Kendal Communities Development Company, which then built a retirement community and nursing facility. Kendal at Ithaca opened in December 1995; wags commented that among the residents, many of them retired faculty, were the makings of one the best physics departments in the country.

REPORT OF THE PRESIDENT, 1980

The university at its best stands for more than the discovery and transmission of information. It stands for knowledge, the personal knowledge that is the transforming power both for individuals and for society. And because it stands for knowledge, the university community also stands for those ancient qualities that provide the foundation for knowledge: for openness in a world of suspicion, for commitment in a world of cynicism, for patience in a world of casualness, for partnership in a age of privatism, for hope in an age of despair.

It is not the task of members of the university to dictate meaning or to legislate purpose, but it is our task to encourage individuals to seek and pursue them. It must be the task of the university community—this University—to nurture the individual, the vision, the compelling impulse, to encourage our students to weave goals of such intrinsic beauty and significance that we are united in a common cause.

—Frank H. T. Rhodes, Cornell University pamphlet, January 1981

The 1980s saw continued litigation. Several cases in 1987–88 involved charges of sexual abuse, and three disputes with the new unions ended in court. In 1989 Cornell and sixty other colleges faced an antitrust case regarding tuition and financial aid schedules. Regulations now covered a broad array of situations between employer and employee, between employee and administrator, and between the sexes.

Some of the disputes reveal a serious deterioration in the relationship between the university and City of Ithaca officials. The problem centered on the tax-free status enjoyed by Cornell and the city's need to raise revenues to meet its expanding budget. Town-gown relationships in Ithaca, as elsewhere, rise and fall with some regularity. The issue in the late 1980s had festered since 1969, when Ithaca first sought voluntary payments in lieu of taxes. Even the Village of Cayuga Heights had requested a financial contribution from the university because parcels of Cornell-owned land were within its boundaries. That year, in addition, some students had focused on Cornell's perceived lack of concern about local poverty and need; they charged the university with lack of social conscience.

Over the years, Cornell contributed land or money or other support to community enterprises, such as Tompco and Better Homes of Tompkins County, two not-for-profit organizations attempting to improve housing. Cornell had participated in the redevelopment of Collegetown in 1984, and it supported the creation of the Ithaca Child Care Center on Warren Road in 1987. And it had given the city money to defray costs incurred because of the university's presence, especially those stemming from a traditional student prank—that of pulling alarms on the city's fire boxes. These efforts were not generally recognized and did little to ease the growing town-gown rift. In 1990, Benjamin Nichols, a retired professor of engineering, became mayor of Ithaca and demanded greater direct contributions from the university to the city. The atmosphere between the two entities became frosty and were not improved by student parties in Collegetown that involved alcohol consumption, rowdy behavior, and trash on city streets.

The university administration braced each year for spring activism on campus. Students disliked tuition hikes, fought for disinvestment in South African companies, and complained about closed trustee meetings. This last issue smoldered until 1981, when a court ruled that trustee meetings must be open whenever the discussion touched on the needs and concerns of the statutory colleges. In March 1979, representatives of the senior class requested that the trustees approve an "outside distinguished speaker at commencement." The trustees, however, voted to "con-

tinue tradition": Cornell commencement would "be a family party with the President being the principal speaker."

Regarding the university's broader "family," there were ongoing negotiations to better define Cornell's relationship with the state and with other schools in the state university system operating under the arrangements legislated in 1948. In January 1980 Cornell proposed a bill to the state legislature to clarify the appropriate interaction between the university and the State University of New York system. There were, in addition, discussions relating to the state budget, especially concerning scholarship aid for the increasing number of students whose families could not afford Cornell tuition.

Dragon Day parade going past Uris Hall.

Frank Rhodes carefully picked his way through this thicket of activism, litigation, rising tension with the city. He was most successful in meeting with alumni groups around the country, bringing them news of the university and urging their involvement and financial support, and he traveled to meet with alumni in Asia as well. The Cornell Campaign, aimed at raising two hundred and thirty million dollars, moved steadily toward that goal.

Following the 1989 massacre at Tiananmen Square, Cornell lobbied for the extension of visas for the approximately 300 Chinese students on campus who sought to remain in the United States. Alumni in Taiwan funded a professorship in honor of Hu Shih, an outstanding Cornell graduate, class of 1914.

BRUCE WANG

Frank Rhodes and the Dalai Lama, 1991.

Frank Rhodes suggested that his role at Cornell was analogous to that of leader of a jazz band. He might have a baton but he needed to recognize the improvisational bent of his musicians, the way one section dominated the music for a time, then receded as another took over. In such an ensemble, a lack of direction is deliberate and necessary, because "independence, scholarship, commitment" were the qualities that the university wanted from its faculty—a group of independent-minded individuals not easily herded. While the faculty played on, Rhodes considered the overall academic program and found some courses that were "undersubscribed." Was the expense of these small classes justified? He speculated that perhaps Cornell offered too many courses, leading to "fragmentation and pulverization of knowledge to a degree inappropriate for undergraduates." He also urged the faculty to seek a "balance between the joy of learning and the discipline of scholarship, between the autonomy of the student and the direction of the teacher, between the requirement of impartiality and that of personal conviction, between the need for linkage and the danger of premature synthesis." Along with other university presidents, he worried about grade inflation, a problem attracting national attention.

Contrary to the trend toward fragmentation of knowledge and overspecialization was an impetus toward interdisciplinary activity. Multidisciplinary programs brought faculty, researchers, and students of allied interests into collaboration.

Cornell teamed with centers, some of long standing, others of more recent origin; most of the affiliated organizations were in the sciences but they spanned the alphabet from the Aegean and Near Eastern Dendrochronology Laboratory to the Waste Water Management Institute. Their scope reflects the broad reach of faculty and students and indicates the many avenues of research. These provided links between departments, across departments and schools, and between East Hill and scholarly endeavors around the world, all tapping new technologies and research activity. They represent, too, additional needs for facilities, staff, and funding.

Increasingly heard on campus was the phrase "teaching across the disciplines." Common interests of faculty from a variety of departments brought about the creation of a Department of Science and Technology Studies, located in the College of Arts and Sciences; it was the result of a merger of the History and Philosophy of Science program with the interdisciplinary program Science, Technology and Society. Centers and programs evolved into more organic bodies, confirming the fact that knowledge is not a bulk commodity that can be packaged into tidy categories but is more like a liquid, always seeking connections, extensions, and common ground.

The university's commitment to academic programs and opportunities for undergraduates assumed new forms. The Learning Skills Center opened in 1983. Cornell Abroad, which began with programs in Hamburg and Seville in 1985, added a Rome-based program in 1986 and others thereafter. Cornell in Washington, started in 1980 and based near Dupont Circle, places students in government and nongovernmental internships in Washington while providing specialized coursework. Project Ezra, begun with an eight-million-dollar grant from IBM in 1985, proposed to make Cornell a leader in microcomputer technology, and that year, the library began to automate its circulation functions and holdings. In 1986 a grant from the John R. Knight Foundation funded the establishment of the Knight Writing Program, which focuses on excellence in writing and helps students investigate subjects by "writing in the disciplines." The program has won numerous national awards.

Cornell continued to extend its teaching function beyond Ithaca and under its land grant mandate began extensive inner-cities programs for a new group of nontraditional students. In 1983, Industrial and Labor Relations established an

EZRA AND ANDREW

· ·

The Ezra in me . . . spends his hours fixing fences, building and cleaning out barns, admiring a neighbor's ability to make a log splitter out of salvaged parts, and trying to understand the mysteries hidden beneath the hood of an old Case tractor; the Andrew in me is concerned with books and ideas and the mysteries of value and meaning contained within a specific literary text.

—James R. McConkey, professor of English, quoted in CORNELL UNIVERSITY ANNOUNCEMENTS: INTRODUCING CORNELL, 1983–84

The Cornell Theory Center, Frank H. T. Rhodes Hall, 1991.

extension program in New York City. Pioneering in adult education, the Cornell Alumni University, later the Adult University, expanded from summer offerings to off-campus and year-round domestic and international programs. The university calendar shifted and January classes were eliminated to help conserve energy, but the January weeks were soon filled with winter session offerings.

Environmental issues at home were a new challenge. In 1984 the university had to remove asbestos from the Johnson Museum and other campus buildings. In 1985 emissions from the university boiler did not meet standards set by the Department of Environmental Conservation, and in 1986 the disposal of chemical wastes provoked local protests. In 1987 environmentalists strongly opposed the siting of the new Theory Center so close to Cascadilla Gorge, but the issue was settled by curving the building along Hoy Road. The university also took up defense of the environment when it opposed a landfill proposed by Tompkins County to be sited along the Fall Creek watershed in Dryden, arguing that it would have an adverse impact on Cornell's water supply. It also sought to have Fall Creek named a wild, scenic, and recreational river to prevent the construction of a hydropower plant at Ithaca Falls. The county landfill went elsewhere, the plant was not built.

New student housing grew up along Jessup Road. The Robert Purcell Community Center, named for the chair of the Board of Trustees, featured student dining facilities, meeting rooms, and two residential towers, including space for faculty apartments. Across the road, townhouse facilities varied the living options on campus but still could not meet the demand for dormitory space.

When Frank Rhodes was hired, the committee reviewing the field of candidates hoped to find an articulate leader of the university "within" who would also "interface effectively with outside constituency groups." What the committee in 1977 could not have known was how much time would be needed by the ninth president to pursue corporate relations and development and to manage litigation of many sorts. Rhodes was most appreciated by alumni—to whom he gave a great deal of time—and trustees, whose role, he observed, was "to have their noses in and their fingers out." Yet he remained attentive to the teaching mission of the university "within." Cornellians, who love to point to the Nobel and Pulitzer prize winners teaching undergraduate and even introductory classes, all recognize what Rhodes defined as the ideal professor: the coach, guide, and role model "who encourages, trains, inspires, and prepares the student for the contest; who establishes the goals, initiates the team into both the rules and the spirit of the game, designs and calls the plays, and develops intensity, commitment, and spirit; who instills confidence in the ability and skills of his or her team; and who brings out the best in both individuals and the team."

M. H. Abrams summed up what it meant to be a professor of literature at Cornell. "Suppose," he wrote, "one were now to imagine an ideal place for writing a work on Romantic literature. He might envision a study in a commodious old university building surrounded by the studies of scholars, generous of their learning, whose provinces include both ancient and modern literatures and philosophy; a minute's stroll distant there would be a major research library with a notable collection in the age of Wordsworth, reached by a path commanding a Wordsworthian prospect of hill, wood, lake, and sky." This, insisted Abrams, was his own situation in Goldwin Smith Hall, where he wrote, met students, and taught. This is what makes a university a community, he observed, and what makes a university great. Harry Levin, dean of the College of Arts and Sciences, remarked that "our aim is to get the best faculty and then turn them loose. They must be totally independent, responsible only to the quality of their teaching and their scholarship. All we ask of them is that they be geniuses."

Chapter Eleven

WATCH AND WARD FOREVER KEEPING

There is always a *frisson* of anticipation as a university welcomes a new administration. Frank Rhodes had been an eloquent spokesman for the university and for the cause of higher education, and he was tremendously successful raising funds. Several new buildings under construction stood as proof of Cornell's expanding programs. How would the new president approach the position? For what would his administration stand?

If Rhodes was the alumni president, as some have asserted, his successor Hunter Ripley Rawlings III was his opposite: he was not disinterested in alumni—no president could be that—but he would be the faculty's and students' president. A classics scholar and student of Thucydides, Rawlings arrived on campus in summer 1995. He brought to Ithaca experience as president of the University of Iowa and a keen interest in the quality of the undergraduate experience. His inaugural speech set forth a broad agenda, calling on Cornell to build bridges among the academic offerings on campus, across the gulf between a student's intellectual and residential life, and spanning the odd divergence of experience between students living on the North Campus and those on the West.

Still, when asked by a student what it took to become Cornell's president, the six-foot-seven-inch Rawlings replied, "You have to be tall." At that height, it was hard not to be seen, and Rawlings was seen everywhere: at lectures, in seminars, in classrooms, talking with faculty and students, eating hotdogs from the vendor in front of Day Hall.

One of the first bridges Rawlings built was between Cornell and the larger community. Almost immediately, Rawlings and Alan Cohen, the newly elected Independent mayor of Ithaca, changed the language and the tone of discussions between town and gown, bridging the gap between the university and the City of Ithaca. In October 1995 the two leaders announced a memorandum of understanding affirming "mutual recognition that their futures are inextricably entwined." Cornell acknowledged the importance of the health and vitality of Ithaca to its mission and for its employees and their families. The city, for its part, recognized the importance of the university to its growth, and to that of the county. As Martha Armstrong of the Tompkins County Area Development Office observed, in 2001 Cornell University accounted for twenty-three percent of the economy of the county and approximately fifty percent of the money that comes into the local economy from outside.

The inauguration of Hunter R. Rawlings III (president, 1995–2003), from left: James Perkins, Frank Rhodes, Deane Malott, Rawlings, and Dale Corson.

Frank conversation has only infrequently guided the affairs of academic institutions and the communities in which they are located. Rawlings and Cohen, however, created a working group with the goal of analyzing issues of common concern and making recommendations and proposals for both parties to consider. The university pledged to increase its long-standing voluntary contribution to the city, in lieu of taxes, from two hundred twenty-five thousand dollars in 1995 to one million dollars in the year 2007. Cornell and Ithaca agreed to cooperate on creating a countywide transportation system, the bus service known as Tomtran, and Cornell pledged support for local economic development efforts, a joint electronic futures project, and increased faculty and student involvement in the community. Other evidence of new cooperation involved the city school district, a university-leased office building to be built in the heart of Ithaca, university support for the Hangar Theater (Center for the Arts in Ithaca) and the innovative Sciencenter discovery museum for children, and in 2002, the Paleontological Research Institute and its new Museum of the Earth.

MEMORANDUM OF UNDERSTANDING
BETWEEN THE CITY OF ITHACA AND CORNELL UNIVERSITY,
OCTOBER 5, 1995

As is true with many long-term relationships, the intensity and quality of the interaction between the City and the University have varied over time. Both parties have faced, and continue to face, significant fiscal and regulatory pressures from the outside, particularly from the state and federal governments. Both parties are similarly affected by changes in the local economy and beyond. These pressures make it all the more important that both parties understand and accommodate their respective interests in furtherance of the common good of the entire community.

The City of Ithaca recognizes that Cornell's ability to succeed as a leading national research university is essential for the long-term economic and social health of the City and its residents. Without question, the presence of Cornell enhances in many ways the quality of life in the City and in all of Tompkins County. Cornell faculty, students, and staff provide thousands of hours of voluntary services each year to various community and social service agencies in the City. As the largest employer in the City of Ithaca and in the county, Cornell's students, faculty, and staff contribute to the area's economic vitality; their local expenditures constitute a significant share of the sales tax revenue generated in the City and in Tompkins County, and the thousands of visitors attracted to our local community by virtue of the presence of the university make a like contribution. The

capital construction and renovation programs of the University similarly play a major role in the enhancement of the local economy, with the prospect of tens of millions of dollars being spent locally over the next decade. The civil life of the community also has been enhanced through the participation of many University faculty and staff on City boards and commissions, and indeed on Common Council, as well as through the provision of continuing ad hoc advice and consultative services to this and other municipalities.

Cornell recognizes that its presence also creates demands in the community for municipal services, particularly in the area of fire protection. The city's police and fire services, its well-maintained streets and bridges, its many youth and recreational programs, its affordable housing initiatives, its extensive park system, and its attractive neighborhoods and civic centers, among other resources, all help to provide the healthy surrounding community environment necessary for Cornell's well-being. Cornell was among the first universities in the nation to make voluntary payments to its local municipality in support of public services, and it remains committed to doing so within the availability of its financial resources.

—PROCEEDINGS OF THE BOARD OF TRUSTEES OF CORNELL UNIVERSITY, 1995–96

On campus, Rawlings focused upon Cornell's teaching mission, with an enthusiasm for classroom discussion—in which he frequently participated—and communication across disciplines. He brought faculty together in intellectual discourse. He created a position of vice provost for undergraduate education and placed in it Isaac Kramnick, a popular professor of government. He proposed to expand research opportunities for faculty and students and created a program of Presidential Research Scholars in all the disciplines for undergraduates who would undertake independent research projects, each student-researcher paired with a faculty adviser.

Rawlings had a vision of the university functioning as an informed dialogue among its many parts. His priorities were to build academic strength through program and tenure review and to nurture a more cohesive intellectual community on campus by improving the living and learning environment, concentrating especially on all aspects of the freshman year. Dormitories would become residential units with live-in faculty, faculty associates, and an academic component.

His objective was to maintain student enrollment and faculty at current levels while raising quality and reallocating necessary funds to financial aid. He made a commitment to reduce administrative costs because, he insisted, in terms of wise use of funds, the student comes first. Next are the acquisition and retention of quality faculty members, the "single most important asset in attracting students to Cornell and preparing them for a rapidly changing world." The physical and administrative infrastructures would be upgraded in support of student and faculty activities.

In 1996 Rawlings and his administrative team announced a new approach to residential life, intended to address the many rifts visible on campus between religious, ethnic, and racial groups and even academic programs, all of which divided students from one other. Rawlings set out

Mews Hall, one of the new first-year student residences on North Campus, 2001.

CHARLES HARRINGTON

a long-range plan to move all upperclassmen who chose to live in dorms to the West Campus and house all freshmen on the North Campus, where new residence halls and a commons would be erected. Included in this sweeping design was a plan for greater and even more intellectually focused interaction between faculty and students. Construction began in March 2000, and a year and a half later, in September 2001, freshmen of the class of 2005 found new and renovated facilities awaiting them on North Campus.

Housing all first-year students together was one way to provide a common experience. Another was to create a shared intellectual experience. Well before the fall 2001 semester began, faculty and others on campus and all members of the class of 2005 received a package containing Jared Diamond's book, *Guns, Germs, and Steel* (New York, 1999), presented as a reading to be discussed on campus. That September, the book became the focus of discussions, seminars, arguments, debates, a lecture by the author, excitement, and a goodly undercurrent of complaints and even some outrage at the university for "intruding" on the summer. The administration considered the seminar discussions and the large gatherings a success, and the reading initiative continued. In September 2002 the assigned reading was Mary Shelley's *Frankenstein*, and in 2003, *Antigone*, the reading to be augmented by a performance of Sophocles' play in the Sheila W. and Richard J. Schwartz Center for the Performing Arts.

With the completion of the North Campus, attention turned to the West Campus dormitories, many of which had been erected after World War II as temporary housing. Those fifty-year-old West Campus buildings are to be replaced by residence halls primarily for sophomores who elect to remain in university housing. There will be five residences, each housing three hundred fifty students, and each with a commons, library, and guest suite. Although the West Campus initiative will not completely solve Cornell's housing problems, it will provide attractive alternatives to Collegetown apartments, co-ops, and fraternities. The students who live in the West Campus residential units will remain affiliated with their houses while at Cornell, even if they leave for other living arrangements. Groundbreaking for the first of the West Campus residential halls, named to honor Prof. Alice H. Cook, was on April 30, 2003, with completion scheduled for 2008 or 2009.

Obsolescent equipment and government regulations forbidding the use of chlorofluorocarbons led the university into a construction project that generated heated local response and some alarm. Cornell proposed to draw cold water from the depths of Cayuga Lake to cool buildings on campus. Some environmentalists and local activists protested this "tampering" with water from the lake and

ROBERT BARKER

**S. C. Johnson
Graduate School
of Management,
with restored tower,
1998.**

predicted thermal pollution; engineers and other environmentalists lauded the program as innovative and beneficial to the environment, since it would drastically cut energy usage and emissions. In 1999, after extensive review, state and local approvals were granted and Cornell began building its Lake Source Cooling plant on East Shore Drive, at a cost of nearly sixty million dollars. By 2001 the design and operation of the plant had attracted attention and nine major environmental and design awards. The university, the Town of Ithaca, and a group called the Cayuga Lake Defense Fund monitor the quality of lake water.

For much of Rawlings's tenure, there seemed to be construction everywhere, especially along Tower Road, as Kennedy Hall, Seeley G. Mudd Hall, and Dale R. Corson Hall appeared. Sage College, opened in 1875, had fallen into a dreary old age. Although some spoke of demolition, the Johnson Graduate School of Business Administration decided to build a new home within its old walls, and to everyone's delight, the tower, which had been damaged by lightning in the nineteenth century and removed completely in the 1950s, reappeared to change the skyline on campus. Perhaps the 1990s was a time of return: also restored was the mansard cap on the tower of Franklin Hall, renamed Tjaden Hall and home to the Art Department of the College of Architecture, Art and Planning.

The greatest alteration to the campus skyline came on the morning of October 8, 1997, when a giant pumpkin appeared on the spire of the McGraw Tower. The reaction was amazement, wonder, and something akin to joy. From the ground, it looked like an oversized scoop of orange ice cream. Everyone stared and pointed. Who had placed the pumpkin at the top of that steep slate roof 173 feet above the ground? How had they done it? The *Sun* ran a daily "Pumpkin Watch," recording the number of days the pumpkin remained on high. As the weather worsened, the campus grew accustomed to the enchantment, though never bored. Administrators feared that the pumpkin might hit someone if it fell. In March, Provost Don Randal went skyward in a bucket on a giant crane and brought the pumpkin down. It had withstood an Ithaca winter, but despite Cornell's best efforts to preserve this trophy, it fizzled in its vacuum-sealed container.

The pumpkin on McGraw Tower, 1997.

For three years there was no answer to the question of how the pumpkin came to sit on the spire. Then the editor of the *Sun* received an e-mail from someone who said he knew the pranksters. He reported that the instigator had once planted a squash on a church spire in his hometown. On coming to Cornell and seeing the library tower, he knew: "he was put on God's green earth just to decorate the steeple." And so he and two other rock climbers went forth with duct tape, wire cutters, rope, and a cored pumpkin from a local farm stand. The leader "climbs up to the peak. He tugs on the rope to let them know he's up there. They send him the pumpkin on the rope . . . he jams it on the damn thing, and then he climbs down." When he was safe inside the tower, the three "laughed their asses off for fifteen minutes and went and had a beer." So that's how.

Cornell is a university unique in its identity and scope. As Carl Becker well said, "In the process of acquiring a reputation, Cornell acquired something better than a reputation, or rather it acquired something which is the better part of its reputation: It acquired a character." Cornell's character, though difficult to define precisely, comprises at least the following elements: a burning desire for intellectual freedom; a brashness that stems from its relatively recent founding; a skepticism, even iconoclasm, that delights in upsetting convention; and a moral vigor that challenges received opinion. Those qualities, taken together, give Cornell the robust and rigorous character of a private Ivy League university with a public land-grant mission.

Cornell's scope is remarkably broad: it encompasses a wider range of academic disciplines than almost all other private universities, and most publics as well. From its founding, when A. D. White envisioned a university that combined the classical curriculum and the new pragmatic learning in agriculture and the "mechanic arts," Cornell has successfully blended the liberal arts with practical and professional education. As a result, it attracts students from a wide variety of backgrounds and from all over the world, who are drawn by a superb faculty with expertise across the spectrum of knowledge. Cornell, in other words, has more intellectual capital than any other institution of higher learning. With its robust character, it makes intense use of that fund of knowledge and thus insures that the next generation will carry it still further.

—Hunter R. Rawlings III, 2003

Other innovations at Cornell that fall were procedural—and less enchanting than the pumpkin. The Faculty Senate replaced the Faculty Committee of Representatives, and the Employees' Assembly began meeting. The Board of Trustees, once sixty in number, having reduced itself in 1987 to forty, grew back to sixty in 2002, but this time with two-thirds of its members appointed by the board itself. Provost Don Randal, leaving Cornell to become the president of the University of Chicago, observed that the relationship between Cornell and the other schools in the State University of New York system would always be somewhat off-kilter. Despite tighter financial constraints, Gov. George Pataki provided what support he could, funding some research initiatives and contributing to the renovation and replacement of obsolescent buildings, including Bailey Hall, Cornell's concert hall, which for more than forty years had begged for attention. In 2000 the university presented the state with a royalty check for $452,786.91, money earned by Cornell from projects created in the Biotechnology Building and in Rhodes Hall, both built with state funds. The royalty was certainly not equivalent to the state's outlay, but it was the first time the state had received royalties for research conducted in state-financed buildings.

In winter 2001 university officials began to use the term *contract* rather than *statutory* to describe the College of Veterinary Medicine, the College of Agriculture and Life Sciences, the College of Human Ecology, and the School of Industrial and Labor Relations. Although these institutions were created by state statute, they are run under contract with the state. Rawlings chose the word *contract* to more accurately portray the nature of this special relationship. Rawlings stated frequently that Cornell University was a "totally private institution" receiving funding from a variety of sources, including the State of New York.

Technology created interesting possibilities for expansion of Cornell's teaching mission. Cornell had begun buying computers in the 1960s. In 1996 distance learning began, first as electronic links between the Ithaca campus and the Medical College in New York City. A year later, several campus programs and colleges began using electronic resources to expedite faculty grant applications, explore donor potential, and pioneer "video streaming" between the medical school, the School of Hotel Administration, and the veterinary school. Electronic communication also facilitated meetings between faculty in Ithaca and those at other Ivy League institutions. Prof. David Lipsky of Industrial and Labor Relations regarded distance learning as the "next step toward the fulfillment of the University's core mission in teaching, research and extension," consistent with its land grant mission. By 1999 Cornell was ready to create a separately incorporated for-profit corporation to consolidate all distance-learning courses in non-degree-granting programs. At the same time, the trustees created the position of vice president of information technologies to ensure campus-wide familiarity with the new technologies and coordinate their use on campus. Technology allowed Cornell to capitalize on its "brand name" and gave rise to eCornell and the development of CyberTower, a program to link alumni and university friends with various academic subjects and programs on campus. The initial results were less glorious than the proposals, but distance-learning courses became available along with some specialized training. Cornell's presence on the Internet expanded

NICOLA KOUNTOUPES

A. D. White Professor-at-Large Jane Goodall, speaking at Sage Chapel, 2002.

DALE R. CORSON

Ho Plaza, photographed from McGraw Tower, 1998.

with its frequently consulted site, the Legal Information Institute of Cornell University, which established an important database of all Supreme Court cases from 1990 to the present along with selected historic cases.

Continuing the tradition begun in 1901, students celebrated Dragon Day, now the Thursday before Spring Break, with ever more ambitious constructions. Some dragons have stood as high as 30 feet before being burned by the engineering students on the Arts Quad. In 2000 members of the Phoenix Society built a giant phoenix that shot projectiles at the architects' dragon.

The turn of the century witnessed other impressive actions at Cornell. Trustee Stephen Weiss had long called the Cornell Medical College "Cornell's treasure." In April 2000 Joan and Sanford I. Weill donated one hundred million dollars—the largest single gift received to that date by the university. In recognition, the university renamed the medical school the Joan and Sanford I. Weill Cornell Medical College. At the same time, the school's dean, Antonio M. Gotto, Jr., announced the formation of a branch of the medical school in Qatar, giving Cornell a unique presence and mission in an area of the world where medical training is relatively limited. This provided an opportunity "to do what no other major university has done," said Gotto. The new branch will not only bring state-of-the-art medical training to Qatar to be taught by a first-rate faculty, thus significantly expanding opportunities for medical education in the Middle East, but will also adhere to the same admission and graduation standards as the rest of Cornell University.

Cornell's expanded presence at home includes the Cornell Business and Technology Park, clustered on two hundred acres near the Tompkins County Airport. As of 2003 it employed fourteen hundred people, some by businesses that have moved into facilities along Brown Road, others by the many divisions of the university's development office. Fund raising today requires a large and talented staff rather than the few nonspecialists of earlier times. President Day had first signaled the importance of fund raising when he placed this function under the provost; today it is the responsibility of the vice president for alumni affairs and development. In 1995 the Cornell Campaign ended in success, having raised one and a half billion dollars; a second campaign raising 200 million dollars concluded in 1999.

The university announced its New Life Sciences Initiative in 2002. Duffield Hall on the College of Engineering campus, located at the end of East Avenue, will provide a home for the university's cutting-edge nanofabrication research program. Specialization in genomics, bioinformatics, computational biology, and nanobiotechnology will be concentrated in the new facilities to be built on Alumni Fields.

Not all new developments on campus were scientific. The success of the Society for the Humanities and the strong humanities programs in the College of Arts and Sciences prompted concern about the social sciences. A committee undertook a two-year investigation, and on its recommendation, the university committed funds to create a Center for the Social Sciences, with special fellowship awards and additional faculty. A home for this initiative is to be identified.

The years Hunter Rawlings spent in Day Hall have been described as a period of prosperity, reflecting the national economic expansion of the late 1990s. There were problems, however, that roiled the atmosphere on campus. A sign hung from Morrill Hall demanded that the dean and not the Division of Modern Languages be dissolved; there were several shifts in the administration of the colleges and ripples in one department or another. As a place that fosters intellectual activity, an ivory tower can never be a serene retreat—even if it is as remote as the university on East Hill.

During Rawlings's tenure, even as the endowment more than doubled, the number of applicants increased, and so did the proportion of minority applicants. The cost of tuition also rose, and more and more incoming students sought significant financial aid. At the same time federal and state programs, two sources of student support, diminished or terminated funding. Supporting needy students became a priority under the university's needs-blind admissions policy.

A profile of the students is instructive. The trends set in 1995 continued, and by 2001 there were 98 American Indians or Alaska Natives enrolled at Cornell, 761 African American students, 981 Hispanics, 2,713 Asians, and 2,906 foreign citizens. Total enrollment that year was 19,420. The faculty numbered 1,550 in 2001–02, down 43 full-time permanent positions from its peak in the previous decade. Women in 2002 represented twenty-three percent of the faculty and held important offices throughout the administration.

Memorial service on the National Day of Prayer and Remembrance, September 14, 2001, with twelve thousand people on the Arts Quad.

In 2002 officials of the United Auto Workers approached Cornell graduate students with a proposal to create a union. Some graduate students saw work-related reasons to create an affiliate of the UAW; elsewhere, certainly, teaching assistants were seeking union representation. But the union drives at other universities had led to strife, mean-spiritedness, and at New York University, a lawsuit. Cornell's administrators favored a different approach. As Henrik Dullea, vice president for university relations, explained in an article in the *Chronicle of Higher Education,* "We pledged to ensure that Cornell's graduate students would be able to debate the issues openly and extensively." Arguments pro and con were aired through discussions, debates, and letters and e-mails to the editors of all local newspapers, and the university sought to provide timely and accurate information. The campaign was waged fairly and with mutual respect, without creating a students-versus-the-administration battle. The union, Dullea wrote, "was unable to present convincing examples of the exploitation of graduate students under the existing structure." The vote, on October 24, 2002, was 581 in favor and 1,351 against. Without rancor, the question of a union died away—at least for the moment.

On the morning of September 11, 2001, President Rawlings was at a Knight Writing Seminar devoted to the history of the university. The topic under discussion was Carl Becker's essay "Freedom and Responsibility." In searching for words with which to address the students gathered on the Arts Quad that afternoon, Rawlings turned to Becker's belief that a university, even in war or under terrorist attacks, was a place of humane and rational values, which are essential to the preservation of democratic society and of civilization itself. Democratic society, like any other society, Becker asserted, rests upon certain assumptions as to what is supremely worthwhile. It assumes the worth and dignity and creative capacity of the human personality as an end in itself. It assumes that it is better to be governed by persuasion than by compulsion, and that good will and humane dealing are better than a selfish and contentious spirit. It assumes that man is a rational creature, and that to know what is true is a primary value, upon which all other values depend. It assumes that knowledge and the power it confers should be employed for promoting the welfare of the many rather than for safeguarding the interests of the few.

When Rawlings next spoke to the Cornell community, at the National Day of Prayer and Remembrance, held on campus on September 14, he identified the core values upon which the United States was founded, stressing "free and open expression for all members of the community; respect for the ideas of others; integrity and responsibility in the search for and the teaching and publication of knowledge." We distill these values, he noted, in the phrase "academic freedom," which might be defined as the "university's version of the civil liberties afforded by our Constitution." Rawlings encouraged the community to "reaffirm Cornell's core value of academic freedom, and the responsibility that goes with it." To bind the nation's wounds, it is important that we all "do what we do best: educate our students in open classrooms and campus-wide teach-ins; conduct our research and scholarship in open laboratories and libraries; and publish our work in open journals and airways. That is the best response to the evil of terrorism, which lives in secret and thrives on hatred. Terrorism is the negation of freedom and responsibility. Cornell is a beacon of freedom and responsibility."

Walter LaFeber, professor of history, who also spoke that day, observed that "we cannot be both ignorant of other peoples and remain free, that we cannot be intolerant of great cultures and races with which we share a shrinking planet and remain free," that we cannot surrender "centuries-old constitutional principles, especially in checks on each branch of government, and remain free."

Rawlings made a comfortable fit with the university. He promoted women and minorities into critical positions: six of his eight vice-presidents were women, as were the provost and the university librarian. He encouraged minority programs. He rewarded teaching efforts and educational innovation. He involved himself as

ONE HUNDRED THIRTY-FOURTH COMMENCEMENT ADDRESS,
MAY 26, 2002

Today's graduates are earning their degrees in a year when events—both domestic and international—have caused enormous change and anxiety. The tragedy of September 11, anthrax-laced letters in the mail, the collapse of Enron and other major corporations, and the Palestinian-Israeli conflict have transformed the world into a more complicated and dangerous place. . . . But on this campus, the center did hold, and the best did not lack conviction: We saw our students, faculty and staff offer support not only to victims of 9/11, but to individuals and groups on campus who had reason to fear they would become targets of revenge. We have witnessed many acts of kindness—some random, others concerted—at Cornell this year, all of them aimed at alleviating fear and instilling confidence in our community . . .

Cornell is a university that creates and disseminates knowledge and instigates debate among all members of our community. It is a place where people extend themselves intellectually by digging into complex and unfamiliar subjects and trying to fit their knowledge into a coherent worldview. . . . Within the "education in depth" you have gained at Cornell is an "ethical literacy" that comes from having confronted serious ethical questions and honed your own critical faculties . . .

As Cornellians, you have lived together on campus in an atmosphere of critical but tolerant confrontation. You have done more than study the roots of global conflict in a detached, intellectual way. You have also affirmed that Cornell is an academic community rooted in a tradition of freedom with responsibility, which, as the renowned Cornell historian Carl Becker memorably said, gives you the freedom to do as you please, but also the responsibility for what it pleases you to do.

—Hunter R. Rawlings III

a participant in teaching and in faculty seminars. Even with some dissent—and at what university is there no grumbling?—there was a campus-wide appreciation of Rawlings's values. The announcement of his retirement in May 2002 therefore came as a surprise and a disappointment. Rawlings will resume the life he prepared for in graduate school by becoming a professor in the Classics Department with a joint appointment in the Department of History. This return to the faculty reflects Rawlings's two intellectual concerns, the world of Thucydides and the era of James Madison, and underscores once again the importance Rawlings, like his faculty, accords teaching, contact with young people, and the life of the mind.

Cornell's eleventh president is Jeffrey S. Lehman '77, the first Cornell graduate to serve in the post and a Cornell legacy as well, his father Leonard having graduated thirty years before him, in the class of 1947. Lehman comes to Ithaca from the University of Michigan Law School, where he was dean and a leading exponent of affirmative action. In an interview given shortly after his appointment was announced, he described his approach to the role of president of Cornell:

ROBERT BARKER

I try always to keep in mind that people who make their careers at great universities have chosen to do so because they want to be part of something that is vitally important. They tend to work very hard, and they tend to care deeply about what they do. That means that an academic leader is less a manager than an orchestra conductor. My role is often to help a group of driven, talented individuals be effective and satisfied in their work while cooperating with one another to serve a larger cause.

Lehman continued: "I expect to arrive at Cornell committed to a set of values that are [already] deeply in the air here in Ithaca." Throughout human history, Lehman noted, race and religion have divided humanity. "In the world today it seems that the dangers of racial and religious conflict remain enormous. I believe great universities have much to teach us about how humanity can transcend those boundaries without eliminating them and how people of different races and religions can live cooperatively." Looking forward, Lehman observed that in 2015 Cornell would celebrate the sesquicentennial of the state legislature's approval of its charter. Lehman asked, "How will Cornell be contributing to the human condition? What can we aspire to?" These are the eternal questions to be asked at the university set upon a hill, an institution that is very much of the land that spreads out below, and way beyond.

Jeffrey Lehman, inaugurated as the eleventh president of Cornell University on October 16, 2003.

Chapter Twelve

ANDREW DICKSON WHITE

1832 ⸺ 19

FRIEND AND COVNSELLOR
OF
EZRA CORNELL
AND WITH HIM ASSOCIATED IN THE FOVNDING
OF THE CORNELL VNIVERSITY
ITS FIRST PRESIDENT 1865 ⸺ 1885
AND FOR FIFTY YEARS A MEMBER
OF ITS GOVERNING BOARD

Ne'er efface the memory

Despite its origins and history of academic innovation, and despite the belief that its traditions cut against the academic grain, many people today—even some at Cornell—regard Cornell as fundamentally similar to other institutions of higher education. Cornell, they say, is not so different from its peers. Of course, defining Cornell's peers is tricky because Cornell is one of the Ivy League schools with which it competes in athletics, academics, and applications, but it also resembles, in the scope of its academic offerings, the great state universities. Some have called Cornell the westernmost Ivy and the easternmost state university.

Defining Cornell depends upon where you stand and what you are looking at. From Harvard or Dartmouth, one sees the College of Arts and Sciences (not Arts and Crafts, as the engineers like to say). From the University of California at Davis, the New York College of Veterinary Medicine is the most noticeable part of Cornell. From schools of design, Cornell's College of Art, Architecture and Planning stands out, comprising as it does both undergraduate as well as graduate programs and encompassing a broader program than is offered elsewhere. To widen the angle of view, from a farmer's field in Mexico, it is the work of the College of Agriculture that is known and appreciated; from a Bangkok hotel, it is the School of Hotel Administration that is admired; those who are ailing turn to the Cornell Medical School. There are many Cornells. But the colleges that constitute this university are much like other schools in the nation, easily compared with one or another by those who rate universities.

Cornell is no longer the exception. In fact, most American universities today are more like each other than they are different. Our universities are large, diverse, and coed; they offer extensive menus of courses from which students make selections. Most have academic requirements; most have more well-qualified applicants than they can admit. All depend upon outside money, from government and foundations and friends, and all are subject to a variety of regulations.

To Ezra Cornell it was important that his university welcome poor boys who could work their way through school in a program of manual labor. Today most Cornell students work during the summers and many work part-time during the academic year to defray the cost of their education. And those in financial need are aided by the university with jobs, loans, and grants and by Cornell Tradition. But financial aid now characterizes most institutions of higher education.

The emphasis on hiring the best instructors, regardless of their creed, and educating students from different backgrounds characterized Cornell from the start. Most schools in this country democratized after World War II, and civil rights legislation has now brought diverse students seeking educational opportunities to all of America's campuses. Most universities have faculty and administration of both sexes and different races and backgrounds. Most universities today have special programs in women's studies and in various combinations of ethnic studies.

As at Cornell in the beginning, research is an important function of American universities today—in the humanities, in the sciences, in practical fields as well as labs that conduct pure research. Many have developed off-campus programs like those Cornell has offered since its earliest years.

Cornell responds to the same issues and problems as other universities—grade inflation, the perpetual quest for adequate operating funds, the unionization of staff and graduate students. It is no longer a radical upstart: it is more like the others than it was in its youth.

If Cornell has lost the distinction of being different, it is *not* because Cornell has modified its character to follow patterns elsewhere, or changed to conform to the standards of others, or reacted to federal legislation promoting sameness. It is because other schools have become more like Cornell. Other institutions—and the times—have finally caught up with what Cornell was at the beginning. President James B. Angell of the University of Michigan warned in 1871 that an institution that was not steadily advancing was falling behind. Professor John Burgess of Columbia University stated in 1884 that he thought there was no future for institutions that chose to adhere to the old collegiate ideals. The new ideals they espoused were to be found at just a few select institutions—notably at Cornell, the University of California at Berkeley (1855), and the Massachusetts Institute of Technology (1859).

At Cornell, students could select from many course options; students were self-governing; students included young men of low social or economic status. Faculty taught and conducted research. Classes were taught in different ways, both in classrooms and off campus. To teach agriculture, Isaac Roberts took his students to walk in fields to see for themselves the choking weeds amid the crops; geologists took students to Brazil and Greenland and into the Ithaca gorges to study rock formations; professors took students to prisons and orphan asylums to examine how society cared for those in need of supervision. Today the classroom has extended far beyond a university's campus buildings, but at Cornell, it always did.

"Person" was the carefully chosen word the founders used in the Cornell charter to refer to the Cornell student, for the founders always expected to matriculate women. If women were treated differently—and in ways they were—it was largely to ease the fears of society at the time. To accommodate the desires of alumni that their daughters be educated, and to meet the needs of women themselves, Columbia, Harvard, and Brown created Barnard (1889), Radcliffe (1879), and Pembroke (1891), but those universities did not become truly coeducational until the 1970s, when they then became more like Cornell. If women expected more than Cornell in its first century was willing to grant—which they often did—they were still granted more than most people at the time expected or thought proper. In 2002, when Margaret Morgan Lawrence '36 and in 2003 former Attorney General Janet Reno '60 returned to campus, students questioning these alumnae became annoyed because neither was in high dudgeon over the inequities women faced during their years at Cornell—the former for her sex *and* her race. Both women, however, were more grateful for what they had gained at Cornell than haunted by constraints placed on them.

Cornell's peers began as colleges and over time became universities. During the twentieth century they modernized their curricula, stressed their research missions, professionalized their faculty. They fell away from regulating morality and promoting particular beliefs, dropping chapel requirements and denominational restrictions. They began to allow students to govern their own behavior, becoming thereafter more like Cornell.

Cornell was once criticized for having courses deemed careerist; now almost all universities have practical courses in their curriculum. Harvard offers a degree in engineering, other institutions offer preparatory courses that lead to professional schools. By including what might be considered practical courses, they have become more like Cornell.

It would be simplistic to insist that it was Cornell and only Cornell that brought about academic change, but Cornell was certainly a leader among the modern institutions that opened higher education to students of all types, offered courses that spanned the educational realm from the sublime to the useful, and recognized that the business of the university was not to serve sectarian goals but to serve the individual and society.

In many ways, the Cornell motto—a university where any person can find instruction in any study—is unfortunate. Not everyone can be a student at Cornell, although as of June 2003, Cornell has awarded 305,975 degrees. And despite the motto, not everything is taught at Cornell. There is no library science, pharmacy, or forest management, and Cornell does not offer a degree in journalism or rhetoric, for which the university was once famous, although there are courses allied to or supportive of these fields. The motto is a myth, but a nice one. It allows and even demands that the curriculum be expansive, which is the way it has always been. At Cornell students can learn chemical engineering and American history, contract negotiations and domestic science. They can learn to become innkeepers or business executives or decorators. Cornell is a place where labor and management are fields of inquiry, and subjects of international importance are explored. At Cornell there are courses on marketing produce and poultry production, on Andean languages, philosophy, and modern film criticism. The motto challenges Cornell to remain open to new areas of interest and exploration.

Cornell remains remarkably true to its founders' vision of what a university in Ithaca should be. What has been constant at Cornell is its democracy, its orientation toward the future, its commitment to a balance between research and teaching, the individual responsibility of its faculty and students, and its freedom of inquiry. Its faculty still considers itself underpaid, the landscape remains thrilling, the weather—rain, snow, sun, cold, heat, wind—is still known as "ithacation" and is always unpredictable.

A university is a living entity. "One cannot be precise about Cornell," Dale Corson observed wryly, for it is an institution that "refuses to hold still." So true. "I believe that we have made the beginning of an Institution which will prove highly beneficial," said Ezra Cornell. He understood that the institution he and Andrew Dickson White created would always be in the process of becoming. As long as this university remains a work in progress, it will be doing its job. It is this tradition of independence, egalitarian creativity, and personal responsibility that has shaped Cornell and will guide it forward.

Sources

Topics concerning Cornell University can be researched in *The Proceedings of the Board of Trustees* (cited below as *Proceedings of Trustees*); these volumes are extensively indexed. The table of contents for the *President's Annual Reports*, which contain the annual reports of each of the units of the university, is also useful. The *Cornell University Register* gives ongoing statistics concerning the university and tracks the growth of the academic program, plus enrollment and student life. All three sources are very helpful in charting the development of the academic mission of the university.

The papers of the presidents of Cornell, as well as those of Ezra Cornell, Henry Williams Sage, and others associated with the university, are housed in the Carl A. Kroch Library, in the Division of Rare and Manuscript Collections (cited as RMC). They are well indexed. Permission from the president's office is required for use of the papers of the previous three presidents. After the first citation, these papers will be cited as Adams Papers, Day Papers, and so forth. RMC has extensive holdings for the entire university and for its colleges, individuals, and activities, and events. The archivists in the department are exceedingly helpful.

Local newspapers are not indexed, but if one knows the date of an event, it is often possible to find corresponding articles. The *Cornell Daily Sun* and the *Ithaca Journal* are available on microfilm. The *New York Times* has an extensive index, which can lead the researcher back into the local papers, using the dates given.

Below, by chapter, are directions to additional sources that have been consulted.

CHAPTER ONE

For information about Simeon DeWitt's possession of the lands at the head of Cayuga Lake, see Carol Kammen and William Heidt, Jr., *Simeon DeWitt, Founder of Ithaca* (Ithaca, 1968), and Kammen, *The Peopling of Tompkins County* (New York, 1985). See also DeWitt's forty-two-page pamphlet, *Considerations on the Necessity of Establishing an Agricultural College and Having More of the Children of Wealthy Citizens Educated for the Profession of Farming* (Albany, 1819).

Cornell's origins are best told in Carl Becker, *Cornell University: Founders and the Founding* (Ithaca, 1943). Becker notes that Indiana sold its scrip for fifty-three cents an acre, netting a profit of $206,700, which if "invested even at seven percent (a possibility at that time) would provide an annual income of $14,469." Although that was a goodly sum in the 1860s, it was hardly enough to create and maintain a university.

For the quote concerning the sale of land scrip, see the Ezra Cornell Papers, 1/1/1, RMC, and for G. B. Lewis to E. Cornell, Aug. 6, 1869, see the Cornell Papers. Ezra Cornell's Cyphering Book is in the Cornell Papers, Box 83. See also Philip Dorf, *The Builder: A Biography of Ezra Cornell* (New York, 1952).

Morris Bishop's book is *A History of Cornell* (Ithaca, 1962). For information about the Morrill Land Grant Act, see Roger L. Williams, *The Origins of Federal Support for Higher Education: George W. Atherton and the Land-Grant College Movement* (University Park, Penn., 1991). The act is in *United States Statutes at Large,* Vol. XII, 503–05.

The documents concerning Cornell's origins can be found in *Laws and Documents Relating to Cornell University 1862–1883* (Ithaca, 1883), which contains a copy of "An Act Accepting the Land Grant. Laws of New York, 1863, Chapter 460" and a copy of the university charter. This book also contains documents pertaining to the money Ezra Cornell paid to the Genesee College at Lima, New York. The New York State Agricultural College acquired a farm of 300 acres in Seneca County on which that college was established. See *Ithaca Journal*, May 25, 1853.

Glenn C. Altschuler's *Andrew Dickson White: Educator, Historian, Diplomat* (Ithaca, 1979) is most useful, but see also Andrew Dickson White, *Autobiography* (New York, 1905), and Robert Morris Ogden, ed., *The Diaries of Andrew D. White* (Ithaca, 1959). And see the Andrew Dickson White Papers, 1/2/2, RMC. White's letter to Gerrit Smith of Sept. 1, 1862, is from the Gerrit Smith Papers, Syracuse University Library; there is a draft of this letter in the White Papers, Box 4.

The quote regarding Cornell's offering his farm is from Waterman Thomas Hewett, *Cornell University: A History* (New York, 1905). Although Cornell University began with what were believed to be ample funds, and more than most institutions had to start with, Johns Hopkins University began with seven million dollars and the Hopkins estate in Baltimore.

White's speech regarding Ezra Cornell's offer of land and money is reprinted in *Speech to New York Senate, March 1865* (Albany, 1865). See also letter from Geo. S. Batchellor to Professor E. W. Huffcut, written from Paris, July 1894, Ernest Huffcutt Letters, RMC. Ezra Cornell's letters are in the Cornell Papers: to his son Alonzo, Feb. 1, 1865, Box 25/13; to his wife Mary Ann, Aug. 4, 1866, Box 28/6; to his lawyer Francis Miles Finch, Jan. 27, 1865, Box 25/12.

Regarding the actions of the trustees, see *Report of the Committee on Organization, October 21, 1866* (Albany, 1867), and also the Minutes of the Board of Trustees, Collection 2/3/74, RMC. In these minutes, White is designated president prior to the vote that elected him Cornell's first president. This collection also contains the proposal that a theological seminary be built in Ithaca in connection with Cornell, and a proposal made by New York City doctors to affiliate a medical school with the university.

One of the attacks on Ezra Cornell was made by the *Rochester Daily Union and Advertiser*, Oct. 26, 1869. This is reprinted in *Laws and Documents Relating to Cornell University*.

See Horatio S. White, ed., *Willard Fiske: Life and Correspondence; A Biographical Study by His Literary Executor* (New York, 1925) for Fiske's letters to White. See also Andrew Dickson White, *The Cornell University: What It Is and What It Is Not* (Ithaca, 1872). Ezra Cornell's letter describing the university in Ithaca appeared in *New York Tribune*, Aug. 15, 1868, 5.

The authority on the building and growth of the campus is K. C. Parsons, *The Cornell Campus: A History of Its Planning and Development* (Ithaca, 1968). For views of the campus as it grew and comparison views today, see *Cornell Then & Now:*

Historic and Contemporary Views of Cornell University (Ithaca, 2003), with text by Ronald E. Ostman and modern photographs by Harry Littell.

The inauguration exercises are described in *Ithaca Journal*, Oct. 13, 1868, and also in the first *Cornell University Register, 1869–70*. A copy of White's inauguration program, on which he wrote his comments, is in the White Papers, Box 8. See also the first issue of *The Cornell Era*, Nov. 28, 1868. By January 1869 the students were asking about the Cornell color. "Why not the bright red of the Carnelian?" suggested one writer in the *Era*, Jan. 30, 1869.

Mary White's comment about Ithaca is in a letter of Oct. 5, 1870, in the White Papers, Box 10. The students also discussed Ithaca. See *The Cornell Era*, Jan. 14, 1881. According to the U.S. Census, the population of Tompkins County in 1860 was 31,409; in 1870 it was 33,178. See Barbara Shupe et al., *New York State Population 1790–1980: A Compilation of Federal Census Data* (New York, 1987), 144. *Norton's Ithaca City Directory for 1888–89* (Ithaca, 1889), 33–34, lists sixteen churches in Ithaca, which became a city in 1888. For a history of the county, see Kammen, *Peopling of Tompkins County*. Ithaca is described in various university publications; see, for example, *Cornell University Register, 1872–73*.

For a discussion of meritocracy, see Morton Keller and Phyllis Keller, *Making Harvard Modern* (Oxford and New York, 2001).

Anita Shafer Goodstein's *Biography of a Businessman: Henry W. Sage 1814–1897* (Ithaca, 1962) describes Sage's belief that he could shape the university to his liking through his donations. It is fairly clear that Sage was not totally in accord with White's ideas about coeducation. Sage believed in the protection of women, along with their getting an education with which they might support themselves or their families if the need arose. Goodstein (223–25) calculates that Sage spent more than a million dollars on Cornell in return for the prestige of giving to a university, since he regarded supporting education as a noble work.

CHAPTER TWO

The Cornell Era's description of the university is from Sept. 16, 1881. The nonresident faculty members are listed in each *Cornell University Register*. See Elaine D. Engst, *125 Years of Achievement: The History of Cornell's College of Architecture, Art and Planning* (Ithaca, 1996). White's statement about the importance of the study of architecture is in *Cornell University Register, 1871–72*, 50–51. The university library is described in

Cornell University Register, 1873–74, 59–60, and the acquisition of the Sparks Library is reported in *The Cornell Era*, Feb. 23, 1872, 295.

The Associate Alumni Association formed as early as June 1872, at the graduation of the first four-year class. Its officers and members are listed by class in *Cornell University Register, 1872–73*. The diversity of the class is noted in *The Cornell Era*, Apr. 3 and May 8, 1869, and Nov. 4, 1870, and in *Cornell University Register, 1869–70*.

The story of Kanaye Nagasawa is almost fabulous. Nagasawa left Japan illegally on an English boat, studied in Glasgow for several years, and was befriended by Lady Oliphant and her son Lawrence, who as disciples of Thomas Lake Harris brought him to the United States. Harris had established a utopian community called The Brotherhood on the shores of Lake Erie, and he sent Nagasawa to Cornell to learn viticulture so that the community might prosper by making wine. When Harris left for California, he took Nagasawa with him, and they established a vineyard in Napa Valley, which Nagasawa inherited when the utopian experiment failed. His heirs lost the land in 1942 when Japanese Americans in California were interned and their land confiscated.

Students' comments about the course offerings at Cornell come from *The Cornell Era*, Nov. 18, 1868, 1–2; Feb. 20 and 27, 1869, 3, 5; Nov. 7, 1873, 68; Jan. 22, 1875, 123; Jan. 16, 1880, 159. *The Cornell Era*, Mar. 12, 1880, 264, observed that the weather station erected by Estevan Fuertes "is not like George Washington. It can and does tell whoppers." Burt Green Wilder's summer school was announced in *The Cornell Era*, Jan. 29, 1876, 118. Comments about Felix Adler appeared in *The Cornell Era*, Apr. 14, 1876, 185–86.

Professor Ch. Fred. Hartt's expedition to Brazil was the subject of an article in *The Cornell Era*, June 1, 1870. The expedition was to last three years, but Hartt contracted yellow fever and died. There is a stained-glass memorial to Hartt in Sage Chapel. Other trips were led by members of the geology department to locations in the United States and Canada. See William R. Brice, *Cornell Geology through the Years* (Ithaca, 1989), 44–73, for trips led by Prof. Ralph Stockman Tarr. In addition, J. B. Sanborn, lecturer in social science, took his classes on trips to public institutions such as the Elmira Reformatory, the County Poor House, the Asylum of Chronic Insane, the Auburn Prison, and the School for Idiots in Syracuse. See *The Cornell Era* during 1884–85 for his activities, especially Apr. 24, 1885, 329–30.

For letters from Henry Wells to Ezra Cornell, especially the one of May 22, 1866, see the Cornell Papers, Boxes 27/16 and 28/2. One of Wells's letters is reprinted in Carol Kammen, ed., *What They Wrote: Documents from the Nineteenth Century in Tompkins County* (Ithaca, 1978), 113. Also in the Cornell Papers, see the letter written by Cornell to his granddaughter Eunice Cornell, Feb. 17, 1867, Box 29/3.

The Reverend Samuel May of Syracuse left his vast collection of abolition materials to the university library. He also had strong opinions about the new institution. See Samuel May to Andrew Dickson White, Sept. 20, 1857, White Papers, Box 2. And see comments in White's *Autobiography*, 397–99.

The speculation about Jennie Spencer and her experience at the university is endless. The notice in *The Cornell Era*, Sept. 16, 1870, that she had been unable to find suitable lodgings and left after one week, however, should eliminate most theories. Regarding women at Cornell, see letter from Martha L. B. Goddard to Andrew Dickson White, May 19, 1872, White Papers, and see White's *Autobiography*, 397–402. A good discussion of women and higher education can be found in Barbara Miller Solomon, *In the Company of Educated Women* (New Haven, 1985), in which the author details some of the reasons given by medical men and others why women would be harmed by education.

The Board of Trustees appointed a committee to study the issue of coeducation. The report was published in Ithaca in 1872; the quote is from page 39. See also *The Cornell Era*, Feb. 2, 1872, 246–47, and June 14, 1872, 491. For the careers of these women, consult the Alumni Files, RMC. The age required of women is announced in *Cornell University Register, 1872–73*, 3, 53. Writers in *The Cornell Era* had plenty to say. See Feb. 16, 1870, 146; Oct. 13, 1871, 55; and Sept. 27, 1872, 22–23. Susan Linn Sage's comment appears in M. Carey Thomas, "Mr. Sage and Co-Education," in *Memorial Exercises in Honor of Henry Williams Sage* (Ithaca, 1898), 54. Thomas '76 went on to get a doctorate at the University of Zurich and returned to the United States to become a professor and then president of Bryn Mawr and later a Cornell trustee.

The Cornerstone Letter is now in Sage Hall Collection 1/1/3251, RMC.

Some of *The Cornell Era*'s complaints about attacks on the university appear on Feb. 16, 1872, 280; Oct. 20, 1876, 46; Feb. 2, 1883; and also in *The Cornell Review*, Jan. 1882, 139, and Nov. 1882, 68–70.

The cost of attending Cornell comes from *Cornell University Register, 1868–69*, 75. In 1870, $275 had a purchasing power equal to $3,767.12 in 2002. Purchasing power, of course, is not the same thing as the cost of an education.

Ezra Cornell stressed the idea that a student could work his way through school, and some students managed to do that. See Cornell's letter in the *New York Daily Tribune*, Dec. 18, 1869, and the President's Report in *Cornell University Register, 1871–72*, 54–55. See also *The Cornell Era*, Dec. 1, 1871, 164–65, and Sept. 13, 1872, 3. When A. L. Rader, a former Confederate soldier from East Tennessee, won the Woodford prize for oratory in 1872, the account of the contest noted that Rader was a "laboring student."

The account of Cornell's and White's testimony appears in *State of New York No. 103, 97th Session, New York Senate, January 1874* (Albany), 246–48.

William C. Russel proved to be a controversial faculty member. See his letters to White, especially that of May 15, 1874, White Papers, Box 16. There are also a number of comments by Sage in his Letterbooks for 1874, Henry W. Sage Papers 1155, RMC.

The Tenth Commencement is recorded in *Ithaca Democrat*, June 10, 1878. See *Ithaca Democrat*, May 13, 1880, for a report on the growth of the university. See also the *Cornell University Register* for periodic reports on the growth of the university.

White's address to the New York Alumni Banquet on Dec. 14, 1883, is reprinted in part in *The Cornell Era*, Jan. 18, 1884, 124–25. See the assessment of White as a family man in Altschuler, *Andrew Dickson White*, 262–65. White's "Farewell Address" was also printed in *The Cornell Era*, May 2, 1879, 311, and White's comments are in Robert Morris Ogden, ed., *The Diaries of Andrew D. White* (Ithaca, 1959), 232.

Carl Becker's reminiscence of visiting White appears in his *Cornell University: Founders and the Founding*, 66–67.

CHAPTER THREE
For comments about Charles Kendall Adams, see *The Cornell Era*, Jan. 27, 1882, 171; March 27, 1884, in Ogden, *Diaries of Andrew D. White*, 236; White, *Autobiography*, 439; and Bishop, *History of Cornell*, 250–51. See also Charles K. Adams Papers, 3/3/356, RMC.

See the long interview with Adams in the *New York Mail and Express*, reprinted in the *Ithaca Daily Journal*, Jan. 16, 1888. His inaugural speech appears on the first page of *The Cornell Era*, Feb. 1, 1889. His advice to students was reprinted in *The Cornell Era*, Sept. 30, 1887. Response to the alumni complaints appears in *Proceedings of Trustees, 1885–86*, 18, 22. Adams published *Cornell University: Its Significance and Its Scope: An Address* (Ithaca, 1886).

The growth of the library under Adams can be seen in *Proceedings of Trustees, 1886–87*, 83–91; *President's Annual Report, 1885–86*, 12, 54, and *1886–87*, 21–22; and *Ithaca Daily Journal*, Jan. 16, 1888.

Prof. Moses Coit Tyler kept a diary, so it is his version of events that has survived. See M. C. Tyler Papers, 14/17/2641, and Jessica Tyler Austin, ed., *Moses Coit Tyler: 1835–1900* (Garden City, N.Y., 1911) 118 and especially 193. See also Bishop, *History of Cornell*, 263.

The relationship between Adams and Moses Coit Tyler began when both were in Ann Arbor, but fell it apart in Ithaca. See Austin, ed., *Moses Coit Tyler*, 249–51. For Sage's comment about White, see Sage Letterbooks, Jan. 23 and Feb. 27, 1883, Sage Papers, RMC. See also *The Presidency of Cornell University. Remarks of Andrew Dickson White, presented in accordance with the unanimous request of the Trustees that he would address them regarding the election of his successor, July 13, 1885* (Ithaca, 1885).

For students' comments concerning the honorary degrees, see *The Cornell Era*, Sept. 17, 1886; for the alumni petition, see *The Cornell Era*, Oct. 8, 1886, 41–42.

Several letters were exchanged between Austin Flint and Charles Kendall Adams regarding the proposed medical school. See especially the letter from Flint to Adams, Jan. 18, 1892, Adams Papers.

Charlotte Williams Conable, in *Women at Cornell: The Myth of Equal Education* (Ithaca, 1977), emphasizes the inequalities in the treatment of women at the university. See also Bishop, *History of Cornell*, "The Girls," 143–52; *Proceedings of Trustees, 1888–89*, 100–105, 223–24; and *The Cornell Era*, May 2, 1879, 392.

Morris Bishop gives a complete account of the romance of Jennie McGraw and Willard Fiske in *History of Cornell*, "The Great Will Case," 224–32. See also Horatio S. White, ed., *Willard Fiske: Life and Correspondence*, especially 399–473.

The account of Sage's firing of Adams is from Bishop, *History of Cornell*, 26. See also *Proceedings of Trustees*, May 5, 1892, where Adams's letter to Sage is reprinted. The minutes of that meeting state, "upon ballot duly had, Dr. J. G. Schurman received twelve votes, the entire number cast." For Adams's subsequent career, see Charles F. Smith, *Charles Kendall Adams: A Life Sketch* (Madison, 1924), and Merle Curti and Vernon Carstensen, *The University of Wisconsin 1848–1925* (Madison, 1949), especially volume 1, chapter XX. An earlier history of the University of Wisconsin is Reuben Gold Thwaites, *The University of Wisconsin: Its History and Its Alumni* (Madison, 1900).

CHAPTER FOUR

The comments about Cornell are from Edwin E. Slosson, *Great American Universities* (New York, 1910). His wife, May Preston, was the first woman to earn a Cornell Ph.D., in 1880.

See Bishop, *History of Cornell*, 353–54. See also *President's Annual Report, 1906–07*, 20–25; *1909–10*, 41, 45; and *1911–12*, 8–11. The American Association of University Professors debated many of these same issues and attempted to define the meaning and nature of "academic freedom." See Richard Hofstadter and W. P. Metzger, *Development of Academic Freedom in the United States* (New York, 1955), 34–55, 456, especially 462 and 609.

Schurman's comments about the law school appear in *President's Annual Report, 1892–93*, 41, 45. For the New York State College of Veterinary Medicine, see Ellis Pierson Leonard, *A Cornell Heritage: Veterinary Medicine 1868–1908* (Ithaca, 1979), 22, 33, and chapter VII, "The Founding of a College," 163–83. The origins of the College of Agriculture are treated in Gould P. Colman, *Education and Agriculture: A History of the New York State College of Agriculture at Cornell University* (Ithaca, 1963), especially 157–70. The Department of Civil Engineering became a college in 1890. See *President's Annual Report, 1895–96*, especially 33–35, and *1919–20*, 5. See also *Proceedings of Trustees*, Nov. 4, 1889, 319, and June 3, 1890, 352. For the report of Dexter S. Kimball, first dean of the College of Engineering, see *President's Annual Report, 1920–21*, xlvii–li. The development of the medical college can be found in *President's Annual Report, 1897–98*, 45, and in reports thereafter, and in Bishop, *History of Cornell*, 317–21, 443–49. See also Ruby Green Smith, *The People's Colleges* (Ithaca, 1949), especially 90–96, and the reports of the heads of each of the university's units in *President's Annual Reports*.

The development of the farmers' reading course can be traced in the *President's Annual Reports* from 1897–98 onward. The earliest of these reports list the nature study leaflets without crediting the women who wrote them. Later, those names appear in the lists of works produced by the faculty. Wayne Wiegand, *Irrepressible Reformer: A Biography of Melvil Dewey* (Chicago, 1996), discusses the Lake Placid meeting at which domestic science at Cornell originated. See also Flora Rose, "Pioneers in Home Economics," in *Practical Home Economics* (Feb. 1947), xx, 116–18 and thereafter.

Martha Van Rensselaer's recollections are in her Faculty Biographical Folder, RMC.

Not all the women teaching at the university at this time were in domestic science. See the annual reports of the dean of the Summer Session in the *President's Annual Reports*, in which some women are listed as instructors (e.g., 1898–99, lxxi–lxxii). Several women graduate students held positions as assistants in natural science, biology, plant pathology, and poultry husbandry. In 1911–12, a Miss L. W. Wing was an instructor in dairy industry, receiving a salary of $750 a year; Ida S. Harrington was an instructor in extension in home economics at a salary of $1,200 a year, and Mary E. Arnold and Mabel Reed were instructors in home economics, teaching without salary. Each volume of *President's Annual Reports* contains a list of the teaching staff.

One of the most interesting characters on the Cornell campus at this time was Liberty Hyde Bailey. See Colman, *Education and Agriculture*, especially 70–90; Andrew Denny Rogers III, *Liberty Hyde Bailey: A Story of American Plant Sciences* (Princeton, 1949); and Philip Dorf, *Liberty Hyde Bailey* (Ithaca, 1956).

As the faculty aged, the university had to consider retirements. See *New York Times*, May 29, 1912, 10; and I. P. Roberts, *The Autobiography of a Farm Boy* (Ithaca, 1946), 297, where Roberts explains that his pension from the Carnegie Foundation was $1,700 a year, more than enough for his needs. Others might not have agreed. Roberts observed that "if all young professors and their wives were as careful as we were," they too might launch their children and still live comfortably. For Schurman's response, see Trustee Minutes, 2/3/74, Box 81, June 21, 1909, RMC.

The honor code is first mentioned in a memoir by John A. Rea, "The Immortal Eight," in *Half-Century at Cornell: A Retrospect* (Ithaca, 1930), 51, 91–92. Rea reports that in class in 1869, Andrew D. White "gave us fifty-two or fifty-three questions to answer. After he had given them to us, he arose and said, 'Gentlemen, I have a faculty meeting at this hour. I put you on your honor,' and he left the room." The current honor code is available at http://cuinfo.cornell.edu/Academic/AIC.html.

The number of African American students is difficult to count because race was not indicated on university forms. On some records, however, the registrar noted "colored student." The 1907 episode is reported in James B. Clark, "Race Prejudice at Cornell," *The Cornell Era*, Mar. 6, 1911, 196–202. The 1911 incident appears in *Cornell Alumni News* Apr. 12, 1911, 314, where Schurman's letter is reprinted. See also these 1911 issues of the *New York Times*: Mar. 13, 8; Mar. 28, 7; Apr. 3, 8; Apr. 11, 4; Apr. 12, 12; and Apr. 14, 10.

In 1903 Ithaca experienced an epidemic of typhoid fever. See *President's Annual Report, 1902–03*, 1–8, which is particularly useful. George A. Soper wrote a long report that appeared in the *Journal of the New England Water Works Association* 18(4) (1905). There was also extensive newspaper coverage; see the *Cornell Daily Sun, Ithaca Journal,* and *New York Times* from February through the end of April 1903. There followed some concern about the conditions in Ithaca's boardinghouses. See Martha Van Rensselaer, "Sanitary Boarding Houses," and Flora Rose, "Some Problems of the Boarding House," *The Cornell Era,* Dec. 1910, 96–100. See also S. P. Lovell, "The Crime of the Boarding-Houses," *The Cornell Era,* Nov. 1910, 47–54; I. Adler, "Boarding-House Inspection," *The Cornell Era,* Mar. 6, 1911, 203–06; and the editorial, *The Cornell Era,* Apr. 11, 1911, 273.

Gertrude Shorb Martin became adviser of women in 1909. See her annual reports in the *President's Annual Report.* The letter from Martha Van Rensselaer to Lucy T. Roberts, Apr. 16, 1908, is in the New York State College of Home Economics Records, 23/2/749, Box 21, RMC. Schurman's comments about women on the faculty appear in his letter to H. D. Mason, Jan. 20, 1914, Jacob Gould Schurman Papers, 3/4/6, Box 26/3, RMC. Louise Brownell had won a traveling fellowship to England and Germany, after studying Greek and English literature at Bryn Mawr (B.A. 1893) and Harvard. When she was hired in 1897 as warden of Sage College and lecturer in English literature, Schurman commented that "by virtue of having studied in universities both at home and abroad [she] might be regarded as the intellectual companion of young women." See *The Cornell Era,* Sept. 25, 1897, 6–7.

CHAPTER FIVE

The incident involving Fred Morelli was not unique. Others report they did not wear Cornell beanie, or forgot to. Harold Gulvin wrote, "I came nearer than I care to go again to a tubing," meaning being dunked in a tub of water, "with my clothes on once when I didn't wear my frosh cap when I went down town." See Harold Gulvin letters to Helen, March 1927 in Harold E. Gulvin Papers, 37/5/2197, RMC. George Lincoln Burr, professor of history, wrote "A Wet Frosh . . . and Something More," for the *Telluride News Letter,* VII, 5 (June 1, 1921). See also *The Critic,* Apr. 26, 1921, and Bishop, *History of Cornell,* 445–46. Morelli met with Acting President Smith and both agreed that he would return another year, when he would not be a first-year man.

It was Willard Straight's widow, Dorothy Payne Whitney, along with Leonard Elmhirst, a Cornell student, who devised the idea of a student union. If Jennie McGraw and Willard Fiske are Cornell's first love story, Elmhirst and Dorothy Straight could be numbered the second.

In 1942, the Cornell University–New York Hospital School of Nursing, then sixty-five years old, became the thirteenth school of Cornell University. Under this new arrangement, two years of college preparation was required of applicants, who would graduate with a B.S. in nursing from Cornell University and a diploma in nursing from the New York Hospital.

The Ithaca Street Railway Company, which began running trolleys in Ithaca in 1884, ceased operating in 1934. After that buses brought students to campus. See Richard D. Kerr, *Ithaca Street Railway Co.* (Forty Fort, Penn., 1972).

The quote from Rym Berry appeared in *Cornell Alumni News,* Oct. 4, 1923, 17; many of Berry's timeless articles were gathered together in *Behind the Ivy* (Ithaca, 1950).

It was Edwin Slosson who quipped that he heard the "cultural value of the Cornell scenery estimated as equivalent to five full professors." See *Great American Universities,* 313.

Regarding the history of the School of Hotel Administration, see Brad Edmondson, *Hospitality Leadership: The Hotel School* (Ithaca, 1996).

The Cornell Era was revived in 1945 and lasted until 1947. See Livingston Farrand, "Sundry Present Problems and Tendencies," in *Half-Century at Cornell* (Boston, 1930). See also the delightful chapter about working for the *Cornell Daily Sun* in Stanton Griffis, *Lying in State* (New York, 1952).

The five troubled freshmen provoked a considerable response. See "Letters," *Cornell Daily Sun,* Dec. 6–17, 1926, some of which are reprinted in David Margulis, ed., *A Century at Cornell* (Ithaca, 1980), 11–18.

There are several folders of letters regarding Prohibition in the Livingston Farrand Papers, 3/5/7, Box 28/44–46, RMC.

The quote by Kenneth Roberts comes from his long essay about Cornell, which appeared in the *Saturday Evening Post,* Feb. 2, 1919.

For letters to Livingston Farrand, see the Farrand Papers. A. W. Abrams to Farrand, Mar. 10, 1924, is in Box 1/1. Letters regarding race—Mrs. F. C. Peyton to Farrand, Jul. 18 and Aug. 2, 1929, and Farrand to Peyton, Jul. 22, 1929; and between M. J. Gilliam and Farrand—are in Box 12. For commentary, see Marcia G. Synnott, "The Admission and Assimilation of Minority Students at Harvard, Yale, and Princeton, 1900–1970," in B. Edward McClellan and William J. Reese, eds., *Social History of American Education* (Urbana and Chicago, 1988), 313–33.

Anti-Semitism was not absent from the campus, either. See letters to Farrand from George Gilson Terriberry, Sept. 12,

1934, and from Professor Vladimir Karapetoff, June 5, 1934, and to Karapetoff from George Munsick, Jul. 3, 7, and 19, 1934, in Farrand Papers, Box 12. All these letters were copied to Trustee R. E. Treman. See also Helen Lefkowitz Horowitz, *Campus Life* (New York, 1987), 82–97, and Paula S. Fass, *Outside In: Minorities and the Transformation of American Education* (New York, 1989), especially chapter 1, 13–35.

The loyalty oath required today is mandated in Section 3002 of New York's Education Law. The text is available at http://cuinfo.cornell.edu/Academic/AIC.html.

Letters from James Lynah to Farrand, including the letter of Nov. 10, 1936, regarding an athletic league, are in the Farrand Papers, Box 19/13–14. See also Robert J. Kane, *Good Sports: A History of Cornell Athletics* (Ithaca, 1992), 144–48, 308–15.

See Ralph S. Hosmer, *The Cornell Plantations: A History* (Ithaca, 1947), especially the documents at the end of the book. Of the several accounts of the origins of ornithology at Cornell, the latest is Gregory S. Butcher and Kevin McGowan, "History of Ornithology at Cornell University," in William E. Davis, Jr., and Jerome A. Jackson, eds., *Contributions to the History of North American Ornithology*, No. 10 (Cambridge, Mass., 1995). See also Mary Fuertes Boynton, ed., *Louis Agassiz Fuertes: His Life Briefly Told and His Correspondence* (New York, 1956).

CHAPTER SIX

Carl Becker delivered his essay "The Cornell Tradition: Freedom and Responsibility" on April 27, 1940; it was published in *Cornell University: Founders and the Founding* and has been reprinted frequently.

President Day's comments at the faculty meeting, Oct. 8, 1941, are in the Edmund Ezra Day Papers, 3/6/8, Box 8/28, RMC. The section of the New York State law under discussion is paragraph 709.

For information about the Cornell Aeronautical Laboratory, see Cornell Aeronautical Laboratory Papers and the Day Papers, Box 29/91, both at RMC.

Those who went to war include faculty, graduate students, and staff on the university payroll. For example, in 1942, the trustees approved a leave for Morris Bishop "at the request of the Office of War Information"; see *Proceedings of Trustees, 1942–43*, 4461. See also the Day Papers, Box 35/7. In 1942 the faculty voted to postpone tenure considerations; they resumed in October 1946. A number of other campus activities were also curtailed: the *Cornell Daily Sun*, for example, published on a weekly schedule for a time and then stopped altogether,

resuming only after 1945. To replace men who went off to war, a number of women teaching assistants were appointed between 1942 and 1945. At the medical school Dr. Ruth E. Jaeger was hired as an instructor in psychiatry, her salary taken from the unused portion of a salary of a man who had entered service. See *Proceedings of Trustees, 1942–43*, 4457. In the Arts College, in 1944, the Department of History hired Dr. Lillian Gates to teach one course in the fall term, at a salary of $700. Her title was acting instructor in history. At the same time, the Department of Mathematics hired five women as instructors or acting assistant professors. They were paid between $265 and $320 a month. *Proceedings of Trustees, 1944–45*, 5311, 5327–28.

In 1947 the Rockefeller Foundation gave Cornell a grant to explore the relationship between civil rights and the control of subversive activities in the United States. See *Proceedings of Trustees, 1947–48*, 7922, and Bishop, *History of Cornell*, 544–55.

In 1948 the five independent libraries on campus—those for chemistry, physics, engineering, and business and public administration, plus the Regional History Collection—were affiliated with the University Library. See *Proceedings of Trustees, 1947–48*, 7662, and also Rita Guerlac, *Cornell's Library*, a pamphlet reprinted from *Cornell Library Journal* (spring 1967, no. 2), 25.

Other developments include the Southeast Asia Program, which grew out of the Far Eastern Studies Program. The New York State School of Industrial and Labor Relations can be tracked in the *Proceedings of Trustees* by year. For the business school, see James W. Schmotter, *Not Just Another School of Business Administration: A History of Graduate Management at Cornell University* (Ithaca, 1992), and see the Day Papers, Box 13/20, 21, 23, 24.

The question of size was important. On May 5, 1948, Day reported to the Board of Trustees that the current student population on the Ithaca campus was 9,000, and he "saw no reason why the University should expand any further than it already has." See *Proceedings of Trustees, 1947–48*, 7870.

Cornell's relationship to the State University of New York system is tracked in the *Proceedings of Trustees*. See the Day Papers, Boxes 18/3; 56/12, 18 and 36; 42/46, 53 and 54; 60/39; 62/29. See also Malcolm Carron, S.J., *The Contract Colleges of Cornell University* (Ithaca, 1948), and O. C. Carmichael, *New York Establishes a State University* (Nashville, 1955).

Instruction in modern foreign languages was a priority at Cornell from the start. The students were amazed at the range of languages available. In 1870 Cornell hired Friederich Ludwig Otto Roehrig to teach French. He was a specialist as well in the Blackfoot language, and he offered courses in Chinese, Japanese, Hebrew, Malayan, Sanskrit, ancient Arabic, and Persian. See *Cornell University Registers* from 1870 through 1876, when the university let Roehrig go, and *The Cornell Era*, Feb. 25, 1875, 146. The innovations in the teaching of languages during the 1940s and afterward were supported by faculty interest and funds from foundations.

CHAPTER SEVEN

De Kiewiet was one of many from the Cornell faculty who became college presidents. Benjamin Ide Wheeler became the chancellor of the University of California, for example, and William Rae Keast left the faculty to become president of Wayne State University. Dean Sarah Blanding became president of Vassar in 1946, and Arthur S. Adams became president of the University of New Hampshire in 1948. In 1951 Asa S. Knowles became president of the University of Toledo. Steven Muller became provost and then in 1971 president of Johns Hopkins University; Lisle C. Carter left Cornell to become chancellor of the Atlanta University Center in 1974; in 1978 Edmund T. Cranch, dean of the College of Engineering, resigned to become president of the Worcester Polytechnic Institute; also in 1978, Provost David C. Knapp became president of the University of Massachusetts. Robert Plane became president of Clarkson University and then acting president of Wells College for a short time in the 1990s. In 1996, Dean Alan G. Merten of the Johnson Graduate School of Business resigned to become president of George Mason University; and Don Randall, professor of music and university provost, assumed the presidency of the University of Chicago in 2000.

Several students from the early years also took on college presidencies. Perhaps the most famous is David Starr Jordan '72, an outstanding alumnus who became president of the University of Indiana and then of Stanford University. Murray Edward Poole, *A Story Historical of Cornell University with Biographies of Distinguished Cornellians* (Ithaca, 1916), cxi–cxii, names others: Theodore Comstock '70 became president of Arizona University; Brant Dixon '70, Newcomb College of Tulane University; Henry Eddy '70, the University of Cincinnati; Daniel E. Salmon '72, the National Veterinary School, Montevideo; Clinton D. Smith, the Agricultural College of Paricicabo, Brazil; John C. Branner '74, Stanford; George T. Winston '74, the University of North Carolina, then University

of Texas, and finally the College of Agriculture and Mechanical Arts in North Carolina.

Other early Cornell graduates who became college presidents were Julia J. Thomas '75, Wellesley; M. Carey Thomas '77, Bryn Mawr; Joseph T. Kingsbury '78, the University of Utah; Phebe Sutliff '90, Rockford College; William J. Kerr '91, the agricultural colleges of both Utah and Oregon; William Blackman '93, Rollins College; Clyde A. Duniway '93, the universities of Montana and Wyoming; Joseph Moore Jameson '93, Girard College; Raymond Pearson '94, the Iowa Agricultural and Mechanical College; Charles Rammelkamp '96, Illinois College; Alexander Meikeljohn '97, Amherst; Ernest Fox Nichols '97, Dartmouth; John Gilmore '98, the University of Hawaii; Albert Hill, the University of Missouri; and Lillian Johnson '02, the Western College for Women.

Cornell figured prominently in the 1950s accusations from Washington. See Ellen Schrecker, *No Ivory Tower: McCarthyism and the Universities* (New York, 1986), and her book that looks at the larger picture, *Many Are the Crimes: McCarthyism in America* (Boston, 1998).

The administration of the university grew under Malott, who added one vice president and a provost, as well as a curator of regional history and a university archivist. A committee to organize the centennial was appointed in 1960, and to mark the occasion, the university published the newly discovered *Diaries of Andrew D. White*, edited by Robert Morris Ogden (Ithaca, 1959). See Deane W. Malott Papers, 3/9/651, RMC

The author of the article on the responsibilities of industry to higher education was Alfred P. Sloan, Jr. A copy is in the Malott Papers, Box 3/55.

Cornell owned the Cornell Aeronautical Laboratory in Buffalo. In 1955 its business netted more than ten million dollars in "fundamental and applied research in the aeronautical field, contracting about 95 per cent of its business with military agencies of the U. S. government." See Cornell Aeronautical Laboratory Papers, RMC, and report in the *Proceedings of Trustees, 1955–56*, 4. The Cornell Research Foundation was self-supporting, owned by the university; its income derived from royalties from licenses and patents awarded to university staff. Its budget for 1955–56 was ten thousand dollars and its income, five thousand, which was distributed by a faculty committee to support fundamental research. *Proceedings of Trustees, 1955–56*, 4.

Jacob Reck's letter to Malott, May 29, 1955, is in the Malott Papers, Box 22/19.

Dating the Ivy League is more difficult than one might expect. The first use of the term in print occurred in an article by Caswell Adams in the *New York Tribune,* in 1937, but that was somewhat premature. At Cornell the idea was discussed in letters to and from Edmund Ezra Day. There are copies in the Malott Papers, Box 64/49 and 71. An early agreement was struck in 1952 with consequences for the fall season and only for football. The agreed-upon date for the founding of the Ivy League is 1954, when the Ivy Group Agreement was signed. See the Malott Papers, Box 20/59–61 and www.not-rocket-science.com for a "Brief History of the Ivy League." See also Ronald A. Smith *Sports and Freedom: The Rise of Big-Time College Athletics* (New York, 1988), especially the epilogue, 213–28. A copy of the quote, from an undated notice issued by the Office of Public Relations and Information, is in the Malott Papers, Box 3/55.

Acting President Wright was quoted in *Cornell Alumni News,* July 1, 1951, 1. For information about Deane Malott and the U.S. House Un-American Activities Committee, see a fine unpublished senior thesis by Michael Ullman, "Caught in a Cross Fire," RMC. See also the Malott Papers, especially Box 3/57–59 and Box 8/1. Several faculty members, in addition to Morrison and Singer, were threatened by Senate investigations during this era. See also the letter from Malott to Austin Story, July 1, 1954, Malott Papers, Box 4/1. Douglas F. Dowd's statement, made to the Committee on Academic Freedom and Tenure of the Cornell Constituent Assembly, May 1969, is reprinted in Immanuel Wallerstein and Paul Starr, eds., *The University Crisis Reader, Volume II: Confrontation and Counterattack* (New York, 1971), 63–64. See also Charlotte Pomerantz, *A Century of Un-Americana* (New York: 1963), 70, quoted in Ullman, "Caught in a Cross Fire," 14.

For Malott's statement about the importance of freedom of speech at Cornell, see Malott's letter to Edward J. Welch, MD, June 30, 1953, Malott Papers, Box 4/1. The article by Robert Cushman, professor of government, appeared in the *Cornell Daily Sun* and was reprinted in the *Ithaca Journal.* A copy is in the Malott Papers, Box 3/59. For letters from and about Cushman, see the Malott Papers, Box 3/58 and 12/93; from Konvitz, Box 24/69; from Singer, Box 23/27–38.

Regarding Vladimir Nabokov, see the letter to Malott from C. B. Kelley, Jan. 20, 1959. For letters to Nabokov, see the Malott Papers, Box 22/2. And see Brian Boyd, *Vladimir Nabokov: The American Years* (New York, 1991), especially chapter 16, "Lolita Explodes," 357–89.

Malott's letter to Victor Emanual, Nov. 28, 1951 regarding Howard Fast's visit, is in the Malott Papers, Box 4/4; for information about Pete Seeger's visit, see the Malott Papers, Box 18/32.

From 1917 to 1978 Cornell was the only university that allowed faculty representation on its Board of Trustees. It was one of ten universities that allowed faculty to nominate deans, and one of twenty-seven that gave professors the right to participate in determining educational policy. The faculty representatives on the board could participate in everything but the vote. This was called the Cornell Idea. See Hofstadter and Metzgar, *The Development of Academic Freedom,* especially 456, describing Cornell as a "university at the democratic extreme."

For information about Cornell students, see Rose K. Goldsen, Morris Rosenberg, Robin M. Williams, Jr., and Edward A. Suchman, *What College Students Think* (Princeton, 1960), 64–80. What the students were thinking about at Cornell was protesting, and in spring 1958 they did just that. See the *Cornell Daily Sun,* which reported the students' complaints and actions; some of these articles appear in Margulis, ed., *A Century at Cornell,* 210–20. For newspaper accounts and alumni letters, see the Malott Papers, Boxes 22/19–29; 23/70, 73; and 24/54–60, especially the broadside in Box 22/20 created by students who complained, "for almost a century the tone of the Cornell Community has been perpetuated by the undergraduates in common accord with the faculty and administration of the university. Carl Becker delineated this policy with the three words 'Freedom with Responsibility.' These three words upon which student life at Cornell has had its foundation *no longer have meaning.* President D. W. Malott has seen fit to break faith with the founders" of Cornell, with alumni, and with students themselves. "The atmosphere of a *University* in Ithaca is fast disappearing," the students continued, and ". . . edict after edict has recently been issued from the administration completely disregarding all suggestions of all student organizations on campus. So completely have our solutions to our own problems been ignored by the power that are that for the first time in memory of most, the students, in complete frustration, have turned to riot and demonstration."

The response to the demonstrations can be found in the Malott papers, Box 22/20. In 1958, the trustees approved the appointment of a vice president for student affairs to find ways of improving the university's disciplinary procedures. See the *Cornell Daily Sun* and the *Ithaca Journal* for newspaper coverage.

See also Conable, *Women at Cornell,* 120–26, 142–44.

CHAPTER EIGHT

The new Division of Biological Sciences drew its core faculty from existing schools, leaving the applied biology faculty and programs, such as plant breeding in the College of Agriculture, within their original colleges and departments. Other divisions followed the same pattern. See the James A. Perkins Papers, 3/10/1022 and 3/10/3158, RMC, and the Dale Corson Papers, 3/11/1665, RMC on these developments. See also James A. Perkins, *The University in Transition* (Princeton, 1966), especially 19 and 80. Students also became involved in educational questions. See "Communication to President Perkins," from the Steering Committee, Students for Education, Apr. 21, 1965, Perkins Papers, Box 9/45.

Altering the name of the College of Home Economics to the College of Human Ecology proved significant: after 1969 the pattern of enrollment changed. It should be remembered, however, that there had been men in the College of Home Economics when the hotel school was part of that program. When the School of Hotel Administration became an independent entity in 1950, the students remaining in Home Economics were almost all women.

The papers of the COSEP program are in RMC; see also the Perkins Papers, Box 32/43 especially.

Mary D. Nichols '66 is quoted in *The Troubled University* (Boston, 1965).

The episode of *The Trojan Horse* can be traced in RMC. Copies of the offensive issue with the long excerpt from David Murray's journal are in the Corson Papers, Box 18/26.

Several important books deal with the events of April 1969 and all that led up to them. See George Fisher and Stephen Wallenstein, Cornell students, who wrote an unpublished manuscript entitled "Open Breeches: Guns at Cornell." A copy is in RMC. There was also the *Report of the Special Trustee Committee on Campus Unrest at Cornell* (Ithaca, 1969), and Cushing S. Strout and David I. Grossvogel, eds., *Divided We Stand: Reflections on the Crisis at Cornell* (New York, 1971). In addition, the events were covered in the *Cornell Daily Sun,* the *Ithaca Journal,* and the *New York Times.* Interviews with some participants are available in RMC.

An important addition to this literature is Donald Alexander Downs's scholarly book *Cornell '69: Liberalism and the Crisis of the American University* (Ithaca, 1999), which gives a thorough account of the events leading up to the takeover of Willard Straight Hall. The book contains a very useful chronology (pages 309–15), a cast of characters, and complete citations. Dale Corson is quoted on the book jacket: "every student of campus crises of the 60s and 70s will see here, in stark perspective, how the issues played out at Cornell." Downs is a professor of political science at the University of Wisconsin.

Important letters are preserved in the Perkins Papers. See Perkins to Nicholas H. Noyes, June 12, 1967, Box 10/30, and letters from Provost Dale Corson, Box 9/43. The letter from Professors of Philosophy David Lyons, Norman Malcom, David Sachs, Keith Donnellen, Sydney Shoemaker, Richard Sorabji, and John Canfield to Perkins, letters from E. Grant Perl to Perkins, and a letter from Andrew Duff to Gov. Nelson Rockefeller are in Box 9/43. Perkins's letter to "Those Who Wrote Me about the Recent Student Events at Cornell," dated June 22, 1965, is in Box 9/45.

See also Wallerstein and Starr, *The University Crisis Reader, Volume II,* 410. These authors reprint the statement of the thirty-one faculty members, Tom Wicker's editorial in the *New York Times,* Apr. 27, 1969, and Milton Konvitz's article from the *New York Times Magazine,* Apr. 27, 1969.

The original copy of George McT. Kahin's address in Barton Hall on April 25, 1969, is in the Kahin Papers, 14/27/3146, RMC; it is reprinted in Strout and Gossvogel, eds., *Divided We Stand.*

An aide to Perkins prepared a statement entitled "Some Achievements of James A. Perkins during His Tenure as President of Cornell (1963–1969). Among those listed: completing a one-hundred-million-dollar fund-raising campaign; organizing the Cornell Centennial Celebration; providing the initiative for the Division of Biological Sciences; securing funding for the Johnson Art Museum and the services of I. M. Pei as architect; increasing admission of black students but "with a lack of success in their integration into the campus"; establishing Andrew D. White visiting professorships; holding the Latin American Year; instituting an office of regional planning at Cornell, "an enterprise that did not survive Mr. Perkins' departure"; and establishing a committee on the future of the arts at Cornell.

CHAPTER NINE

See Dale Corson Papers, 3/11/1665, RMC. The collection includes speeches to trustees and alumni groups, especially those in Box 133, folders 206 and 229. See letters to Corson from Provost Robert A. Plane; from Professors Peter Auer, John S. Harding, and Arthur Spitzer; and from Ellen Emanuel, student, in Corson Papers. Corson's Trustee-Council Weekend address, October 11, 1974, is also in the Corson Papers.

Regarding the era, see Caleb S. Rossiter, *The Chimes of Freedom Flashing: A Personal History of the Vietnam Anti-War Movement and the 1960s* (Washington, D.C., 1996), especially Book I. Thomas Sowell observed in the *New York Times Magazine* (Dec. 13, 1970) that Cornell was "skipping over competent Blacks to admit 'authentic' Ghetto types." For accounts of the first ten days of April 1970, see the *Cornell Daily Sun*, the *Ithaca Journal*, and *Proceedings of Trustees*.

See RMC for records of the Cornell's Women's Studies Program and the Africana Center. Sheila Tobias has written a memoir of the origins of Women's Studies at Cornell that appears in Florence Howe, ed., *The Politics of Women's Studies: Testimony from Thirty Founding Mothers: The Women's Studies History Series: Vol. 1* (New York, 2000). For both programs, also consult the index to the Corson Papers.

For students' preferences, see Eleanor Macklin, "Cohabitation on Campus: Going Very Steady," in *Psychology Today* (November 1974: 53–59). William D. Gurowitz was vice president for Campus Life.

In 1974 the Sloan Institute of Hospital Administration became the Sloan Program of Hospital Administration in the Graduate School of Business and Public Administration. Ten years later, there was discussion of moving this program to the College of Human Ecology, which happened in 1987.

Robert Wilson's exchange with Sen. John Pastore first appeared in print in the AEC Authority Legislation 1970 Part 1: Hearings before the Joint Committee on Atomic Energy, Congress of the United States, Ninety-first Congress First Session on General, Physical Research Program, Space Nuclear Program and Plowshare, April 17 and 18, 1969, Part 1, printed for the use of the Joint Committee on Atomic Energy, U.S. Government Printing Office (Washington, D.C., 1969). It can also be found on-line at www/fnal.gov/pub/ferminews00-28/p3.html.

For Nicholas Noyes, see *Proceedings of Trustees, 1970–71*, and the memorial statement in *Proceedings of Trustees, 1977–87*. For actions concerning the School of Nursing, see *Proceedings of Trustees, 1975–76, 1976–77*.

The quote about the faculty is from Earl Simonson, "Cornell and the Co-ed," *The Cornell Era*, May 1911, 279. Comments about Title IX are from Robert J. Kane, *Good Sports: A History of Cornell Athletics* (Ithaca, 1992), 164–65.

CHAPTER TEN
See Frank H. T. Rhodes Papers, 3/12/2905, RMC. For the presidential search, see Presidential Search Committee Records,

2/6/1872 and 2/6/2262, RMC. The columnist quoted was Marty Robinson, writing in the *Cornell Daily Sun*, Feb. 11, 1977, 2.

Figures about enrollment from 1986 are available online at http://www.ipr.cornell.edu/FactBook/Enrollment/Total/IthacaRE. The information about the New York State Veterinary College is noted in *Beyond Traditional Boundaries: Veterinary Medicine at Cornell in the Twenty-first Century* (Ithaca, 2000).

The 1979 Bakke Case, stemming from an admissions decision at the University of California–Berkeley, was argued before the U.S. Supreme Court, whose ruling ended quotas established at some universities to ensure diversity in their classes. Thirty-five anti-Semitic and anti-Asian posters were found in seven academic buildings; see *Proceedings of Trustees, 1991–92*. The trustees' action on equal education and employment appears in *Proceedings of Trustees, 1977–78*, and the provision for equal opportunity officers is described in *Proceedings of Trustees, 1981–82*. See also the Rhodes Papers and http://www.supct.law.cornell.edu/supct.

The discussions of divestment in South African companies are documented in *Proceedings of Trustees, 1978–79* and thereafter. The faculty vote was 323 to 72 in favor of divestment. The Sullivan principles, devised by the Reverend Leon Sullivan, a director of General Motors Corporation, asked American employers in South Africa to eliminate segregation of races in all eating, comfort, and work facilities; to institute equal and fair employment practices for all employees; to provide equal pay; to develop training programs for blacks and other nonwhites; to increase the number of nonwhites in management; and to work to improve the quality of employees' lives outside the workplace.

Retirement is discussed in *Proceedings of Trustees, 1978–79*, and the policy was amended by the Board of Trustees on December 7, 1982, with the statement that "every member of the instructional and research staff except those with indefinite tenure and all executive, administrative, and academic administrative officers . . . shall terminate . . . on June 30 following their 70th birthday." The trustees considered creating a retirement home for faculty in 1988–89 but nothing came of it at the time. See *Proceedings of Trustees, 1988–89*. In March 1992, Savage Farm was sold to the Kendal Communities Development Company, and Kendal at Ithaca opened in December 1995. *Proceedings of Trustees, 1991–92*.

Each year to 1991, the Report on the Status of Minorities and Women (later the Affirmative Action Report, and finally the Diversity Report) was included in the *Proceedings of Trustees*.

After 1991, the reports were mentioned in the minutes but not included.

The Cornell Eleven were denied class-action status by review of the U.S. Department of Labor, which ruled that there had been no discrimination against women as a class or group at Cornell. The case was dismissed. See *Proceedings of Trustees, 1979–80* and *1982–83*; the Rhodes Papers; and Cornell Eleven Records, 4197, RMC.

Discussions concerning the modernization of the buildings of the New York State College of Agriculture began in 1980. Historic Ithaca, Inc., requested that the City of Ithaca enact protective legislation by declaring landmark status for the Agricultural Quadrangle. In December 1986 a court ruling allowed demolition of Roberts, East Roberts, and Stone Halls.

Benjamin Nichols ran as a Democrat and served as mayor of Ithaca from 1990 to 1995. During this time the city repeatedly challenged university building projects, and relations between the city and the university were strained. See letters from Nichols in Rhodes Papers, Box 257/37–41 and 277/27. See also the *Ithaca Journal*, Sept. 20 and 21, 2002.

In 1981 the courts held that the trustees were required to open meetings to the public when its "deliberations and actions concern the Statutory Colleges."

See Frank H. T. Rhodes, *Creation of the Future: The Role of the American University* (Ithaca, 2001), for his comments about institutions of higher education.

The Cornell Alumni University (CAU) was the product of conversations between alumni and James Perkins. The alumni, according to Ralph Janis, director of CAU in 2003, wanted Cornell to "provide them with a way to maintain relationships with faculty throughout their lives and to introduce their children to the university." The first one-week course was held in summer 1968. By 2003 CAU was offering thirty-six courses in four summer sessions in addition to a program for youngsters ages three through sixteen. Cornell's program is "by far the largest one of its kind in the country," according to Janis, and much emulated. The first off-campus program, led by Cornell ornithologists, began in the 1970s, and the first foreign study tour was to China in 1980. Frank Rhodes led the first cruise program in 1981. CyberTower, which began in June 2001, offers on-line alumni education; see http://www.cau.cornell.edu.

The quote from M. H. Abrams is from the preface to *Natural Supernaturalism: Tradition and Revolution in Romantic Literature* (New York, 1973). Harry Levin is quoted in *The Cornell Idea*, a book of pictures and comments published by Cornell Publications Services (1976).

CHAPTER ELEVEN

See the Hunter R. Rawlings III Papers, 3/13/2843, RMC. See Nicole Neroulis Scrapbook, History 126 Scrapbook Collection, 37/5/2891, RMC, for the question to President Rawlings.

Regarding town-gown relations, see Dan Higgins, *Ithaca Journal*, March 16, 2002, 3A. Tompkins County has more than 80 companies, small and large, created by or staffed by former Cornellians.

See www.town.ithaca.ny.us/lake_source_cooling for the Cayuga Lake Defense Fund and information about the project to air-condition university buildings with lake water.

The pumpkin came down from McGraw Tower on March 14, 1998. There were continuous news stories about it in the *Ithaca Journal* and in papers all over the country, and many articles about the prank appear in scrapbooks kept by freshmen for History 126. See Scrapbooks, History 126, RMC. A pumpkin watch was kept in the *Cornell Daily Sun*, and see "How the Pumpkin Got on the Tower," *Cornell Daily Sun*, Nov. 1, 2000, or http://www.cornelldailysun.com/articles/909.

The word *contract* is first used instead of *statutory* in *Proceedings of Trustees, 2000–01*, 143.

The Legal Information Institute site, http://www.supct.law.cornell.edu/supc, includes U.S. Supreme Court and other court decisions as well.

Henrik N. Dullea's account of the unionization drive at Cornell appeared in *The Chronicle of Higher Education*, January 17, 2003, B16.

For enrollment figures, see http://ipr.cornell.edu/FactBook/Enrollment. Comments about Rawlings's retirement appear in the *Ithaca Journal*, Mar. 16, 2002; the *Cornell Chronicle*, Mar. 21, 2002; and the *New York Times*, Mar. 16, 2002.

For a copy of Lehman's first press conference in Ithaca, see the *Cornell Chronicle*, Jan. 16, 2003, 7. See also the *New York Times*, Dec. 15, 2002, 60. Not everyone was enthusiastic about Lehman's appointment. The lead story in *The Cornell Review: The Conservative Voice at Cornell*, Feb. 7, 2003, by Paul Eastlund, was headlined, "Cornell's New Liberal Chieftain: Affirmative Action's Poster Child Is Coming to Cornell." In the same issue, regarding Rawlings's departure, a heading read, "Good Riddance: Rawlings' Disappointing Stint." See also "Special Commemorative Supplement," *Cornell Daily Sun*, May 2, 2003, and "Standing Tall," in *Cornell Alumni News*, May/June 2003.

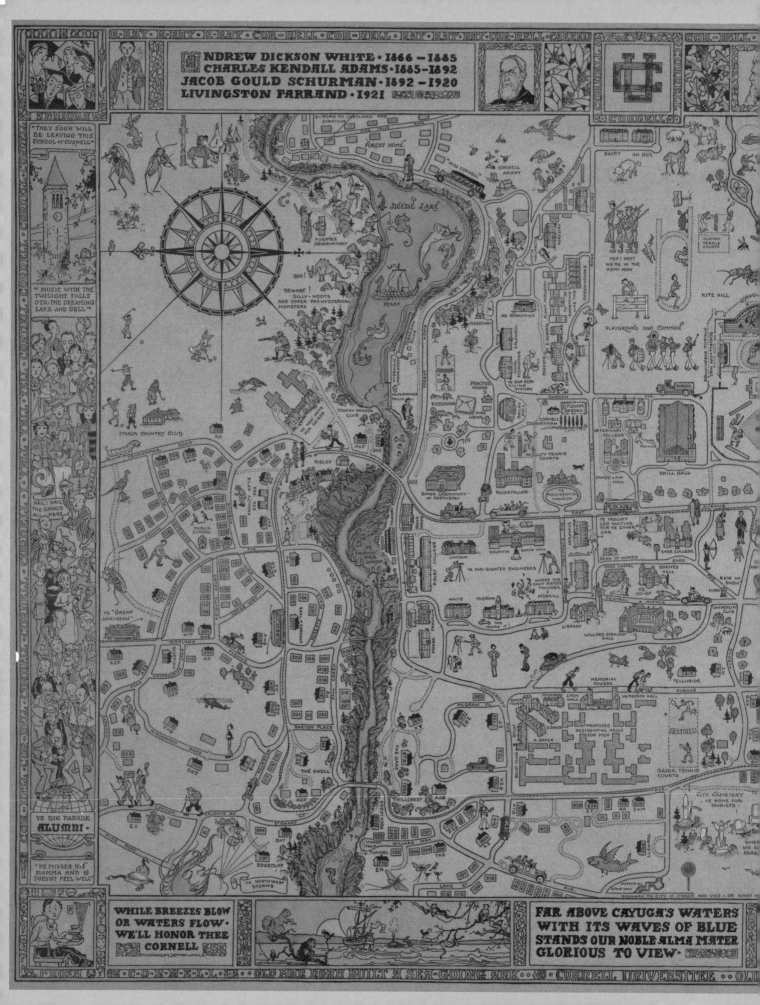